Other Cultures, Elder Years

An Introduction to Cultural Gerontology

Lowell D. Holmes

Wichita State University
Wichita, Kansas

Burgess Publishing Company
Minneapolis, Minnesota

Editorial: Jeff Holtmeier, Janilyn Richardson, Elizabeth Weinstein
Production: Judy Vicars
Compositor: Gloria Otremba
Cover photo: Lowell D. Holmes

© 1983 by Burgess Publishing Company
Printed in the United States of America

Burgess Publishing Company
7108 Ohms Lane
Minneapolis, Minnesota 55435

All rights reserved. No part of this book may be reproduced in any form whatsoever, by photograph or mimeograph or by any other means, by broadcast or transmission, by translation into any kind of language, or by recording electronically or otherwise, without permission in writing from the publisher, except by a reviewer, who may quote brief passages in critical articles and reviews.

Library of Congress Cataloging in Publication Data

Holmes, Lowell Don, 1925–
   Other cultures, elder years.

   Bibliography: p.
   Includes index.
   1. Aging–Cross-cultural studies. 2. Gerontology–Methodology. I. Title.
HQ1061.H574   1983   305.2'6   82-70921
ISBN 0-8087-4715-0

J I H G F E D C B A

To my parents, Marie and Emmit Holmes,
octogenarians and going strong

Contents

Foreword vii

Chapter 1   The Anthropological Perspective   1

Chapter 2   Research Interests: Status, Community, and the Life Cycle   11

Chapter 3   Retirement, Personality, and Applied Anthropology   32

Chapter 4   Longevity   54

Chapter 5   Shangri-las   68

Chapter 6   Varieties of Aging Experience   84

Chapter 7   Universals in Human Aging   112

Chapter 8   Minority Aged in America   134

Chapter 9   The Aged and Cultural Change   166

Bibliography   186

Index   199

Foreword

This is a pioneering effort to produce a book on the anthropology of aging, or, as Dr. Holmes prefers to title it, cultural gerontology. Dr. Holmes has been in the forefront of the effort to apply the skills and insights of anthropology to the field of aging for more than 15 years. My collaboration with him began when he invited me, a sociologist, to appear with him and several other anthropologists on the program of the Central States Anthropological Association. Out of that initial tentative experiment emerged the idea that led to *Aging and Modernization*.

That volume was essentially an anthology of cultural case studies in which, for the first time, the primary question was: What happens to older people in these societies? After assembling the case studies, we sought meaningful patterns and eventually found them by arranging the cases in order of modernization and tracing the relationships between that independent variable and the various ways of regarding and treating their elderly members. The finding of such a strong tendency for the status of the elderly to be low in the modernized societies provoked me to spend much of the following two years in an effort to discover why. This led to the rather elaborate restatement of the theory that is summarized in the chart on page 177 of this volume.

Since publication of *Aging and Modernization*, a number of other anthologies of anthropological works on aging have appeared, although most of the contributions are specialized in their treatment of specific cultures; few attempt the type of *holistic* perspective Dr. Holmes and I sought to portray in the cases we collected for that book. Still, the appearance of these volumes attests to the growing attention of anthropologists to matters pertaining to the elderly members of the societies they study. This is an auspicious development. Not only does it enrich and broaden the field of anthropology, but it provides wider perspectives for all the rest of us as well, helping us to overcome the cultural myopia and ethnocentrism that is a ubiquitous tendency. Other social scientists and gerontologists with other specialties are finding these materials of great value, and planners and practitioners are being alerted to alternative strategies and programs.

After 15 years of accumulating cultural case studies, though, it is time to begin to integrate and synthesize what we have learned. It is time to raise anew the questions: What does all this mean? Are there some broad principles and generalizations that emerge from the enlarged sample of cultures now available to us? In other words, it is time for the development of a systematic summary, evaluation, and theoretical statement of the field of cultural gerontology. That is the pioneering task that Dr. Holmes has set for himself in this volume.

He first reviews some of the major concepts and perspectives of cultural anthropology and relates them to gerontology. Then, in Chapter 2, he reviews the comparative studies of status and role of older people in various societies, studies of age-segregated communities of elderly people, recent research on social networks of aged persons, historic reports by anthropologists on age grades and age sets in various parts of the world, his own research on a home for the elderly in Samoa, and work done by anthropologists on life-cycle analysis.

Chapter 3 provides an anthropological and historical perspective on retirement and the general process of disengagement, including an intriguing discussion of "deculturation" as the anthropological analogue of the sociological process of disengagement. Here also are treated the topics of ethnicity and aging, creativity and productivity of the aged, culture and personality in relation to aging, and applied anthropology as related to gerontology.

Chapter 4 deals with variations in longevity, using the concepts of life span and life expectancy and some operational measurements of each. Since life span is presumed to be the ultimate limit of biological aging, the chapter closes with a review of current biological theories on aging. Chapter 5 is titled simply "Shangri-las." It is a balanced review of current facts and myths about four contemporary reputed utopias noted for extreme longevity—the Abkhasians of the Caucasus region of the Soviet Union, the Hunzas of West Pakistan, the village of Vilcabamba in Ecuador, and Paros, Greece.

Chapter 6 contrasts the aging experience in three widely different societies—the Eskimos, the Samoans, and the United States. Chapter 7 searches for and illustrates some universals in human aging. Chapter 8 outlines the variations in the aging experience of American minorities, including blacks, American Indians, Mexican Americans, Chinese Americans, Japanese Americans, and four American minorities from Pacific islands—Samoans, Pilipinos, Guamanians, and Hawaiians. The last chapter discusses the aged and cultural change. It reviews modernization theory and applies it to the materials of this volume.

Dr. Holmes is to be congratulated for his initiative and courage in exploring this new intellectual territory. The resulting volume provides the rest of us with an integrated perspective on aging around the world, helping us to make sense of the disconnected case studies that have been our fare up to now. I commend the reader to this introduction to cultural gerontology.

Donald O. Cowgill
Professor Emeritus
Department of Sociology
University of Missouri, Columbia

CHAPTER 1

The Anthropological Perspective

The author of this volume is an anthropologist—a cultural anthropologist who, because of his training and scientific interests, looks at the contemporary world in all its cultural complexity and variety and attempts to understand and interpret human behavior. A book on gerontology written by an anthropologist may seem unusual, because most gerontologists are sociologists, psychologists, or social workers. Anthropologists have long been interested in the aged, but unfortunately mostly as sources of information on a non-Western culture as it was when they were young or before the coming of the white man and Western civilization. When Franz Boas (the father of American anthropology) sent out his Columbia University graduate students (Margaret Mead, Alfred Kroeber, Ruth Benedict, Melville Herskovits, and others) with instructions to seek out the elders first as major sources of cultural information, it apparently never occurred to him or his students that they might also ask what life was like for the elderly. Many anthropologists are doing that today, and anthropology is bringing new information and a new way of looking at aging to the science of gerontology.

THE DISCIPLINE OF ANTHROPOLOGY

Anthropology is the study of human beings—total human beings. No other science or humanistic discipline examines the human animal as thoroughly. Anthropology addresses itself to the study of the physical makeup of humans, to their social and cultural behavior in the contemporary world as well as in historic and prehistoric days. It is the science concerned with the evolutionary development of humans as animals, with their patterns of group interaction, and with the nature of their cultural traditions in industrialized as well as tribal and peasant societies.

Anthropology maintains a broad, holistic approach to the study of mankind but, like other social scientists, anthropologists tend to specialize. The anthropological fraternity includes physical anthropologists, archeologists, linguists, and social/cultural anthropologists. Physical anthropologists study people as members of the animal kingdom, recognizing that they are vertebrates, mammals, primates, and finally, because of their superior brains and culture-building capacities, *Hominids* or human beings. Physical anthropologists concern themselves with human evolution, demography, population genetics, and human variation (race), and they are valuable contributors to knowledge in such gerontological and geriatric areas as morbidity, mortality, health, longevity, and the genetic basis of aging. Since there are both hereditary and environmental components to aging, these scholars can be expected to contribute heavily to gerontological science.

Archeologists also contribute to our knowledge of aging, particularly in the area of longevity. In cooperation with physical anthropologists, archeologists specializing in paleodemography study life expectancy and maximum life spans of prehistoric populations. Archeologists generally are concerned with reconstructing the life-styles of past cultures through excavation and analysis of artifacts such as weapons, tools, and ceremonial objects, but paleodemographers calculate the age of death of human skeletons, figure mortality rates, and construct survivorship curves and life tables. An excellent example of this kind of study is that of Douglas Ubelaker (1974), who documented the demographic characteristics of a Late Woodland Indian population in Maryland through analysis of skeletal materials in two ossuaries (communal burial places). His results appear in Figure 1-1 and Table 1.1.

Anthropological linguists also have a potential role in gerontology. These scholars specialize in language analysis, with interests ranging from the history of language development to the study of language structure and semantics and to the use of language as a reflection of class, ethnic, or sex differences within a society. The branch of linguistics known as *sociolinguistics* has demonstrated that our language reflects American racism and sexism, and it is now recognizing agism in our patterns of communication. For example, synonyms for "old" and "aged" tend to be more negative than positive, and evidence indicates that once-positive references have become abusive through time. According to David Fischer, "Most of our pejorative terms for old men began to appear first during the late eighteenth and early nineteenth centuries" (1978:90-91). The word *gaffer,* for example, had originally been a term of respect (a contraction of godfather), and *fogy,* before 1780 meant "a wounded military veteran." *Codger,* which originally was a slang term meaning "to beg," began being applied to old people in the late eighteenth century with a connotation of meanness and stinginess. Old women have fared less well than old men. This may be the result of a combination of sexism and agism. *Hag, crone,* and *old maid* date back nearly 400 years, but derogatory terms for elderly men did not appear before about 1800. The process of coining new words of derision for old people continues even today, and Fischer notes, "Praise words invented for old people are quickly turned the other way—euphemisms such as *senior citizen* are often laden with a heavy freight of sarcasm" (1978:94).

Social anthropologists (who specialize in studies of social structure and social interaction) and cultural anthropologists (who study cultural traditions and systems) consider the many societies of our planet to be multiple experiments in human adaptation and survival in a wide variety of physical environments. The customs evolved by the societies represent their *cultures,* or systems of traditional behavior. One of the

The Anthropological Perspective

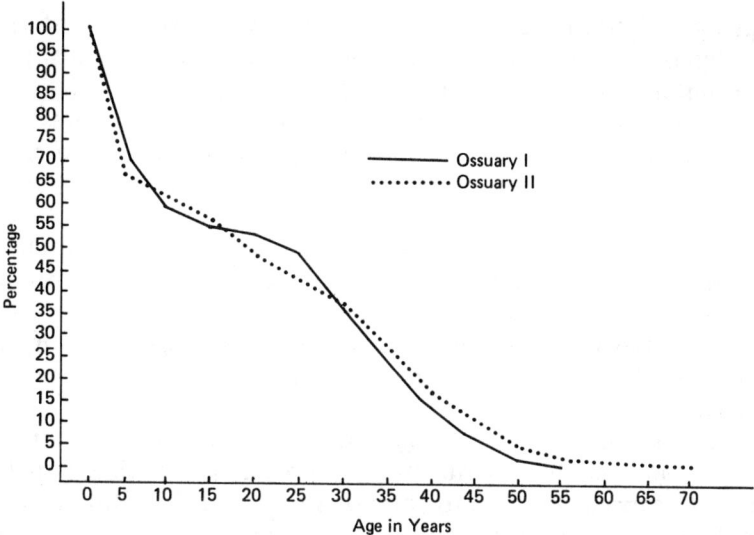

Figure 1.1. Survivorship curves calculated from skeletal remains in two ossuaries in Maryland. These curves show the percentage of a theoretical original population of 100 persons still living at the end of each five-year period. (Redrawn from Ubelaker, Douglas H., *Human Skeletal Remains*, Chicago: Aldine, 1978.)

Table 1.1. Life Table Reconstructed from Skeletons in Ossuary II in Maryland

Age Interval (x)	No. of Deaths (Dx)	% of Deaths (dx)	Survivors Entering (lx)	Probability of Death (qx)	Total Years Lived Between X and X + 5 (Lx)	Total Years Lived After Lifetime (Tx)	Life Expectancy ($e°x$)
0	56	29.79	100.00	.2979	425.525	2297.900	22.98
5	12	6.38	70.21	.0909	335.100	1872.375	26.67
10	7	3.72	63.83	.0583	309.850	1537.275	24.08
15	14	7.45	60.11	.1239	281.925	1227.425	20.42
20	9	4.79	52.66	.0910	251.325	945.500	17.95
25	12	6.38	47.87	.1333	223.400	694.175	14.50
30	21	11.17	41.49	.2692	179.525	470.775	11.35
35	20	10.64	30.32	.3509	125.000	291.250	9.61
40	13	6.91	19.68	.3511	81.125	166.250	8.45
45	11	5.85	12.77	.4581	49.225	85.125	6.67
50	8	4.26	6.92	.6156	23.950	35.900	5.19
55	4	2.13	2.66	.8008	7.975	11.950	4.49
60	0	0.00	0.53	.0000	2.650	3.975	7.50
65	1	0.53	0.53	1.0000	1.325	1.325	2.50
70	0	0.00	0.00	.0000	0.000	0.000	0.00

SOURCE: Ubelaker, Douglas H., *Human Skeletal Remains*, Chicago: Aldine, 1978.

traditions that all societies have evolved concerns how the problem of growing old is to be handled by the society and by the aging person. The ways this problem is approached are infinitely varied around the world.

Anthropologists not only specialize in specific subjects, but most of them also specialize in a particular part of the world. Although some choose to remain at home and study their own people, a considerable number take a special interest in the peoples of the Pacific, Africa, Asia, or the Middle East. Some may be American Indian specialists. Since anthropology is dedicated to studying all peoples in all times and to documenting their infinitely varied configurations of customs, anthropologists often feel they must live among foreign peoples—often for extended periods of time. Anthropologists investigate the value systems, world views, and cultural norms of people in far-off lands because they wish to test hypotheses about the nature of human beings in a worldwide laboratory.

Ethnographers are cultural anthropologists who engage in field studies, and *ethnography* is the term used to describe the empirical, fact-finding activities—observation and interview—carried out by anthropologists in the field. Ethnography is literally the science of describing cultural phenomena. Accurate documentation of human ways of life is considered of vital importance in this social science, but it is also considered important to carry the fact-finding activity one step farther to the level of ethnology. *Ethnology* is a comparative activity, where cultural descriptions (ethnographies) are compared and generalizations then made about human nature.

Fully understanding the nature and cause of the problems and adjustments in regard to aging in a given society (let us say our own) is important, but it is also important to gain the wider perspective which embraces all societies in all times and in all places. Worldwide comparisons allow us to bring our own problems into sharper focus and they may suggest new solutions to common problems or new adjustments to meet unique needs.

Not only the broad scope of anthropology establishes it as a useful discipline in studying gerontological phenomena; it is also its unique perspective. That perspective may be described as being (a) comparative, (b) holistic, (c) concerned with *emic* and *etic* viewpoints, (d) relativistic, (e) case-study oriented, and (f) committed to process or dynamic analysis.

Before we can deal with the nature of these various approaches, we must realize that these are all ways of analyzing culture, and that culture is a major concept of reference in anthropological analysis. *Culture* is defined as the shared patterns of values and behavior that are characteristic of a society because they are passed on from generation to generation through symbolic communication. Once transmitted through teaching and learning, culture shapes the lives of individuals and gives form and stability to societal behavior.

Although aging is a biological phenomenon, our attitudes toward the aged and our own aging, the treatment our aged receive, the evaluation of the importance of the aged, and the roles considered appropriate for the old are more a matter of cultural tradition than of physiology. As Gregory Bateson put it, "Man lives by propositions whose truth depends upon his believing them. If he believes that the old are no good, weak, stubborn, whatever terms of abuse he likes to attach to them, then to a great extent that will become true of the old in the population where that is believed, and the old themselves will believe it and will reinforce the general belief that it is so" (1950:52). Culture lies at the heart of all anthropological thought and investigation, and the cultural perspective represents an important factor of insight for gerontology.

COMPARATIVE ANALYSIS

Anthropology was once known as the science that studied "primitive" or "nonliterate" peoples. However, in these waning years of the twentieth century, cultural change in the form of industrialization, urbanization, and Westernization has made it increasingly difficult to find such preindustrial peoples. But anthropology does not require the existence of "primitive" people to be a relevant social science discipline. More and more anthropologists are turning to their own culture or to subcultures within it for their studies, and simple, isolated, preindustrial societies no longer dominate the interest and subject matter of anthropology. The science does continue to be comparative and cross-cultural, however. Not only are *synchronic* studies (those comparing many cultures) important, but so are *diachronic* ones (where single societies are described at various time periods).

In *The Counterfeiters* Andre Gidé describes a particular species of fish that, because of its unique biological makeup, must swim at a particular depth in the ocean. It has never been able to descend to the bottom nor has it ever been able to rise to the surface. Such a fish, suggests Gide, has no insight into the nature of its watery environment since it has experienced neither sand nor air. Human beings who know only their own culture are in danger of this kind of provincialism. If one has never experienced another culture—through residence or reading—then there is a good chance that person does not fully understand the significance of what is happening in his own society.

Comparative analysis is frequently used in anthropology to determine whether a particular form of behavior—such as competitiveness, pugnacity, mother love, or acquisitiveness—is cultural behavior (and therefore learned) or whether it is a product of the human biological heritage (and therefore passed on genetically). In 1961, Cumming and Henry proposed that it was "natural" and beneficial for elders to disengage socially and economically. Since such disengagement was presented as "natural," anthropologists might expect to find the phenomenon in all cultures. They have not. In fact, they found that disengagement was quite common in Western industrial societies but almost unknown elsewhere.

Cross-cultural comparison has been tremendously helpful in investigating the concept of human longevity. Although the relative importances of nature and nurture are difficult to determine precisely, comparison of dietary differences, variations in work and play patterns, and differences in supportive social structures and respect patterns in various societies shed important light on some of the cultural influences on long life. And we know that the aged are more esteemed and more conscientiously served in agricultural than in industrial societies, by extended rather than nuclear families, and in rural rather than in urban communities.

HOLISTIC PERSPECTIVE

Anthropologists think of culture as a configuration of interrelated traits, complexes, and patterns, and they believe that one aspect of culture cannot be effectively studied without taking the totality into consideration. As Ruth Benedict so aptly phrased it, "All the miscellaneous behavior directed toward getting a living, mating, warring and worshipping the gods, is made over into consistent patterns in accordance with unconscious canons of choice that develop within the culture" (1934:48). Since life is really merely a series of events and people interacting we must realize that to categorize human behavior as "economic," "political," or "religious" is to arbitrarily divide up human behavior for the convenience of study. Distortions occur when facts are taken out of context, and there has been a long history of faulty thinking that has resulted from this practice. Racial, economic, biological, and other forms of determinism are reductionist, oversimplified forms of analysis that have stressed one causal factor to the exclusion or underemphasis of others. Comparative and holistic analysis has proved to be a valuable weapon against this kind of reasoning.

Although anthropology recognizes a great advantage in specialization, it is more interested in the total configuration of culture—in its organic wholeness—than in documenting every minute detail of every facet of human life. If forced to do so, the anthropologist will sacrifice detail for a comprehension of form.

Not only have anthropologists stressed the interrelationship of all aspects of culture, but they have also emphasized the biocultural totality of human experience. Human behavior is partly a response to physical or animal needs and partly a following of established traditions. Although mankind is one biologically, there are almost as many kinds of culture as there are societies. To consider one factor without the other is to distort human nature. People require a given amount of nutriment to survive, but whether they receive it in two meals a day or five or in the form of raw fish or sauerbraten is a cultural matter.

EMIC-ETIC PERSPECTIVES

Any cultural situation can be viewed from the *inside* and from the *outside*. Anthropologists believe that much can be gained by attempting to see the culture as its participants see it. This approach, sometimes called *ethnoscience,* attempts to discover "folk" or local categories of thought and reality. This insiders' window on the world is referred to as the *emic* perspective, and this term comes from the word *phonemic,* which refers to the combination of meaningful sounds unique to a particular language. Therefore, *emic* is not a universal reference to language but a specific reference to a particular language. The *etic* approach deriving from the word *phonetic*), on the other hand, is the scientific perspective that the well-trained anthropologist brings to the analysis. This comprises his or her cross-cultural frame of reference and is an objective and controlled procedure for weighing and sifting facts and theoretical viewpoints. Its approach to human behavior is a general, *outsiders'* approach, just as *phonetics* is the term for the science of all human speech production.

The best way to distinguish between *emic* and *etic* perspectives is to imagine the difference in perceptions of a worshipper and an art historian who are both observing a great stained-glass cathedral window. The window undoubtedly represents something very different, very personal, and very meaningful for the worshipper, who would include the window in his total complex of worship. The window might move him spiritually as well as artistically. The art historian, on the other hand, might be moved by the window's beauty but not by its connections with worship. He would analyze it coldly and objectively in terms of other great cathedral windows and in terms of established scholarly criteria for judging such architectural or artistic features.

RELATIVISTIC PERSPECTIVE

Because of anthropology's insistence on a cross-cultural perspective and because several generations of anthropologists have lived among their foreign subjects and have come to respect them and see the wisdom of their lifeways, anthropology has come to be dominated by a kind of philosophical stance known as *cultural relativism.* Cultural relativism is both a *methodological* tool that ensures objective data collection and a *philosophical* and *theoretical* principle that calls for open-mindedness in accepting cultural diversity. It emphasizes the idea that no single culture can claim to have a monopoly on the "right" or "natural" way of doing things. From this standpoint, anthropologists who study gerontology believe that the meaning of old age and the effectiveness of solutions to the problems of old age can only be understood and evaluated in terms of the cultural context in which the aged reside. Although mankind's common biological heritage and the inevitability of senescence create elements of common experience, anthropologists are extremely cautious about declaring that the customs in one society are more acceptable or more honorable than those in other societies. Who is to say that locking the elderly up in nursing homes is more humane than allowing them to wander off on the ice flow and freeze to death as Eskimo elders are sometimes permitted to do? Cultural behavior that may imply low status for the aged in one society may mean something entirely different in another.

Cultural relativism also warns that cultural institutions within one society may not easily transfer to another. Proof of this was observed by the author in American Samoa, where a Meals on Wheels nutrition program was attempted. To begin with, Samoa is not a society that understands volunteerism, a major factor in Meals on Wheels success elsewhere. In Samoa, *families* serve the elderly—not neighbors or strangers who volunteer. Thus, when the government's planning began, Samoans suggested that food or money be distributed among families who would then make sure that their elderly got proper nourishment. American government officials (mostly white contract employees) objected to this on the grounds that other family members would perhaps get the food intended for the elderly. After long consideration (with each other but not with Samoans), the government officials decided that the food should be cooked in the kitchens of the 26 consolidated elementary schools where food was already being prepared by kitchen personnel for government-subsidized hot meals for the schoolchildren. The elderly could simply go to the school for lunch. This solution led to the demise of the nutrition program for elders, because it did not take into consideration appropriate age-status and role behavior, particularly in respect to titled chiefs who maintained that it was beneath their dignity to go to school and line up like children just for a midday meal. Also, the usual time for Samoans to eat is not noon but at 10 A.M. and 7 P.M.

Cultural relativism is a difficult concept to apply, because all peoples in all places tend to be *ethnocentric,* which means that they believe that their own values, customs, and attitudes are superior to those of people in other societies. Although respect for one's own cultural system and loyalty to one's own group is necessary and worthwhile, social scientists in particular must realize that there are many effective and efficient ways of doing things, and no one way of life is either "natural" or necessarily best. In fact, no technique of qualitatively evaluating cultures has ever been discovered.

CASE-STUDY APPROACH

Anthropology's use of the case-study method is similar to that found in the field of social work. A case study is a detailed and comprehensive report on a person, a society, or a social situation. Just as social workers go into homes to observe and document the life-style of families in their case loads, so anthropologists go to communities or other cultures to investigate the circumstances of the peoples they wish to understand. The title of the largest and most popular series of ethnographic monographs used in college courses, *Case Studies in Cultural Anthropology,*[1] is an indication of the fact that anthropologists consider their monographs cultural case studies.

The holistic approach is characteristic of case studies, and in their book on case-study method, the Committee on the Family (1970) maintained that in studying the family, four determinants of family functioning must be considered. They are (1) the cultural, (2) the interpersonal, (3) the psychological, and (4) the biological. This manual for social workers elaborates on the determinants:

> The cultural area includes the profile of value orientations associated with cultural affiliation of the family and the belief systems that pattern all role activities, including domestic roles, as well as the structure of the nuclear and extended family. The interpersonal area is composed of overt, day-to-day interactions between family members in maintenance of their role relations—their communications, alliances, and coalitions; expressions of feeling; ways of reaching decisions; methods of child rearing and control; handling of illness, finances, education, religion, recreation and losses through death or separation. The intrapsychic processes of individual members, including their unconscious cognitions, emotions, defenses, and object relations, comprise the psychological area. The biological area embraces the physical constitution of family members, including their age and sex, the state of their physical health, and the patterning of biological functions in nutrition, sleep, excretion, and motility. (1970:258-259)

The above prescription for a case study for social workers could easily, with minor changes, serve as a guide for anthropologists studying cultures or cultural situations. Like social workers, anthropologists are not always sure what they will find, what aspects of the situation they will be required to document, or exactly what methods they will have to use in collecting their data. But they know there will undoubtedly be some difficulties in establishing rapport, in comprehending the value systems of their subjects, and in understanding the complexities and subtleties of communication.

---

[1] Edited by George and Louise Spindler and published by Holt, Rinehart and Winston, 1960-1982.

Because of these challenges, the anthropological investigator normally moves into the situation for an extended period of time and carries on *participant observation*. That is to say, the investigator attempts to participate in the life of the subjects as much as permitted to get the feel and flavor (the emic perspective) of the culture.

PROCESS ANALYSIS

Anthropology's interest in change and process is perhaps older than any of its other interests. Beginning with speculations about the principle of cultural evolution before anthropology was even an established scholarly discipline, anthropologists have, for more than 200 years, attempted to understand the reasons for and ramifications of change under such headings as evolution, revolution, innovation, discovery, acculturation, diffusion, and modernization. Anthropologists interested in gerontology have particularly been interested in *modernization influences* in developing countries and the effect that they have on elderly status and roles. The general assumption has been that the influence of Western industrial culture will destroy the traditional values and agencies of support and recognition for the aged and that the status and authority of the aged will be reduced, despite a general increase in the number of elderly.

Special research interests can also help explain the trends in the gerontological writings of anthropologists. An analysis of the anthropological literature on aging reveals a number of trends in research interests that undoubtedly grew out of the nature of the discipline and the perspectives of its scholars. They are:

1. Studies of status and role, often relating to ecological or modernization factors

2. Community studies, particularly of age-homogeneous or age-graded situations. The bulk of this pertains to our own culture

3. Life-cycle analysis and definitions of age

4. The concepts of retirement and disengagement in cross-cultural analysis

5. Studies of ethnicity and aging

6. Longevity studies—both in terms of hereditary and cultural factors

7. Studies of artistic creativity and productivity of the aged

8. Personality and culture studies that primarily emphasize ongoing personality development throughout the life cycle

9. Studies of physical changes associated with advanced age

10. Studies of death and dying among the aged

11. Applied or practical studies directed to solving specific problems associated with aging or the aged.

SUMMARY

From this brief treatment of the nature of anthropology, its interests, and its potential for gerontological research, we can see that anthropology's concern for cultural, biological, and historical dimensions of mankind makes it unique among the sciences that deal with aging. Even though anthropology has only recently developed its interests in aging and the aged, its somewhat different approach can profitably supplement the work of sociologists, psychologists, social workers, and biologists. Since it concerns itself with all peoples at all times in history and prehistory, anthropology is specially equipped to deal with universal problems of aging, and through its comparative data, is able to shed valuable light on the relative adequacy or shortcomings of solutions to gerontological problems in America. The following two chapters survey the work of anthropologists in the 11 areas of gerontological research listed above. These are followed by chapters providing anthropological perspective and data on longevity, universal problems of aging, ethnic variation in aging experience, and the impact of change—particularly modernization—on the elderly.

CHAPTER 2

Research Interests: Status, Community, and the Life Cycle

STATUS AND ROLE

Anthropological interest in gerontology did not really begin until Leo Simmons (actually a Yale University sociologist) published *The Role of the Aged in Primitive Society* in 1945. An earlier encyclopedic volume by J. Koty, *Die Behandlung der Alten und Kranken bei den Naturvolkern,* had been published in Stuttgart in 1933, but it had little or no impact on American research interests. Simmons' book purported to be a "report on the status and treatment of the aged within a world-wide selection of primitive societies," and it addressed itself to such questions as What in old age are the possible adjustments to different environments, both physical and social? and What uniformities or general trends may be observed in such a broad cross-cultural analysis? Simmons' study was unique in its day, because it used elaborate and complicated statistical measurements; one reviewer described it as the "first systematic comparative analysis of the role of the aged in primitive society" (Kimball, 1946:287).

Simmons selected 71 widely distributed preindustrial societies and carefully analyzed the monographs in which they were described with an eye to differences in environment, level of technological development, and degree of cultural complexity. One-hundred nine cultural traits pertaining to (1) habitat and economy, (2) religious beliefs and practices, and (3) social and political organization were correlated with 112 traits dealing particularly with status and treatment of the elderly. Among the latter were traits pertaining to property rights, food sharing practices, community and family support, ceremonial roles, and political authority. Although some reviewers objected to some of Simmons' statistical procedures, they generally applauded his attempt to establish universals and variables of aging. Solon Kimball conceded that the book did have value as a "reference work," but he criticized Simmon's methodology on the grounds that "there is the ever-present danger that the use of isolated cultural facts, called 'traits,' outside their context may produce distortion of meaning" (1946:287). Even though this pioneer work may have contained methodological problems, Simmons must be applauded for creating a great deal of interest in aging and for laying some important groundwork for future investigation. He established, for example, that old people the world over seek (1) to preserve life as long as possible, (2) to be released from wearisome exertion and to be protected from physical hazards, (3) to maintain active participation in group affairs, (4) to safeguard prerogatives—possessions, rights, prestige, and authority—and, (5) to meet death honorably and comfortably.

Simmons further established that the status of the aged had a tendency to stem from the force of tradition and from the special skills and knowledge that they possessed. To a large extent their security, he thought, was derived from their control of property, and in many cases food for the elderly was assured either through communal sharing, through kinship obligations, or through food taboos from which the elderly were exempt. The general welfare of the aged was at least in part seen as resulting from the routine economic and personal services they perform for their family or community, and from their ability to wield civil and political power either because of individual ability or because of a combination of social and cultural factors. Simmons found that old people usually have high prestige in preindustrial societies, the only exceptions being in very rigorous climates that require great energy and stamina to survive.

Although Simmons was technically a sociologist, his methods of cross-cultural analysis in this study were certainly more anthropological than sociological. The same can be said for his earlier life history study of a Hopi Indian, *Sun Chief* (1942). Also of an anthropological nature was the work of Western Reserve University sociologist Irving Rosow, who in 1965 used much of Simmons's data in assessing the cross-cultural factors that seem to contribute positively to the treatment of the elderly. Rosow's analysis revealed that the position or status of the aged is higher if (1) they own or control property that younger people depend on; (2) their experience gives them a vital command or monopoly of strategic knowledge of the culture, including the full range of occupational skills and techniques, as well as healing, religion, ritual, warfare, lore, and the arts; (3) they are links to the past and to the gods in tradition-oriented societies; (4) the extended family is central to the social structure; (5) the population clusters in relatively small, stable communities where the governing values are sacred rather than secular, where roles are formally age graded, and where contacts are face-to-face; (6) the productivity of the economy is low and approaches the edge of starvation—the greater the poverty, the relatively better off old people are by the standards of their group; and (7) there is high mutual dependence within the group—the greater the interdependence among members, the greater the reciprocal aid in meeting survival problems.

Following both Simmons's and Rosow's suggestion that the aged are generally revered in preindustrial society because of the traditional knowledge they command, Robert Maxwell and Phillip Silverman (1970) hypothesized that societies value their aged in varying degrees, depending upon the amount of useful information they control. In their study, which they described as using the "general rubric of system theory," they analyzed data from 26 widely distributed societies, directing their attention to such aspects as information control among the aged, treatment of the aged, rate of institutional change, and ecological factors affecting the aged. Analysis of the key variable—information control—was directed at such aspects of social participation as roles in feasts and games, consulting, decision-making, entertaining, arbitrating, and teaching.

As anticipated, Maxwell and Silverman found a strong correlation between control of useful information and good treatment and high status of the aged. They stated, however, that rapid institutional change (as found in industrialized societies) generates a high rate of information obsolescence and therefore leads to an eventual deterioration of prestige for the elderly.

Another study that assessed the impact of change and technological development on the status and roles of the elderly was that of Donald O. Cowgill and Lowell D. Holmes, *Aging and Modernization* (1972). Modernization in this study was equated with industrialization, urbanization, and westernization and was analyzed as a major factor affecting the fortunes and activities of elderly men and women in 14 societies ranging from what traditionally have been called "primitive" to those of Western Europe and the United States.

Although cross-cultural in its emphasis, the study differed from those of Simmons or Maxwell and Silverman in that aging was considered entirely in terms of complete cultural contexts. The contributors to this study—eight anthropologists, seven sociologists, two psychologists, and a social worker—had all conducted extended, in-depth studies in the societies on which they reported. Cowgill and Holmes had provided each with a list of topics to discuss to ensure uniformity and continuity in the several studies, but the contributors were totally ignorant of the general theoretical propositions that their data would be used to test. The theoretical orientation for the study consisted of a number of hypotheses on the way the aged would be affected along a societal continuum from primitive to modern. A general hypothesis was that there is an inverse relationship between status of the aged and the degree of modernization, but the study also set forth 30 propositions, eight labeled "universals" and 22 identified as "variations" (to be considered in terms of unique social and cultural contexts). The uniqueness of the contexts was in this case related to the society's place on the primitive-modern continuum.

Although the data generally supported the hypotheses, a few exceptions—Russia, Israel, and Ireland—provided an interesting and unexpected challenge to the hypothesis. In general, the researchers concluded, "The theory with which we began this study has survived the test for the most part. In some cases we did not get adequate or relevant evidence. A few of our propositions were found wanting and must now be deleted or modified. These were more than balanced by serendipitous findings which we have not anticipated and were not looking for. Thus our theory has been extended and strengthened and is now ready for further testing" (1972:321).

Status considerations were also paramount in the study of Middle-American aged carried out by Irwin Press and Mike McKool (1972). Here the investigators isolated four prestige generating components in a select group of meso-American and perhaps all societies. These components are *advisory, contributory, controlling* and *residual.* The advisory component involves the extent to which the advice and opinions of the aged members of the society are heeded; the contributory component concerns the degree to which aged are allowed to participate in and contribute to ritual and economic activities. The control component concerns the degree to which the aged have authority over the behavior of other persons, institutions, or ritual processes, and the residual component pertains to the degree to which the elderly continue to retain prestige from roles performed earlier in life.

Press and McKool concluded that at least in meso-America the aged are disadvantaged in societies featuring economic heterogeneity, diversity, and discontinuity in father-son economic interests and occupations. Status of the aged was also found to be low where achieved rather than ascribed roles, nuclear families, and independence from larger kin structures are emphasized, and also where there is an early turnover of family resources. Aged status also declines in societies marked by ritual, political, and judicial bureaucracies and where modernization forces are potent.

Status and modernization forces among the Baganda of East Africa were the subjects of a gerontological study by Nina Nahemow and Bert Adams in 1974. In this society, 115 elders between the ages of 60 to 90 years were interviewed along with 1,699 secondary school students "to address the question of the salience of traditional roles for modern life and the position of the aged today" (1974:151). The Baganda are a particularly interesting society in which to conduct such a study, because the aged have no tradition of societal leadership, although it has been customary for them to give advice, serve as storytellers, and try to be "good grandparents" (1974:164). Nahemow and Adams relate that the Baganda system emphasizes individualism over familism, and personal achievement and change are viewed in a positive light. Rights over land are established through political affiliation and not through kinship. Interviews with secondary students indicated a general tendency toward negative stereotypes of the aged and they definitely rejected the idea that the aged should, merely because of their age, have any special position of authority. The investigators discovered that even the traditional role of advisor-storyteller has lost its significance under the impact of modern education. Although Baganda elders appear to have lost their function as repositories of tradition, they continue to be honored and valued as good grandparents. This is possible because of the high degree of rapport between grandparents and grandchildren. This rapport results from their sharing a common traditional value system that has always revered individualism, personal achievement, neolocality, and minimal lineage ties. In other words, modern and traditional values are so much the same that grandparents and grandchildren agree on intergenerational relations and definitions of family obligations. For example, they generally agree "that it is legitimate to criticize parents and grandparents; that grandparents should not 'spoil' grandchildren; and that each individual has a responsibility to both descending and ascending generations in terms of providing for them" (1974:161).

The Baganda example should impress us with the value of approaching every situation in terms of the total cultural context. A superficial analysis of the Baganda situation might very well result in the conclusion that modernization has been highly detrimental to the aged, but a more holistic analysis (of values and social structure) would reveal that the present situation in which the Baganda aged find themselves is not particularly out of character with tradition.

Generational problems associated with modernization were the focus of Charlotte Ikels' study "The Coming of Age in Chinese Society: Traditional Patterns and Contemporary Hong Kong" (1980). Ikels' research dealt with the ideal of filial piety and the realities of everyday family life in overcrowded Hong Kong. Here she found that the veneration of age, so often identified with Chinese culture, was mostly enjoyed by the well-to-do. One of the reasons that the concept of filial piety is breaking down is that many of the supporting features—such as family property—do not exist in the urban setting. Also, the percentage of aged in Hong Kong is far greater than in rural areas. Because of increasing strain in intergenerational relations, Chinese elders have adopted a practice of carefully selecting and cultivating the child who will willingly respond when parents need support. Although Ikels' study confirms the fact that filial piety and respect for the wisdom of the aged remain paramount within the Chinese value system, she maintains that such ideas are difficult to carry out where population density approaches 400,000 per square mile.

Still another study of age status using a world sample was produced by Tom Sheehan (1976), who investigated the relationship between esteem for elders and the economic and political nature of the societies of which they were members. Forty-seven societies representing three levels of societal complexity were studied to determine elders' decision-making authority in interpersonal relationships and over offices and material or intangible property. The types of societies compared were (1) geographically unstable—that is, semipermanent bands ranging from people who periodically relocate their villages to complete nomads; (2) various tribes inhabiting fairly large, permanent villages; and (3) nucleated peasant communities with an economic base of agriculture or animal husbandry.

Esteem for the aged, defined by Sheehan as "the intersection of decision-making role or resource control and quality of received behavior" (1976:433), was definitely found to correlate with societal type. For example, Sheehan found that the lowest esteem for the aged is found in societies with the simplest and smallest socioeconomic structures. He reasons that "they have the fewest material resources and human relationships available for control and are usually located in harsh environments favoring youth and vigor" (1976:436). The highest esteem for elders was enjoyed in large-landed peasantries with highly developed social organizations. Although Sheehan was not specifically interested in change and its effect on elders' status, he did comment that the decline in status or esteem often observed in societies involved in modernization may result from a weakening of the social structure and it therefore represents, in effect, a return to a less complex societal level. The author explains:

> The community turns away from extended family living or kin loyalties. With different emphases, both capitalist and socialist structures replace familial orientations with other-directed individualism on a mass level. A partial return is therefore made to the ideology of the nomadic band: old age and seniors are not accorded special status. (1976:437)

Although the majority of the studies dealing with status and role of the aged have tended to dwell on societal conditions or cultural factors, Virginia Kerns (1980) reports on a society, the Black Carib of Belize, where elders through individual activity and appropriate interaction affect their own status. To begin with, Kerns found a great gap between the ideal and the manifest in regard to intergenerational relations. Obligations to parents and affection for elders are values and sentiments universally espoused but not always realized, and there is a great range in societal observance. What is found is a great deal of pragmatic behavior on the part of elders to ensure their security within the kinship and village structure. Older women, for example, work at making themselves indispensable within kin relationships. Kerns explains, "The parent-child relationship is the central social bond" (1980:120), and what is significant about this relationship is its reciprocal nature. Therefore, the quality of support of the elderly depends greatly on the quality of the parent-child relationship throughout life. Parents strive to establish themselves as someone to "bank on," someone to call upon for help when it is needed. Elderly parents also control their security by using potential public opinion as a source of pressure on errant adult children.

In summarizing the significance for gerontology of her Black Carib experience, Kerns writes:

> There is no denying that the ideal of filial responsibility is an important one to the Black Carib, but certainly the efforts that aged parents must make to enforce this ideal are equally worthy of attention. These efforts argue against the popular conception of the elderly as passive dependents. (1980:124)

The impact of modernization on the status of Samoan aged was the focus of a research project carried out by Ellen C. Rhoads (1981) in three Samoan communities in 1976-1977. This research represented a test of the Cowgill-Holmes (1972) hypothesis that modernization and status of the aged are inversely related. Samoan society was chosen because of a strong tradition of respect and special care for aged, plus the fact that Samoa has been rapidly modernizing since 1963 and many Samoans have emigrated to the United States. Focusing on four areas of modernization cited by Cowgill (1974)—health technology, economic technology, urbanization, and education—as having special relevance for determining the status of the aged, Rhoads carried out participant observation and interview in the isolated village of Ta'u in Manu'a; in the main port and government center, Fagatogo; and in the Samoan migrant community in the San Francisco Bay area. Comparisons were also made with data obtained by Holmes in a 1962 study of Samoan aged.

Rhoads discovered that although the three research sites represented progressive levels of modernization, the Samoan aged have managed to retain relatively high status in all three settings. This, she claims, is primarily due to the continuing strength of the Samoan extended family system (*aiga*). Although her findings appear to question the Cowgill-Holmes hypothesis, Rhoads believes that there are indications of pending problems that could, with time, cause a change for the worse. She writes, "The time factor cannot be overlooked and should be taken into consideration in future theorizing on the effect of modernization on status of elders. In Samoa, the fourteen years since the beginning of modernization may be too short a time for the development of the predicted effects. To my knowledge no one has said much about how much time is needed to produce a decline in status" (1981:147).

Although neither Erdman Palmore nor Kenneth Manton are anthropologists, their cross-cultural study on modernization and status of the aged (1974) has direct bearing on much of the anthropological research described on the previous page. In a study that used data from 31 societies (including non-Western ones, such as Ghana, Indonesia, Malaysia, Korea, Costa Rica, and Honduras) Palmore and Manton first established an index of modernization based on (1) gross national product per capita, (2) percentage of labor force in agriculture, (3) percentage literate, (4) percentage of youths in school, and (5) percentage of population in higher education. Status of the aged was then measured in terms of a so-called Equality Index of employment, occupation and education. Regarding the EI the investigators write:

> The lower the employment EI, the lower the rate of employment of the aged compared to the nonaged, which indicates lower income and greater dependency among the aged. Similarly, the lower the occupation EI, the less the employed aged are in the same kinds of occupations as the major part of the work force, which usually indicates less of the aged in the better paying and more prestigious business and professional occupations. The lower the education EI, the less the aged are in the higher levels of education because of generally increasing levels of education among younger persons. (1974:206-207)

What Palmore and Manton discovered in regard to the relationship between old age status and modernization was a "J-shaped" pattern. That is to say, they found that status of the aged fell during the early stages of modernization but bottomed out and began to climb in the advanced stages. They conclude that during early stages of modernization there are great discrepancies in the behavior and attitudes of the aged and the nonaged, but as societies "mature," rates of change level off and the discrepancies between young and old begin to decrease. Palmore and Manton's findings were, of course, acquired by comparing societies at various levels of modernization and not by studying the progress of modernization and its ramifications within a single society. They suggest that "longitudinal analysis of changes in status of the aged within modernizing countries are needed to test the applicability of these theories to specific countries" (1974:210).

COMMUNITY STUDIES

During the 1960s a burning gerontological issue was whether old people should be segregated in age-homogeneous retirement residences or whether they should remain integrated in society and participate in activities without reference to age. Some elders are extremely happy sharing life with people of their own age, but one survey (TIAA Cref, 1974) revealed that just as many volunteer such advice as "Don't hole up in a senior citizen enclave or retirement home until you must. Stay where you can get mad at the school kids cutting across your lawn."

Of course, the question of what kind of community is best for the elderly is important, because such matters are often important government policy concerns or involve private-sector capital investment. When bureaucrats and real-estate developers initially turned to the social scientists for answers, the social scientists had to admit that they frankly didn't know what kind of community situation would best meet the physical, psychological, and social needs of the elderly.

Although the majority of researchers in gerontology were sociologists in the 1960s, a number of anthropologists were particularly interested in this question. Community study was not new to anthropologists, because most of them had worked in small isolated communities in preindustrial societies and had evolved a methodology appropriate to this kind of research. Also, they were especially interested in the *nature* of community. Robert Redfield had produced a classic study, *The Little Community and Peasant Society and Culture* (1960), as well as documented the characteristics of "The Folk Society" (1947). Redfield defined community in terms of distinctiveness and group consciousness, size (small enough for ongoing interaction), homogeneity (sharing common goals and values), and self-sufficiency. Arensberg and Kimball (1968) had suggested that "community" is not a thing, but a process and that it must be understood in terms of ongoing human interactions—adjustments, compromises, and cooperation. Therefore, when anthropologists turned to an analysis of communities of aged they were interested in an applied problem: What is the best residence for the elderly? They also addressed theoretical aspects: What is community? How does it develop? What are its functions for the elderly?

One of the first anthropologists to take an interest in the aged community question was Jerry Jacobs. Jacobs not only produced a detailed ethnography of a retirement community in southern California which he facetiously titled *Fun City* but he also analyzed the characteristics of several others. In *Old Persons and Retirement Communities*, Jacobs contrasted three different kinds of retirement residences with the goal of "providing some initial insight into the question of retirement and retirement settings and a basis for a grounded theory of aging" (1975:vi). Jacobs was not only interested in the quality of life for elderly in a variety of retirement settings but he was also interested in exploring the theory of "disengagement," which holds that as old people grow older they tend to disengage from social and economic relationships and that this is beneficial to them and to their society.

Jacobs looked first at High Haven, a 21-story retirement residence of "well elderly" located on a university campus in a middle-sized eastern city. The facility was originally established under a federal grant to the university, and the school, along with the city housing authority, administered a program specially designed to promote interaction between elderly residents and university students living in adjacent dormitories. Interaction was supposed to take the form of eating together in the university dining room, sharing a snack bar, attending a film series together, and attending holiday parties. It was anticipated that this arrangement would result in greater intergenerational understanding and that the students and the elderly residents could assist one another in solving their respective personal problems.

Neither the 420 residents nor the students were informed that they were social science guinea pigs in an experiment in intergenerational living, and very little interaction took place. Segregation by age is, after all, a predominant pattern in American life. Some aspects of the experiment were put into operation, but after a time the university's grant ran out and the administration of High Haven became the sole responsibility of the municipal housing authority. The snack bar closed for lack of business, the elderly found the dining facility too expensive, and attendance dropped at the film series. The elderly residents, unhappy with their campus environment, began haranguing one another; cliques developed and this resulted in some people becoming recluses. Several residents attempted suicide, and alcoholism became a major problem. Thus, the experiment in creating an artificial intergenerational community proved to be not only nonproductive but nearly a disaster.

Jacobs next contrasted his High Haven findings with his findings from Fun City, an age homogeneous community that he studied much as he might have studied an exotic tribal society. Fun City was a specially planned tract-home town of 6,000 white middle- and upper-class elderly. It was a relatively isolated (90 miles from a metropolitan area) community located in a warm (often hot) valley in California. The name *Fun City* was coined by Jacobs because of the stress developers had placed on the community's many recreational opportunities. Fun City, however, had no young people (except visiting family members), no people of color, no people of less than middle-class means, no hospital, no fire department, and no security force. Jobs, for those who sought to relieve boredom with parttime employment, were limited, and shopping facilities were less than adequate. The two so-called supermarkets and a coffee shop actually had more social value than they did as a source of food and other supplies. Shopping became a valued means of meeting people and breaking the boredom. Although the people of High Haven had a multitude of problems and complaints, Jacobs believed that they fared better than the people of Fun City, since they were able to be in contact with friends and relatives constantly, while the isolation of Fun City rarely permitted its residents to maintain close ties with either family members or former friends.

The third old-age residence described by Jacobs was Merrill Court, a community of 43 elderly welfare recipients living in a small apartment building in San Francisco. Rent was only $55 a month, provided the tenants did not have an income of more than $3,000 a year. Merrill Court was not isolated like Fun City but it too had no black or Jewish residents. Nearly all were widows. Although they had little in the way of planned activities, they are described as relatively happy and generally in good health. Merrill Court residents appear to have developed greater participation, reciprocal aid, and social involvement than was true of the residents of either High Haven or Fun City. Arlie Hochschild, who did the original study of this community in 1966-1969, believes that the study shows that old people who live among other old people make more friends than old people who live among young people (1973:28-29).

Based on his somewhat limited but diverse sample of retirement homes, Jacobs concluded that these are not just unique examples of retirement communities and that they are important in understanding a number of basic theoretical issues. He believed, for example, that "it may be more fruitful to consider not so much the merits of this or that kind of retirement setting, but the pattern of social interaction within these various settings." Moreover, he believed that "similar settings may produce very different interaction patterns and that this is best understood not only with reference to the kind of setting, but also with respect to special characteristics of the individuals comprising it" (1975:121-122).

A study of a public housing project for the elderly in Milwaukee produced results that somewhat paralleled those of the Merrill Court project. This study showed that age-homogeneous housing can have a positive influence on the mental and physical health of residents. Eunice Boyer (1980) found that residential homogeneity did not produce a ghetto of the rejected aged, but rather it allowed residents to overcome mobility limitations (thereby permitting greater social participation), gave them a greater opportunity for leadership, reduced isolation, allowed a more vigorous social life to develop, and gave greater opportunity for mutual aid and exchange of helpful services. Because they had less anxiety about need satisfaction and because they had increased social activity and opportunity to play useful community roles, the residents had a decidedly positive perception of their own physical and mental health and well-being.

A special issue of *Anthropological Quarterly* in 1979 was devoted entirely to papers on age-homogeneous communities. The issue, edited by Jennie Keith, focused on cultural differences in communities comprised of elderly with a variety of class and ethnic backgrounds. For example, it described styles of community participation among Cubans, blacks, Sephardians, and whites and attempted to identify factors that promote or obstruct community formation among old people. Researchers touched on such aspects of group behavior as the *affective* (we-feeling), and the *structural* (social interaction and shared norms) and an analysis of *boundary* (relationship of the new community to the surrounding society).

The editorship of this special volume was for Keith a continuation of a career-long interest in the concept of community and how it is manifest in a variety of settings involving the aged. Beginning with her doctoral dissertation and continuing through a recent book (1982) Keith has been concerned with the analysis of community formation and functioning. A comparison of eight widely varied retirement communities has resulted in her formulation of a set of characteristics common to all. They are (1) a common shared territory, which is jealously protected against encroachment by outsiders, (2) a strong sense of in-group/out-group differences, (3) shared norms and common goals, and (4) clearly defined roles and statuses, that is to say, a social system. Keith believes, however, that the real meaning of community rests not in models or prerequisite functions but in flesh-and-blood relationships. She writes:

> All of these old people have turned to each other for many kinds of social needs. They are friends, lovers and factional adversaries; they protect each other in illness and emergency; they laugh, dance and mourn together. They evaluate each other in terms of the life they share, rather than according to the status ladders of the outside world where they are guaranteed a place on the bottom rung. That outside world is seen as dangerous in many ways: physically, financially, socially and psychologically; the community of age-mates is a refuge from all of these threats. (1977:192)

Although anthropologists traditionally seek cross-cultural perspective in their study of human behavior, the bulk of age-homogeneous community study has been done in the United States. An exception to this pattern is the study of Les Floralies, a retirement community located in a Paris suburb. This study, also conducted by Jennie Keith (Ross), focused on community formation and maintenance in a French working class retirement home and then compared it with what the "west end of Boston, a trailer park in northern California, and a band of Pygmies in the Congo have in common" (1977:4-5).

Les Floralies is the major focus in Keith's study of community, although she goes on to compare it with a variety of retirement home settings in the United States in an attempt to understand such important gerontological issues as: Under what conditions does "community" develop in a residence for old people? What is the relationship between patterns of social life inside and those of the wider society outside? How do people learn to participate in this new kind of community? How does this community made up exclusively of old people differ from more heterogeneous ones?

Keith's study reveals that community creation among the aged is not materially different from community creation among any other group of people, but perhaps studies of the aged reveal important factors that are taken for granted or overlooked in other groups. Keith observes, "Friendship, love, conflict, power, laughter at 'in' jokes, support in the face of common fears and sorrows, and roles to structure time and action are the stuff of everyday social life, so necessary that most of us take them profoundly for granted. To the old, they often become both scarce and precious. By preserving these possibilities for each other, older people join in a kind of communal conspiracy to continue living like human beings" (1977:198).

Thus Keith concludes that common age can become a context for community; social interaction appears to be greater in age-homogeneous groups, and this increased contact between age mates means that morale is usually higher.

NETWORKS

Anthropologists can no longer expect the communities they study to have clearly defined boundaries, particularly if they are working in their own society. When anthropologists studied mainly in preindustrial societies, they observed people who lived together in a limited area (usually a village) and who interacted in a daily face-to-face relationship. Many communities composed of aged are still like this, but in areas where old people do not live in special segregated housing their communities are not always clearly defined. Because of this, anthropologists have had to resort to network analysis to identify communities, because sometimes viable communities exist only as chains of social and economic linkages, or cliques, of interacting individuals. According to Barnes, "The study of networks calls for information about a plurality of persons who are in contact with one another, and consequently the traditional methods of selecting respondents individually are inadequate" (1972:23).

Network analysis has been used effectively by Sokolovsky and Cohen (1978) in analyzing degrees of isolation of inner-city elderly, particularly those living in single room occupancy (SRO) hotels. Studies of elderly living in such environments have stressed their isolation, anonymity, normlessness, and lack of communication resources. Sokolovsky and Cohen contend that this perception is incorrect and is "distorted by a tendency to study social linkages within the context of formal institutional structures rather than viewing the social matrix as culturally significant in itself" (1978:324). Their work, as well as recent anthropological research on SROs in New York and San Diego (also using network analysis), reveals that considerable social interaction takes place within and outside SRO hotels. One study (Cantor, 1975) reports that 80% of the hotel residents sit and talk with neighbors in front of the building or in nearby parks, and two-thirds of them have a visiting relationship with neighbors. Some investigators have found a real sense of community within these inner city hotels, although personal networks may be temporary. Extensive personal networks operate during the day but there is a drastic curtailment of interpersonal contact at night. This is, of course, due to fear of street crimes and assaults. This threat has resulted in an increase of neurotic symptoms associated with the night in both SRO hotel and inner-city tenement dwellers.

SRO residents are often called loners, but Sokolovsky and Cohen believe that such designations do not accurately describe SRO behavior, because many of these "loners" have larger than average personal networks. *Loner* does, however, describe a world view that appears to have adaptive utility in a difficult inner-city milieu.

Network analysis also proved useful in a foreign culture where Linda Cool (1980) used the technique to identify and analyze a community of elderly Corsicans living in Paris. She found a very effective structure of kinship and friendship bonds being used to combat feelings of loneliness and homesickness and to solve a variety of personal problems. Cool writes, "All but a few elderly Niolans can find the assistance they need in special situations—someone to talk to about difficult problems and someone on whom they can rely in an emergency. Sixty-nine of the 74 sample members report that they have a confidante, either relative or friend. All but one of the elderly Niolans feel they have someone to call on in case of an emergency. Seventy individuals know of people on whom they could rely if they were sick, even for an extended period of time" (1980:158).

Network analysis also has its uses in discovering channels of interaction and interdependence within an age-homogeneous community. Jonas and Wellin (1980) found the method valuable in studying ways in which problems of transportation, health care, and household maintenance were solved by elderly living in a public housing project in Milwaukee. Although the housing unit itself represented a kind of community, the investigators were particularly concerned with who does what for whom, why, and how often. In discovering this kind of data, Jonas and Wellin learned how social and mutual-aid networks develop and function and to what extent they serve as effective ways to meet old people's needs. They found that peer responsibility for long-term support of disabled friends greatly relieved pressures on relatives, deferred institutionalization, and reduced demands on public-assistance programs. Not only did reciprocal aid by peers meet physical needs, but it also permitted the aged a degree of independence since it allowed them to continue living in their own apartments and gave them a measure of self-esteem because they could contribute to the needs of others.

Network creation was cited as a valuable procedure in organizing self-help among the aged in San Francisco (Ruffini and Todd, 1979). Here an organization known as Senior Block Information Service (SBIS) was organized and operated by Services to Seniors (San Francisco Council of Churches) to develop leadership and to promote peer aid among the elderly in the Sunset and Richmond districts. Even though organizations of this type are not particularly unique in American cities, the program had a number of special features that could be reproduced elsewhere. By establishing block-based networks, volunteers can have modest and limited duties that require no transportation. They are called on to aid only their neighbors and only when necessary.

Agencies often expect too much of their elderly volunteers, suggest Ruffini and Todd, and therefore they recommend this network approach where large numbers of people (neighbors) can be recruited for limited, close-to-home service. The alternative, which is more often put in operation, is the so-called community action system wherein a few active people are called on to provide a great deal of service to strangers. The network system not only reduces personal obligation, but it also serves as a means for acquiring new neighborhood friends who are likely to share similar goals.

AGE GRADES

Retirement communities, we have noted, are often called *age homogeneous,* although they may include people who range in age from 60 to 100 years. *Age homogeneous* is an adjectival phrase that could better be used to describe the elderly in some non-Western cultures, because many such societies have what is known as an age-grade or age-set system. Approximately three-fourths of societies that age grade are in Africa, where about 15% of the tribes have this feature.

A good example of an age-grade system is that of the Nandi of East Africa. According to A.C. Hollis (1909), the social system of the Nandi has three age categories for males (boys, warriors, and elders) and two for females (girls and married women). A circumcision ritual marking the advent of manhood takes place about every 15 years, accommodating boys varying in age from 10 to 20 years. Although there are only three major age divisions for males there are actually some seven age sets in all—each composed of all those who underwent their initiation into manhood together. Before this ritual, the boys must spend two years in military instruction, because after the initiation they are officially warriors. After several years as warriors, when they concentrate on making war and making love, they graduate to the status of elder and as such are expected to settle down, marry, and raise a family. The elder category contains several age subdivisions, and eventually if a man lives long enough, he, along with his surviving age mates, serve their society as statemen and tribal advisors. Age-graded societies are often labeled gerontocracies, but it is also possible to have a gerontocracy (society governed by the elderly) without an age-grade system.

While anthropologists have long been interested in age-graded societies, only recently have anthropological perspectives focused on age stratification in our own society. Of particular note is the work of Asmarom Legesse (1979), who looks at the American retirement community as a kind of age grade and compares its social structure with that found in African societies.

Although African age grades and retirement communities differ in many ways, they have a number of common features. First, Legesse points out that a process of resocialization is inevitable as an age group enters each new age status, and he maintains that this is clearly observable in American elderly as they become assimilated into retirement communities. He writes, "The intolerance toward noisy children, the heightened intolerance toward authority figures, the elimination of pre-retirement status distinctions or symbols, and the establishment of egalitarian peer relationships are all examples of behavior changes" (1970:63).

Second, Legesse suggests that initiation rituals that are frequently found in non-Western age-graded societies find a parallel in American retirement residences in "the seductive advertising, the encounter with the manager, the screening procedures, admission into the community, the purchase of a lot, the taboos attendant on membership . . . . All these steps strike one as fairly elaborate role induction procedure and are perhaps the modern functional equivalents of rites of transition" (1979:63).

Several years ago, S.N. Eisenstadt postulated that "age-homogeneous groups tend to arise in those societies in which the allocation of roles, facilities and rewards is not based on membership in kinship units and criteria" (1956:54). Legesse wonders if, according to this idea, the strength of ties within the retirement community and the strength of ties with people outside the community are related. Cross-cultural data cast doubt on the Eisenstadt hypothesis, however, and data from other gerontological studies show that "the more friends an individual has among the elderly, the more likely he or she is to maintain family ties outside the community" (1979:63).

Legesse also contends that age-set systems universally seem to be marked by egalitarianism in their organization and values, but that the relationship between age sets is that of a pecking order. Within the age set, peers support one another but tend to be intolerant of outside authority figures. Similarly, our age-homogeneous retirement communities "lack in internal hierarchical organization and are extremely intolerant of bosses of any kind . . . who supervise the communities. Even the informal governments that emerge in retirement communities are fairly broad based and democratically recruited" (1979:65).

Another similarity between age sets and age-homogeneous communities is that members of both behave like novices when entering a new phase of the life cycle. Legesse writes of our age-homogeneous group residents, "They behave like novices who are not entirely sure as to how to form the communities and what rules should govern their new lives. They are supervised in this process not by their elders but by a *younger* group of men and women who hold positions of authority because of their expertise" (1979:66).

This reversal of what is normally found in age-graded societies the world over—elders being initiated by younger people—is unnatural at least in age-grade terms and may be responsible for many of the problems encountered by residents and administrators alike.

Legesse's comparison of age grades and retirement communities also calls attention to the subject of group competition. The retirement community, on the one hand, exists within a pluralistic society and therefore may include a variety of racial and ethnic representatives. Data concerning age-grade societies, on the other hand, reveal that they have much less sociocultural diversity and therefore little or no deviance that can threaten the structure. One wonders if American ethnic variations can be successfully reconciled or if the normal age-grade tendency toward forcing members into a narrow mold will prevail, perhaps to the destruction of the group. Although these questions pique our academic interest, comparisons of retirement communities with age-grade systems may also prove to be a fruitful approach to understanding the dynamics of age-homogeneous living. Regardless of where we look in the world, all societies tend to have a number of common organization and transition problems.

Unlike families, both age grades and retirement communities are transitory and must draw on a different method of achieving unity and cooperation. Age-grade analysis is a good example of how the findings of anthropologists in non-Western societies can be brought to bear in promoting a clearer understanding of the nature and functioning of our own social institutions.

CROSS-CULTURAL STUDIES OF HOMES FOR AGED

Descriptions of retirement residences in other cultures are relatively scarce in the anthropological literature. To a certain extent, this is because the traditional pattern among nonliterate peoples has been that the elderly were invariably cared for in the home by the family. However, in 1951 Albert Abrams reported on "Trends in Old Age Homes and Housing for the Aged in Various Parts of the World" in a New York legislative report on aging. Abrams' survey of 68 countries revealed that "the old age home is common in most of the western world," but "is uncommon or completely unknown in some near-Eastern and small Central American countries" (1951:268).

Examples of societies where old age homes were completely unknown in 1951 included Iran, Lebanon, Pakistan, Thailand, Liberia, Ethiopia, Nicaragua, and Costa Rica. Generally, he found a positive correlation throughout the world between high industrialization and urbanization and the existence of old age homes. On the other hand, he found an inverse relationship between cultures stressing family responsibility and the existence of homes for the aged. There were, however, a few notable exceptions to this. Cultures that stress family responsibility but are in the process of changing from an agricultural-based to an industry-based economy are beginning to find a need for old age homes. Such has been the case in Japan, Korea, Burma, Ceylon, China, Saudi Arabia, and Mexico. Some countries such as India, which had a national life expectancy of 27, had relatively little need for old-age residences since only a small percentage achieved elderly status.

Abrams also discovered that relatively long life span and scarcity of inexpensive domestic help were consistently associated with the existence of homes for the elderly in non-Western cultures. Apparently inexpensive and readily available domestic help takes some of the strain off the family who can hire people to help them meet their obligations to elders.

Gerontologists generally believe that as societies become more modern, responsibility for the aged shifts from the family or clan to the society as a whole, with specific responsibility being placed on either the local or national government. While this is generally true, many of the homes for aged in developing, non-Western countries are church, industry, or philanthropic group supported. If the homes are supported by national or local governments, they are financed through general taxation or lotteries.

MAPUIFAGALELE: SAMOAN HOME FOR THE AGED

In some cases, studies of old people's residences in societies that have traditionally cared for the aged within the family provide important insights into the problems associated with modernization or other forms of cultural change. Such is the case in Western Samoa, where a home known as Mapuifagalele (haven of peace) was established

Western Polynesia's first home for the aged, Mapufagalele (Photo by Lowell D. Holmes.)

by Cardinal Pio and the Little Sisters of the Poor in 1975. A report on this institution by Rhoads and Holmes (1981) describes this home outside the port town of Apia as the residence of 83 Samoans (38 men and 45 women) whose average age is 75. Although Samoa is a place where people vehemently insist that families should and do take good care of their own elderly, Rhoads and Holmes maintain that changing economic and social conditions are creating problems that seem to necessitate institutional care. They write:

> The economic picture in Western Samoa, along with shifting value emphases, appears to be a major factor associated with the development of the institution. There is very little industry and wages are generally low. Education has become increasingly important to Western Samoans, but it is not free. It is the opinion of some informants that the emphasis of education and the concomitant cost of tuition for families with several school-aged children has resulted in a shift in priority from the aged to the young. (1981:132-133)

They further suggest that the migration of substantial numbers of young adults to New Zealand in recent years has also affected the structure of the family and may have contributed to the care problems of some elderly.

LIFE-CYCLE ANALYSIS

Margaret Clark once pointed out that "anthropologists have long claimed the study of cultural patterning of the human life cycle, with its various phases, transitions, and rites of passage, as one of their special concerns" (1968:433). Crane and Angosino maintain that "every complete ethnography should give the reader an understanding of the life cycle of the people in question—what it is like to be born, to live each phase of life, and to die in that particular society" (1974:74). Unfortunately, however, the focus in anthropology has been on the earlier years in the life cycle—infancy, childhood, adolescence, and early adult years. Only since Simmons (1945) have the final years of life received any great amount of attention.

Anthropological gerontologists have found a number of interesting questions associated with the life cycle: When does old age begin? How is one supposed to behave when identified as old? Do all cultures use the same criteria in determining the onset of old age? Of course, all societies in the world recognize a number of phases of the life cycle. Shakespeare's seven ages of man is but one of many systems of dividing up life. Regardless of how the life cycle is divided, all societies recognize old age as a definite status.

Most societies also believe that certain kinds of behavior are appropriate to the different life stages, and most societies have well agreed on markers by which to recognize the beginning of old age. In the United States and in much of the Western world, one becomes old at age 65, regardless of one's biological condition. That is when most individuals are given their gold watch for long and faithful service to their employers and told to go home, retire, and start collecting their pensions and Social Security. This system of determining the onset of old age is based on an arbitrary sum of years (65) and bears no relationship to the individual's personality, vitality, biological condition, or mental acuity. Such a system is *chronological*.

The alternative method of reckoning age, and the one used by most non-Western cultures is a *functional* system. That is, a person is considered old when he or she is no longer able to be a fully productive, participating member of society. A person who has reached this stage does not necessarily command less respect, but special considerations are forthcoming from fellow societal members. People who are considered old are given the right to work at their own speed, to engage in special kinds of duties, or perhaps to do nothing at all, having already put in a lifetime of productive labor.

Various circumstances seem to determine how and when old age is recognized. Cowgill and Holmes postulated that "the concept of old age itself appears to be relative to the degree of modernization" (1972:7). That is to say, as societies become more modern, the age at which one becomes old goes up. Moreover, in some areas where the elderly were eligible for government assistance or Social Security, evidence indicated functional definitions for old age had been completely replaced by a chronological one.

Christine Fry (1980:42) conducted a study of age markers and appropriate age behavior in the United States, and she sought answers to such questions as: What makes us old, culturally? How is age differentiated and structured into a cultural system? What are the expectations and standards of acceptable behavior for different age groups? Fry used an ethnoscience (involving establishment of emic categories) approach to age cognition. Believing that aging is more than a series of birthday celebrations, she developed a methodology for understanding aging in terms of certain kinds of life-cycle events or conditions related to involvement and responsibility in domestic, career, and public spheres. When she approached cultural aging in terms of such dimensions as engagement-responsibility, reproductive cycle, and encumberment, Fry discovered that the following was characteristic of the American life cycle:

> As the life time becomes longer, the statuses are marked by increasing responsibilities and engagement in the social system. This progression is then "intersected" by further responsibilities with the possible arrival of children and then their maturation. Finally, the horseshoe is complete as the sequence of statuses is marked by an increasing withdrawal primarily from occupational engagement. (1980:53)

In general, Fry found the typical American life history to run something like this: Before the age of 25 role changes are frequent and marital status is likely to change from single to married. Between 25 and 35 Americans establish their major work commitments and are involved with preschool and beginning schoolchildren. Ages 35 to 50 are marked by highly productive job activity; family households contain high school children but during this period the "empty nest" becomes a reality. Beyond 50, reference to children disappears and widowhood and retirement become typical. Approaching aging as something multidimensional rather than unidimensional (in terms of years) permits the investigator to discover "how age is interlaced with basic issues that must be resolved by all cultures" (1980:44). Fry believes her cross-cultural approach could be fruitful in understanding "the underlying cultural organization, the commonalities and variations, of an issue which is universal for all humankind—aging" (1980:61).

In a study that in some ways resembled that of Fry's, Bradd Shore asked informants in Western Samoa in 1975 to associate age-appropriate behavior or associations with recognized age categories. That is to say, informants were asked to match such descriptive phrases as *free life, protected, sits, evil behavior, respected, peaceful, stupid, dignity, does chores, evil behavior* with the age divisions *pepe* (0-3 years), *tama'ititi* (4-12), *tagata talavou* (13-20), *tagata matua* (30-60), and *lo'omatua* and *toea'ina* (over 60) (see Table 2.1).

Dianne Kagan carried her interest in indigenous age designations to the peasant village of Bojaca, Colombia, where she found the life cycle divided into "babies," "children," "young people," "adults," and "old people." Although informants had no trouble conceptualizing the stages, they also warned that chronological boundaries could not or should not be assigned to these age grades. One informant pointed out, for example, that many Bojaca females of 15 are married, have children, and function as responsible adults. Although a precise number of years could not be assigned to old age, the greater share of local inhabitants believed that the elderly should be given

Table 2.1. Survey on Aging in Samoa: Cultural Associations with Stages of Maturation

	0–3	4–12	Age (years) 13–30	30–60	Over 60
Free life	142	120	18	20	63
Protected	171	88	50	23	49
Controlled	4	21	66	162	74
No judgment	86	144	45	9	2
Evil behavior	0	110	121	16	4
Smart	6	52	114	91	29
Sits	71	126	6	23	173
Serves	36	29	163	105	6
Does chores	—	124	183	54	6
Roams about	12	152	58	10	11
Respected	2	4	17	139	142
Works	—	16	183	88	7
Stupid	69	48	7	6	46
Stays at home	61	5	1	22	200
Runs the family	—	2	3	154	132
Lives happily	95	145	54	19	30
Peaceful	142	72	6	16	77
Hard life	4	7	72	98	32
Dignity	—	1	16	137	127
Strong	53	65	146	63	6
Difficulties	46	82	56	36	44

SOURCE: Data from Bradd Shore.

NOTE: Informants were asked to place an X in the column under the age category that each description in the left column best suggests and to use only one X for each descriptive phrase.

greater deference and respect than those in other age categories and that old age is a period marked by greater dependency. They did not see old age as a period of idleness but rather as one where active contributions could be made to community life in such areas as religion, food preparation, manual skills, folk medicine, horticulture and nature lore, personal counseling, and advice on questions of justice.

The Bojaca model was found to be one where during the life cycle "the aging adult experiences increasing degrees of biological change and psychological change as he or she passes from middle years into old age. The aging individual must also come to terms with the changes in the manner in which he or she is perceived by others.... The older person is often expected to drop former roles and activities and assume new ones more appropriate to the new category" (1980:77).

Although those in Bojaca occasionally disagree over age-appropriate behavior, both young and old share values that preclude any identity crisis that might be experienced by anyone just entering the category of *vejez* (old age).

One of the more unique approaches to the life cycle is that of Myerhoff, Simic, and others in their book *Life's Career—Aging*. Here aging is presented as a *career* or a life's work. The authors explain their perspective as one that

> stresses old age as a period of activity, participation, self-movement, and purposefulness. It holds that aging cannot be understood in isolation but rather must be conceived as the product of a building process involving the entire life span. Old age is not a passive state but one evoking dynamic responses. To live each day with dignity, alertness, control over one's faculties, and mobility necessitates the output of tremendous energy, and in the most general sense of the word, it is a kind of *work*. (1978:240)

The volume brings together the research conclusions of five anthropologists, each of whom considers old age and aging in relation to a particular cultural tradition, including the Chagga of Tanzania (by Sally Moore), the slum residents of Mexico City (by Carlos Velez), the Mexican Americans in East Los Angeles (by Jose Cuellar), the Yugoslavians in central Europe and the Yugoslavian-Americans in northern California (by Andrei Simic), and the Jewish Americans from east Europe living in Venice, California (by Barbara Myerhoff).

The study has three major focuses: continuity, sexual dichotomy, and aging as a career. *Continuity* emphasizes process and relates to exploring the way events and ideas of one period are tied to those of the next. It concerns stability of ideas, values, and symbols and the permanency of interpersonal relations through time. Although all human beings value continuity, the authors propose that for those approaching the end of their lives, interconnectedness becomes a dominant theme and "that there is a tremendous impetus toward the maintenance of continuity, and where it is lacking, toward its reestablishment" (1978:236).

Sexual dichotomy relates to the way society defines appropriate areas of influence, responsibility, and behavior for men and women. These change during the life cycle, and it is important to understand how men and women pass from one status to another and how power peaks and wanes at various periods in life.

Finally, viewing *aging as a career* provides an alternative to the usual conception that growing old is simply a series of losses to be endured. On the contrary, it introduces the idea that although "losses do occur with the passing of years, gains are clearly accrued as well. However, these gains are not distributed equally to all, and the analogy to a career in its everyday sense of the meaning also suggests the idea of differential success . . . . In every society the rewards possible in old age depend to a great extent on the individual ability, resourcefulness, good judgment, and luck at every point during the life cycle" (1978:241).

SUMMARY

Beginning with Leo Simmons's study of role and status of the elderly in primitive society in 1945, anthropologists have explored this area with considerable interest, considering the relationship of role and status to such factors as control of useful information, ecological circumstances and subsistence patterns, ritual participation, societal structure, and long-term value orientations such as filial piety. More recently investigators have assessed the influence of modernization and westernization on senior status and have described the impact of migration, technology, urbanization, and education.

Anthropologists have always been comfortable studying small homogeneous communities (particularly in non-Western societies), and it is not surprising therefore that they have been partial to research on retirement residences and communities. In the many studies that have been undertaken, their interests have centered on such questions as what community is, on the evaluation of quality of life in a variety of institutional settings, and on the more basic question of whether elders should live in a community of their age peers or in the society at large. The study of community in complex urban America has, however, presented researchers with methodological problems, and in many cases they have been forced to turn to network analysis to locate "community" and study its patterns of interaction and interdependence.

Retirement communities have often been termed "age-homogeneous" groupings, and some theorists have compared them to age-graded societies in other parts of the world. Actually, age-graded societies and age-homogeneous communities have much in common in regard to attitudes and interaction patterns of members. In spite of these behavioral similarities, the retirement home is a uniquely Western phenomenon. A few nursing homes and senior citizen residences have been established in non-Western countries like Samoa which are experiencing the disorganizing influences of modernization, but usually these establishments have been initiated by people from outside the culture, such as missionaries or religious orders. Most third- and fourth-world countries still vehemently insist that the family or clan can take care of its own elderly.

Although life-cycle analysis has always been a traditional phase of anthropological data collection, some anthropologists are now taking a special interest in latter phases of life and are also asking such basic questions as how a society determines when one is old. Criteria for deciding this range from functional analyses of mental and physical performance to simple chronological determination. Or, the question may be decided on the basis of the person's social roles, career situation, or public responsibilities. For some anthropologists the life cycle is best understood as a "career" in aging or a life's work, and therefore they believe it should be studied as a configuration of gains and losses, triumphs and tribulations.

CHAPTER 3

Retirement, Personality, and Applied Anthropology

RETIREMENT AND DISENGAGEMENT

Retirement as we know it in the United States tends to be nonexistent in preindustrial and even in many non-Western industrial societies. Formal retirement, which ends career activities, is associated primarily with bureaucracies that have complex military, civil service, educational, commercial and industrial enterprises. To understand retirement, we need to understand the significance of work in the society in question—how it provides role and status in the society and what kinds of rewards in money, goods, or prestige it yields.

Margaret Clark (1972) suggests that two aspects of retirement deserve study: the cultural and the psychological. From the cultural standpoint, it is important to investigate retirement in terms of its history, form, function, and meaning in a given society. The psychological approach, on the other hand, concerns itself with recording the personal meaning of the institution for the individual. Some cultural systems permit second careers for retired persons and although this occurs only occasionally (as with Colonel Sanders or Ronald Reagan) in America, it is fairly common in preindustrial societies. These societies often have a well-defined category of activities known as "old people's work." These activities may represent modifications of roles occupied by younger people or in some cases entirely different roles that are appropriate to the declining energies of the elderly, but they are seen as no less important than roles occupied by younger people. Examples of second careers are those of elder statesman and political advisor, folk medicine specialist, storyteller, choreographer, or ceremonial director. Although all societies observe sex divisions of labor, age divisions of labor are of consequence primarily in preindustrial societies.

In the United States, the categories of "children's work" and "old people's work" are not significant because neither age category is expected to do much in the way of productive labor. About the only kind of work the elderly are consistently permitted to do is babysitting and domestic work (these tend to be children's jobs also), but even these prestigeless tasks are not reserved for them. Even if Americans were to find the concept of a second career appealing, the scarcity of such employment opportunities for those over 65 would quickly discourage any such notion.

In tribal and peasant societies, the retirement experiences are much the same for men and women, and the situation resembles to a certain extent what has been the situation for women in our own society. In other words, in the United States and in the West generally, men traditionally retire but women do not. This may change in the future as more and more women join the commercial labor force, but for homemakers, the old-age domestic work differs little from what they have done for most of their lives. There may not be children to raise any more, but the cooking, cleaning, mending, laundering, and marketing go on. Men in retirement, however, are completely cut off from the work activities that gave their lives meaning and status. Unless a second career is started, their lives are nonproductive and without purpose. In one investigation of death anxiety (Schulz 1980), work role continuity was found to make women in our society much more accepting of the inevitability of death than men. There is a positive correlation between role satisfaction and lack of anxiety about one's own death, and middle-class men face a real crisis. During their working years, role satisfactions enabled them to repress and deny the possibility of death, but when role satisfaction no longer exists the anxiety over death surfaces.

In preindustrial societies, there is a continuity of useful roles for men also, and they do not expect to cease functioning in productive activities until they are unable to make contributions to either family or community. Most societies of this type believe that the elderly should have the option of enjoying complete leisure if they so desire, but few elders make this choice. Most continue to find satisfaction and personal rewards in productive labor of some type.

Any study of retirement in America must consider American concepts of work, leisure, and work-derived status. For many years, the American work ethic has dominated perceptions of personal worth and status, but evidence now indicates that American values in this sphere are changing. Although America continues to condemn idleness, the work ethic is being replaced by an activity ethic. Activity may be recreational but it must be purposeful. One aspect of our puritan heritage is that recreation and sports are acceptable if the physical activity contributes to physical health and makes more efficient work habits possible. The energy expended on modern-day vacations is often greater than that exerted on the job, and people in the United States often return from vacations a day or two early to rest up before going back to work.

Jerry Jacobs describes, in his monograph on Fun City, what developers have instituted as attractions for potential residents of the age-homogeneous community. He writes, "The weekly community newspaper lists the week's events by date and time of day. A typical week's calendar lists about 150 separate social events, most of which are conducted within the activity center. Approximately 65 of these are morning activities, 60 afternoon, and about 25 evening. Fun City boasts a total of 92 different clubs and organizations" (1974:607). The planned activities include Camera Club, Garden Club, band practice, Bridge Club, American Legion, lawn bowling, golf, chess, checkers, Square Dance Club, Glee Club, Bicycle Club, typing classes, dinner club meetings, Scrabble Club, TOPS (Take Off Pounds Sensibly), ballroom dancing, language classes, Pinochle Club, Canasta Club, art classes, Lapidary Club, jewelry making, sewing, ceramics, woodworking, and Photography Club. Jacobs points out, however, that those who want to work at a part-time job often have to travel outside the community.

Regional as well as urban-rural differences in values affect attitudes toward, work, leisure, and retirement in the United States. An example of this can be found in the phenomenon peculiar to Appalachia (and perhaps some other rural areas), which is known as "retiring to the porch." This behavior is associated primarily with men and involves a set of social arrangements in which a person has over a long period of time won the respect of the community and therefore its support in his retirement. Lozier and Althouse (1975), who have studied this phenomenon, maintain that porch sitting is a way of receiving social attention and care but only if the recipients have established "social credit" by their own lifetime contributions to neighbors and the community in general. It is a form of idleness permitted people who have "paid their dues" and now have a right to dividends (in the form of communication and privilege).

Clark also suggests that it is not possible to understand the full impact of retirement in a society without making some reference to age segregation. America is one of the most segregated societies in the world in regard to class, race, religion, and age, and our industrial system also tends to segregate us in terms of our role behavior. Only on farms do Americans work close to their homes, and children in urban areas often have no idea of the work their father does because they have never seen him on the job. This kind of segregation means that work colleagues are a separate group of people from neighborhood, church, or social club acquaintances. When the American worker retires, he or she not only loses a job that has provided meaning and status but also a group of fellow workers with whom he or she has shared a lifetime of work cooperation. Since men and women in preindustrial societies do not have occupational segregation and since they do not retire, they obviously do not experience this kind of social separation. Loneliness, so much a fear in industrialized societies, is not a serious consideration in less complex ones.

According to Barbara G. Anderson, retirement in America does more than separate people from jobs and colleagues; it is actually a period of *deculturation*. The learning of a culture (by a child or an adult immigrant) is referred to in anthropology as *enculturation*. This learning usually takes place informally in the family and community and formally in school. It is a process vital to the continuity of society since human behavior is not inherited genetically but must be taught and learned. A number of anthropologists—Margaret Mead, Ruth Benedict, Ralph Linton, John Whiting—have carefully researched this period of cultural transmission, but Anderson (1972) is the first to document the process of unlearning culture, which she believes is forced on the elderly in our society. She writes:

> If it is during childhood that the individual comes to learn the given ways of a society so that he can function within it, then in the United States at least, it is through old age that he is made to unlearn these ways so that eventually he can and

does cease to function culturally in it. There is no doubt in my mind that, through a system of conscious and unconscious conditionings, the older American is gradually groomed by his society for total cultural withdrawal. (1972:210)

America today is faced with a dilemma. It now has greater numbers of old people than the society can comfortably support. Since 1900 life expectancy has increased by 24 years. More than 20 million people in the United States are 65 or older, but in spite of this, no appropriate or meaningful life-style for the elderly has been evolved. Anderson maintains that old age in our society is merely a "degenerate extension of middle-years, already negatively valued in a youth-invested, action-oriented culture" (1972:210). When the aged were few in number and the rate of cultural change was moderate, American society seemed to be able to cope with people growing old, but today there is mostly confusion. Mead observes that "we are retiring many men at the height of their creativity. This is one of the slow death-dealing mechanisms of present-day society . . . . Early retirement was primarily based on an attempt to make room for other people in a society built on the kind of productivity that ties together a job and the right to eat. We don't need this any more. We can build a society in which social contribution is not related to keeping someone else out of a job" (1967:36). A few exceptional elderly—artists, judges, professors, statesmen, business tycoons—have been integrated into the system, but the majority of aged have been forced into a condition of statuslessness and culturelessness. Their lives, states Anderson, "are lived outside and apart from the viable body of tradition that constitutes the daily patterns of younger Americans. More accurately, perhaps, they are a lost generation in the sense that they are carriers of a defunct or dying culture. In the thirty or forty years since the world revolved around them . . . the content of our world has changed significantly. Material culture is vastly different . . . . Ways of making a living, the pace and orientation of life—all have changed" (1972:211).

The deculturation process that has been forced upon our elderly is somewhat like the enculturation process in reverse. Society insidiously communicates that in old age acquisitiveness, mobility, creativity, and innovation are improper and that the aged should be content with only modest social involvement. Society demands that the elderly not only relinquish their earlier status and roles but that they also begin to value themselves as the society values them. Just as children begin to value themselves by observing society's approval of their behavior, so elderly learn to devalue themselves as they sense society's disinterest or disapproval of their behavior.

Even social science appears to have contributed to the effort of American society to devalue the aged by its formulation of what is commonly known as the *disengagement theory* (Cumming and Henry, 1961).

Actually, disengagement is a controversial issue in social gerontology. According to Cumming and Henry (1961), withdrawal from societal involvement is a normal and beneficial aspect of aging. "Aging is an inevitable act of mutual withdrawal or disengagement, resulting in decreased interaction between the aging person and others in the social systems he belongs to" (1961:14). The authors believe that disengagement applies not only to industrialized societies but to traditional or "primitive" ones as well.

Although Cumming and Henry insist that disengagement is a universal phenomenon, evidence from numerous anthropological studies conducted in a variety of cultures shows that had the basic theoretical orientation of social gerontology been established by anthropologists (with their cross-cultural perspective and relativistic approach), there would be no such thing as a "disengagement theory." Disengagement would merely be recognized as a phenomenon that may or may not be present in the society, depending on the unique social and economic cultural patterns.

In fact, disengagement is rare in tribal or peasant societies. Most elderly in these groups continue to play important roles in family enterprises and in many cases their value to the greater society increases with age. They tend to be called upon more than ever for decision-making and for advice in those areas where their experience and knowledge of traditional matters are valued. Disengagement in preindustrial society is not a matter of societal pressure but depends entirely on the strength and mental clarity of the individual.

A study by Andrei Simic (1977) that contrasts intergenerational relationships in the United States with those in Yugoslavia reveals that disengagement and deculturation are peculiar to American culture and should not be considered universal phenomena. He does, however, maintain that disengagement and deculturation are culture-specific models that have value in that they provide a contrasting framework for analyzing aging in other societies.

Simic believes that disengagement and deculturation are not simply products of seniority but that they reflect the American values of individualism, independence, and the right to unrestricted freedom in decision-making. What we must understand about America, states Simic, is that "individuals do not suddenly find themselves isolated in their declining years, but are socialized for this role almost from the time of conception in the context of the family and community" (1977:55).

Simic also maintains that American children are socialized toward a goal of independence and Yugoslav children are taught the importance of reciprocal roles that they will play throughout their lifetime with family members and other relatives. Isolation (often verbalized as privacy) is a part of an American's life from the very beginning. Even babies in cribs have their own rooms, each child must have a separate bedroom, and children are not expected to relate as much to family as to peers outside the home. Yugoslavian children, by contrast, live in a social environment where "privacy . . . is notably lacking, and the need to be alone and to control personal space is not culturally recognized in terms of the family group. The Yugoslav child is expected to identify more strongly with other members of the household than with an external peer group" (1977:61).

There are marked contrasts in the world of work as well. Americans labor as a moral obligation to achieve personal, spiritual, and emotional fulfillment, but Yugoslavs work to maintain and enhance familial and other important social relationships.

At every point in the American life cycle, evidence points to a lack of family solidarity, cooperation, or reciprocity. With this kind of ethos, societal members can expect little support in old age either from families or from an independence-oriented society. Although disengagement and deculturation are compatible with "individualism and generational replication," Simic points out that it does not seem to be compatible with the Yugoslavian stress on "kinship corporacy and generational symbiosis" (1977:63).

David Gutmann, whose research has primarily centered around personality change in old age among the Maya, Navajo, midwestern Americans, and the Druze of Israel, has also turned his attention to disengagement as a supposedly inevitable, universal phenomenon. In his article "Alternatives to Disengagement: The Old Men of the Highland Druze" (1976), Gutmann describes an apparent cross-cultural tendency for men over 65 to move from an orientation marked by active production-centered, competitive motives and attitudes to a passive one labeled *magical mastery*.

Even though Cumming and Henry hypothesize that old people move toward a more passive orientation, Gutmann's study indicates "that disengagement need not be compulsory, and it particularly demonstrates that passivity is not inextricably tied to disengagement" (1976:106). Gutmann found that the movement toward passivity and magical mastery among aging Druze men is actually a shift from allegiance to productive and secular-productive life to one concerning traditional Moslem religion and the moral life. Pointing out that elder men have a tendency to move into an active religious role, Gutmann states, "While the religious role fits the special needs of older men, their tendencies toward mildness and accommodation are particularly fitted to the requirements of the religious role" (1976:104). In other words, the Druze elder does not disengage but merely shifts his interests and activities from a life of economic striving to one of religious service. He is no less involved, but now in old age he carries forward the moral rather than the material work of this society. It is not a disengagement but a social rebirth.

Sylvia Vatuk (1980) has worked among the people of India, where social and psychological disengagement are a part of the traditional culture, but even there she does not find the social disengagement described by Cumming and Henry. There is, in India, a pattern of withdrawal in old age known as "dwelling as a forest hermit" (1980:135). Old age is regarded as a period of rightful dependency with the security of the aged dependent on the support of the extended family, particularly the adult sons. But in regard to disengagement there is a great discrepancy between the ideal and the real. As elderly parents increase in age many of their roles are turned over to the young, but the aged do not usually drop out and they do not really become hermits. Activity levels actually are increased, but as among the Druzes, they are in different areas than those engaged in when younger. The situation is much like the second-career situation described earlier. Retirement from household affairs and rejection of attachments to other human beings is sanctioned by age-old sacred Hindu texts and cultural traditions but, in reality, aging brings disengagements from certain roles and relationships. Moreover, aging means forming new relationships and assuming new roles that are more in line with "the activity theory," a concept that holds that successful aging requires maintaining reasonable activity levels and role substitutions in retirement.

A test of disengagement theory in Fun City (Jacobs, 1974) reveals that only about half the residents fit the Cumming-Henry model and then perhaps imperfectly. Jacobs found that about 10% of Fun City's population was clearly engaged and participating in the community's 92 planned recreational activities. These people were actively

Old age in India involves a withdrawal from certain productive roles and household obligations but a greater involvement in religious worship and spiritual leadership. (Photo by Lowell D. Holmes.)

engaged in preretirement and they continued this life-style in retirement. A second group—disengaged both in pre- and postretirement periods—also represented an exception to the disengagement rule. They were never active in clubs or recreational activities, and retirement has brought no change in their lives. These individuals constituted upwards of 15% of the total. A third group—representing about 25% of the population—were happily engaged in pre- and early postretirement periods but were now disengaged, not by choice, but because their health had failed. This group and the two just described represented a total of approximately half of the residents of Fun City and therefore a strong challenge to the Cumming-Henry theory.

Approximately 50% of Fun City's residents do fit the disengagement model. These people have voluntarily disengaged at retirement. They clearly intended to withdraw from society, watch television, do a little reading, play a little cards, and walk the dog. Their life-style was, according to Jacobs, regarded as "vegetating" by the more active members of the community and by outsiders, and they were looked upon with pity. Of this group—the truly disengaged—Jacobs writes, "There is no proof for or against the contention that their disengagement is beneficial, either for them or society" (1974:486). Generally, Jacobs felt, however, that living in Fun City, with all its isolation and segregation, could not be beneficial socially or psychologically.

ETHNICITY AND AGING

Ethnicity is a characteristic of modern pluralistic society. Ethnic groups or ethnic subcultures are entities that differ from the majority population on the basis of shared history and values and/or a racial or national identity. Ethnicity is identifying with a particular cultural group.

Most studies in social gerontology that deal with minority aged tend to be social-problem oriented, with discussions and statistics on such matters as life expectancy, average income, housing conditions, health problems, and average levels of education. Anthropologists, on the other hand, are much more interested in the cultural aspects of minority aging and believe that much of the contemporary life-style of minority aging is related to traditional attitudes and behavior patterns of that group.

Christie Kiefer, in a 1971 article on minority elderly, suggests that it is important for us to understand the effects of ethnicity, social class marginality, and discrimination on the aging process. He further suggests that it is important to investigate the effects of acculturation on minority aged. The meeting of two cultures and the resultant effects on families through several generations is of vital importance to gerontology. Kiefer's own research concerning Japanesse *Issei* (immigrants), *Nisei* (second-generation American-born), and *Sansei* (third-generation American-born) and their intergenerational conflicts and stresses is characteristic of the kind of anthropological research being undertaken. The clash of such values of self-reliance, dependency, filial responsibility, peer orientation, and self-interest (or personal freedom) held by different generations is responsible for the kind of anxiety and depression felt by some minority elderly.

Today, however, a new phenomenon is operative among some ethnic groups. This might be called the "roots" phenomenon, where the young are interested in learning their cultural heritage and are seeking out the elderly as sources of that information. Linda Cool's experience with the Corsican subculture in Paris was that "ethnicity offers the old a continuing identity and source of control which may be compartmentalized during different stages of the life cycle but which remains available for use when needed or wanted. While ethnicity does not guarantee valued friendships for the older person, it does provide a backdrop for shared understandings and values, which are often the foundations of friendship" (1980:168).

Although some ethnic groups do not encourage social participation of the elderly, Cool found a meaningful exchange between young and old among the Paris-dwelling Corsicans. The elderly had knowledge of a cultural heritage that the young wanted to learn, and by imparting it, the elderly gained not only self-esteem but also the satisfaction that tradition would be perpetuated. As one might expect, disengagement is absent in this society where ethnic identity and ethnic membership reduce role loss and isolation of the aged. If anything, Cool found that elderly Corsicans in Paris were being called on as authorities on traditional culture to a greater extent than the elders in Corsica. As often happens with ethnic groups, cultural identity and knowledge of traditional culture had become powerful rallying and unifying devices.

In a similar study, Maria Siemaszko compared a Polish-American sample in Chicago with one in Poland and with one representing the American majority. Siemaszko maintains that ethnicity causes greater heterogeneity among the total aged population of America and suggests that Polish Americans relate differently to the elderly than Americans do. She writes, "Often their children live quite near them and regularly give them both service and financial support. They reciprocate with food and with watching grandchildren, and in cases of emergency. Kin relations are very close in the Polish-American subculture. Of course, one could raise the question as to how this behavior is related to socioeconomic background, and therefore, question future patterns. Nevertheless, at present the data show a great deal of kin interaction" (1980:267).

Knowledge of ethnic values and patterns of support of the aged also have an applied value. The degree to which people rely on community agencies varies from ethnic group to ethnic group, depending on the kinship system and concepts of filial responsibility, and this means that planners and agencies must take these cultural differences into consideration. This does not mean, however, that agencies can completely ignore subcultures with strong family systems, but it does perhaps mean that services to different minorities must be of different kinds.

Trela and Sokolovsky state that while it would be difficult to imagine an enduring social policy for the aged based entirely on ethnic status, "the implementation and administration of policy can be appropriately ethnicity-conscious to the degree that cultural differences are related to the need for and the utilization of services. Bureaucratic structures must be sensitive to cultural differences" (1979:134).

Much of the interest of gerontological anthropologists today concerns the consequences of being poor, old, and of minority status, particularly since the United States is a society with youth-oriented values, with a crisis-oriented public health service, and with patterns of discrimination against a variety of minorities. All of these combine, according to Wilbur Watson, "to form a complex system of oppressive processes in the disservice of the elderly" (1977:65). This is particularly serious in

America's environment of rapid change where even aged majority Americans are looked upon as obsolete, and where the forces of modernization are causing the formerly supportive minority cultural systems to crumble.

LONGEVITY STUDIES

Longevity studies by anthropologists have profited from the fact that anthropology is able to approach the subject from both the biological and the cultural standpoints. Chapter 4 contains a discussion of anthropological investigations into longevity.

CREATIVITY AND PRODUCTIVITY OF THE AGED

For some time America has labored under the misapprehension that middle age marks the end of any capacity for creativity or intellectual growth. Renaldo Maduro points out that "although there has been general interest in both aging and creativity, a more focused consideration of artistic creativity in relation to different phases of the life cycle has been neglected. Anthropological studies of culture and aging have not stressed the expressive symbolic dimensions of human existence" (1974:303). Harvey Lehman, a psychologist, is one of the few behavioral scientists who has been concerned with the idea of creativity and life cycle. While Lehman has stated that "with some dramatic exceptions, our greatest creative thinkers have been long-lived" (1956:333), he also maintains that superior creativity generally rises rapidly to a high point in the thirties and then slowly declines. Wechsler (1958) also supports this position, but Irving Lorge (1963) believes that longitudinal studies might produce counterevidence. One of the main problems with this kind of investigation is a lack of consensus on the meaning of creativity. Artistic creativity, scientific creativity, and creativity as a generalized personality trait are often confused. Much of Lehman's research actually deals with productivity rather than creativity. Tallies were made of the number of symphonies, paintings, books, poems, and scientific discoveries produced by artists, scholars, and scientists at various periods in their lives. Since production was greater in the early adult years of most of his sample, he assumed that those were their most creative years. The problem with these tallies of productivity is that they measure quantity and not quality.

Anthropological data indicate that the capacity to grow intellectually has no bounds, but we also know that both the ability to learn and the ability to create can be greatly influenced by cultural ideas about these abilities. Mead (1967) points out that the capacity to adopt or relinquish roles at different ages is something that is learned within a culture. For example, the Balinese have no concept that age has anything to do with the ability to learn and be creative. If a man who has never carved or painted wants to begin at age 60 no eyebrows whatsoever are raised. A man of 60 may start to play a musical instrument for the first time, or a woman of that age may decide to become a dancer. On the other hand, a child of six may learn to play one of the more important instruments in the village orchestra or even begin to lead it without anyone's objecting or finding it inappropriate.

This disregard for age-grading activities must be considered in cultural context to be understood. Since the Balinese believe in reincarnation, what is begun in one lifetime may be carried on in the next. Perhaps our own popular beliefs about learning and creativity grow out of our Christian tradition where a person has only one life to live on earth. Mead suggests, "We have put an enormous stress on living out a singled individual life, where strength and longevity are related quite differently, and learning is considered to be necessary and appropriate only in youth" (1967:35).

To my knowledge there have only been two anthropological studies of creativity of the elderly: a study of aged jazz musicians in New York and Los Angeles and a study of Brahmin folk painters in West India.

In 1978 and 1979, Lowell D. Holmes and William Thomson studied 15 aged jazz musicians to explore such subjects as creativity, and musician's attitudes toward their life-styles, their assessment of their own capacity to play and create, the effects of age on performance, and their acceptance by younger musicians. The researchers used definitions of *creative* borrowed from jazz composer and performer Charlie Mingus on the one hand and, strangely enough, from cooking expert Julia Child on the other. Mingus maintained that "creativity is more than just being different. Anybody can play weird; that's easy. What's hard is to be simple as Bach. Making the simple complicated is commonplace; making the complicated simple, awesomely simple, that's creativity." Child suggested, "What is new comes out of what is old. Probably, too often, we use the word *creative* when we mean imaginative. To be truly creative involves taking the art form seriously, really learning the basics. It is a lot of work" (1977:31).

When creativity was defined in these terms, neither the researchers nor the musicians themselves felt that creativity must cease or begin a downhill slide in advanced age. Playing jazz was seen as putting together musical ideas in a new and imaginative way, and the larger the stock of these ideas and figures and the more experience one has in putting them together, the more creative the jazz player. All artists interviewed had been around so long and heard and played with so many fine musicians that they could recall an idea from here, borrow an idea from there and in putting them all together could achieve a result that no younger player without equivalent historical depth could accomplish. A particularly interesting example of creative capacity in old age was that of Doc Cheatham, who did not start playing improvised jazz until he joined the Benny Goodman quintet in 1971 at the age of 66. Up until that time he was strictly a lead trumpet player doing section work. John Guarneiri, former pianist with Benny Goodman and Artie Shaw, is in his middle sixties but is constantly experimenting. A few years ago he began playing many of his numbers in 5/4 time instead of 4/4 because of the different effect it produced. He predicted to the researchers, "I think I'm going to do some very interesting things in the future."

In 1974, Renaldo Maduro conducted a study of creativity in quite a different culture—West India. Maduro studied 110 male Brahmin folk painters in Rajasthan to determine whether artistic creativity declines with age. He concluded that in India creativity appears to peak in the early middle age and then remains constant into old age. In measuring creativity, Maduor asked the painters to rank each other along a creativity continuum and they were also given the Barron-Welsh Revised Art Test for scaling creativity. What is most interesting about this study is the relationship between the various stages of the Hindu life cycle and creative activity. For example, the onset of old age is identified as the "forest hermit" stage. This is a time when a man has "met his family obligations and performed his duties to caste and his society. He can turn inward and contemplate the inner light. At this time a man's powers of imagination increase fourfold

In his new role as jazz soloist, Doc Cheatham is one of New York's most sought-after trumpet players. (Photo courtesy of William Thomson.)

because he has learned to reach into himself for light, bliss and balance" (1974:308). The artists maintain that with increasing years they become "more open" to the nuances of intuition, to "conceiving," and to "the unfolding of the self" (ibid.). They are no longer interested in acquiring power or wealth and they are free to grow in new psychological and symbolic directions.

CULTURE AND PERSONALITY

In an article in the *Gerontologist* in 1967, Margaret Clark cited gerontology as "a new area for studies of culture and personality," and she lamented that in spite of a great deal of research in this area by eminent anthropologists little or no attention had been given to the last half of the life cycle. Culture and personality as an anthropological specialization developed originally from a fusion of cultural anthropology and psychoanalytic theory during the 1920s. Its primary function has been to study how personality development is influenced by participation in a given cultural system. Because it focuses on culture (a group phenomenon), this research area differs from psychology in that it concentrates less on individual personality than on the extent to which personality types, or at least traits, are shared within societies. Workers in this field have also concentrated on documenting early childhood experience in order to understand the impact of cultural norms and practices on adult personality. Some of the basic theoretical positions of this school of inquiry are presented by Clark:

> The assumption persists that human beings are basically unchanging, at least in their deeper and "more important" aspects. This orientation has led students of culture and personality to confine their work to four major areas: (1) the enculturation of children and adolescents, and the role of childrearing practices in the determination of adult personality; (2) status personality characteristics, as influenced by sex roles and class or caste differences—these, too, thought to be group differences for which the individual is shaped quite early in life; (3) modal personality and national character, usually derived from studies of young and middle-aged adults (those whose personalities are now assumed by the observer to be "fixed" or "set" into a particular shared pattern through common early life experiences); and (4) individual deviance and its cultural interpretation. (1967:57)

Culture and personality scholars still tend to think of personality as a static commodity, and a significant number of scholars stress continuity of personality types. Clark and a few others believe, however, that personality is "an on-going process of interaction between the sociocultural world and the internal life of the individual—a process that continues throughout the life cycle" (1967:63). Scholars who believe that personality reflects life experience ask, and rightly so: How could forced retirement in America, age discrimination, the necessity for a total reorganization of ideas of goal achievement, leisure activities, changes in residence and ideas of personal worth not affect personality characteristics of those past 65 years of age?

Even though culture and personality studies of the aged are few and far between, there has been some movement in this direction. The study of ongoing personality by David Gutmann is worthy of mention. Although not an anthropologist, Gutmann's approach is cross-cultural, and data were acquired through investigation in the field. Gutmann's study used Thematic Apperception Test (TAT) protocols in the study of perceptions of self and the world at different ages in four cultures—Western Navajo, Mayan, Midwest American, and Druze (Israel). Believing that "important psychological orientation, based around passivity and aggressivity, dependence and autonomy would discriminate age groups within culturally homogeneous societies" (1976:88), Gutmann proceeded to investigate ego states of men between the ages of 40 and 70. In a Kansas City sample of 140 men, he found that between 40 and 54 years men exhibit an ego state that he labeled *active mastery*. This involved a deliberate pursuit of achievement and independence and was marked by an attempt to control external conditions. Men aged 55 to 64 exhibited traits that were labeled *passive mastery*. This involved more internal than external control and a greater tendency to accommodate than was true of younger men. Those men who were 65 or over exhibited an ego state termed *magical mastery*. This life-cycle characteristic was described as featuring self-deception and denial of unpleasant realities. Gutmann believes that he found many similarities in his Navajo, Mayan, and Druze populations. Finding that all four societies exhibit "an age shift away from Active Mastery and towards the Passive and/or Magical orientations" (1976:89), Gutmann believes that ego states are distributed more reliably according to age than according to culture. In other words, he believes that he has found a universal feature of personality change that is immune to cultural influences.

In 1967, Margaret Clark and Barbara G. Anderson studied the consequences of aging on personalities of 435 San Francisco aged. Comprising the sample were 264 "normal" people from the community who were 60 years of age or older, 81 inpatients of the psychiatric ward at San Francisco General Hospital, and 90 former patients of that ward who were now living at home. The focus of the study was adjustment to elderly status, and the variables studied were self-evaluation, morale, status, and level of social interaction. Postulating that the major threats to the mental health and well-being of the aged are weak kinship ties, rapid technological change, relative and absolute increases in the number of aged, and the sacred cows of American culture—independence and productivity—Clark and Anderson suggested avenues of survival that might, in opposition to disengagement theory, be labeled *relaxation*. The researchers concluded that if aging Americans are to achieve positive self-image and morale, they must learn to accept their physical and mental changes, be willing to relinquish certain roles and activities, substitute alternative sources of need gratification for those unavailable to them, modify their basis for self-judgment, and in general, find a new place for themselves in the larger scheme of things. Although the mentally ill seemed to have difficulty distinguishing between circumstances that could be changed and those that could not, the mentally healthy elderly seemed to be "able to meet unpleasant but alterable circumstances with action, and inalterable ones with flexibility and forbearance" (1967:61). There were distinct differences in the level of aspiration of mentally well and mentally ill aged. The former had more modest expectations in life, while the latter seemed to "feel that they must ever strive for perfection. They seem to believe seriously in the Cinderella legend—for them, the life story should have a happy ending, ambition should triumph, and all dreams come true" (1967:61). Clark concludes from her study of healthy and unhealthy adjustment in old age that people must not only learn how their culture defines the proper way to grow up but also the proper way to grow old.

Another study that dealt with culture as a dynamic force in aging perceptions was conducted by Austin Shelton (1965) among the Nsukka Ibo of Eastern Nigeria. Shelton reported a "virtual absence of psychosenility or even a sense of indolence or disengagement" among this eastern Nigerian society's elderly. Shelton suggests that psychosenility has generally been considered to result almost entirely from physiological deterioration associated with advanced age, but that it should be reexamined in terms of the cultural milieu.

In Ibo society Shelton found a distinctly positive attitude toward growing old, coupled with a decline in stress situations. The aged men enjoy an important role in the religious life of the society, because they supposedly have the goodwill of the ancestors, and they have a strong economic position because support is guaranteed by both family and clan. They are past the time when they must face the tribulations of procuring lands, wives, and titles. Gone also is the anxiety over being able to father a son. They have no worries about antagonistic spirits or the need to leave the village to seek employment. Shelton argues against the inevitability of psychosenility and he maintains that among the Ibo elders the ability to perform useful tasks with mental clarity and to thereby command respect is more commonly a matter of culture than of biology.

Malcolm Arth has also devoted considerable time to gerontological studies of Ibo culture and personality. Shelton and Arth see and interpret the Ibo values, culture, and behavior quite differently, however. For example, Arth questions Shelton's claims that the Ibo have a placid old age and he insists that today attitudes toward the aged are ambivalent. Acculturation has tended to increase stresses and differences in values between the young and old, as evidenced by frequent outbursts and conflicts between members of different generations. He maintains that there is an underlying hostility toward the aged, perhaps because they are reminders of human mortality. Arth also questions Shelton's definition of psychosenility. Drawing on data from a study of psychiatric disorders, not among the Ibo but among their neighbors, the Yoruba, Arth reports that "senility is not considered abnormal, and such patients would usually not be hospitalized." Perhaps, Arth suggests, "Shelton's informants were speaking about cultural ideals," whereas he believes his own research focused on the real or behavioral level (1968:243-244).

PHYSICAL CHANGES ASSOCIATED WITH ADVANCED AGE

Anthropologists have discovered that as the aging process continues, the mass of nearly all bones in the human skeleton decreases. The cortex, or compact core of the long bones, diminishes (leaving them nearly hollow tubes), the endplates of vertebrae reduce in thickness and in strength, and the articular ends of bones, which form the joints, shrink in size and in number. Although the terms *osteoporosis* and *demineralization* have been used to describe this process, it is actually bone loss. Stanley Garn maintains that bone mass and weight decrease naturally with age, that they do so in both sexes (although at different rates), and that bone loss is not peculiar to any particular racial grouping over another. It should be noted that this is a natural and not a pathological phenomenon.

Researchers once believed that bone loss did not begin until age 60 or 70, but it is now apparent that the phenomenon begins at approximately 40 years of age, with the tubular bones of the hand being the first affected. Bone loss has been blamed erroneously on long-term inadequacy of diet, decreased physical activity, and hormonal (estrogen or parathyroid) changes. Recent studies have shown, however, that diet is apparently neither the explanation nor the cure for bone loss, and there is little support for hormonal explanations. Montoye (1975) has likewise found little correlation between amount of physical activity and quantity of bone loss. Unfortunately, the present state of knowledge indicates that there is neither a cure nor a prevention for this condition. On the positive side, however, is the fact that adult bone loss may prove to be a valuable model for the measurement of age. Garn writes:

> Adult bone loss so far and perhaps uniquely, seems independent of major differences in activity, diet, and expectations of aging. The rich and the poor, rural and urban, Londoners and Lacandones all share remarkably similar bone loss rates when compared with archaeological populations. The bone loss model allows us to compare loss of bone with declines in other bodily systems, including the skeletal muscle so intimately connected with bone, and with other parameters of aging. (1975:54)

Anthropologists have also shown considerable scientific interest in bone diseases in which age is a factor, such as Paget's disease (bowing of the long bones and deformation of flat bones) and osteoarthritis. Osteoarthritis, a degenerative joint disease, dates back to the time of European Neanderthals and appears to be present in all human populations today. From investigations of a variety of sample populations—black and white Americans, Pueblo, Blackfoot and Pima Indians, and Alaskan Eskimos—it has been discovered that the age of onset, the frequency, and the location of degenerative changes can be correlated directly with the nature and amount of environmental stress. Stress factors that definitely affect the onset and degree of impairment include physical trauma such as fractures or dislocations of joints, presence of foreign bodies in the joint, injury to ligaments, or repeated hemorrhages (Jurman, 1977).

Anthropologists are only beginning to understand the causes of many of the pathologies associated with age. Most have multifactorial explanations involving sex and genetic and environmental variables, but new perspectives are now being acquired that may very well result in valuable preventative and remedial methods.

DEATH AND DYING

Old age is seen as a period of preparation for death in many societies, and senior years are therefore a time for planning, reflecting, and summing up. Although death may occur at any stage in the life cycle, and often does during infancy in preindustrial societies, there is a natural tendency to associate old age with death and dying. If old age is the final act of the human drama, then surely death is the final curtain. Leo Simmons (1945) established the precedent of linking old age and death in his study of roles of elders in preindustrial societies, and most social scientists agree that it is a valid association, since the aged, more than any other age group, have to come to terms directly and realistically with this inevitability. But anthropologists know that the way the elderly handle the prospect of death varies from culture to culture, depending on the society's world view, religious orientation, conception of the hereafter, and extent to which the society accepts or denies the reality of death. Anthropologist/psychologist Ernest Becker, in his book *The Denial of Death* (1973), maintains, for example, that the human fear of death is the source of much individual and institutional behavior—heroism, neurosis, and religion. Geoffrey Gorer (1967) goes so far as to describe the Western attitude toward death as similar to its attitude toward pornography, explaining that we find death disgusting and immoral and yet we have a morbid fascination with it that results in grotesque fantasies and perversions. On the other hand, some social gerontologists (Jeffers and Verwoerdt, 1977; Kastenbaum and Aisenberg, 1972) present evidence that aged Americans handle the idea of death well. Although they are not overly apprehensive, they are more prepared for the event than younger people. Two-thirds of the elderly in America have wills, for example, compared with the national average of one-fourth. While anthropology's interest in death and dying has been as slow in developing as its interest in gerontology, the discipline is now making worthwhile contributions to both areas with studies of funeral and bereavement practices of American ethnic groups and non-Western cultures, the role of the aged as intermediaries between the living and the dead, and attitudes and institutions of our own and other cultures associated with preparation for death.

APPLIED ANTHROPOLOGY

Anthropology, like every other scientific discipline, has its pure (theoretical) and its applied (practical) interests. Just as medicine has its practitioners and its laboratory research people, anthropology has its scholars researching issues to seek knowledge of humankind for its own sake; other anthropology scholars use anthropological knowledge to solve social, economic, educational, and political problems. These applied anthropologists have proved to be of great value in dealing with problems in industry, in public health where minority populations are involved, and in providing answers to difficult problems where services to the aged are involved.

One of the areas in which the applied researchers have brought their anthropological knowledge to bear is the nursing home. One of the first to study the philosophy and operation of such residences was the late Jules Henry. In his discussion of the institutionalization of our elderly in *Culture Against Man* (1963), Henry makes the point that "society has been established primarily for the purpose of guaranteeing food and protection. And from this primitive necessity has emerged the central problem of the human species, the fact that inner needs have scarcely been considered . . . . Although culture is 'for' man, it is also 'against' him" (1963:11-12).

In his analysis of how culture is "against" human beings Henry describes three nursing homes, Muni San (an institution supported by public funds) and two private, profit-making institutions, Rosemont (for paupers) and Tower Nursing Home (for the middle class). According to Henry, "Tower is comfortable and humane, Rosemont is inhumane, and Muni San is somewhere in between" (1963:391). Although the public institution, Muni San, is described as providing adequate if not inspired care and the residents receive proper medical attention and sufficient food, the patients suffer from a sense of being obsolete and abandoned, inferior to the least qualified employee, and nuisances to everyone.

Rosemont, on the other hand is labeled *hell's vestibule,* and it epitomizes America's lack of concern for the aged, particularly the aged poor. Henry's description of the "national character" of the inmates and staff suggests that the institution sees the residents as "child-animals" and treats them accordingly. This is made possible because "in our culture personality exists to the extent of ability to pay, and in terms of performance of the culturally necessary tasks of production, reproduction, and consumption" (1963:440). The fact that the inmates are paupers (who have social security income only) has been impressed on them to the extent that they expect to have no rights. They are both economically and intellectually poor. Their educational level plus the cultural environment in which they have spent their lives provided them with no inner resources for making their lives more bearable. Henry described life for the residents of Muni San as one of "apathy, preoccupation with food and excreta, the adoption of the role of child-animal, . . . and preoccupation with reminiscence" (1963:440-441).

Even Tower Nursing Home, functioning as it does within the American value system, failed to meet the inner needs of its middle-class residents. Although the staff is solicitous and kind, it "seems to maintain an attitude of indulgent superiority to the patients whom they consider disoriented children" (1963:474). The staff is oriented toward bodily needs, not mental ones, but this perhaps is because they do not understand the mental characteristics of the elderly. Because of staff insensibility, patients' lives are marked by anxiety and silent reminiscing, punctuated by outbursts of bad temper. Social life is minimal and although there is a desire for communication, there is an inability to achieve it. Henry maintains that the fault does not necessarily lie with the nursing home director or the staff but with the values of the culture. Through the use of cross-cultural comparison, Henry brings the characteristics of American culture into sharp focus:

> In many primitive societies the soul is imagined to leave the body at death or just prior to it; here, on the other hand, society drives out the remnants of the soul of the institutionalized old person while it struggles to keep his body alive. Routinization, inattention, carelessness, and deprivation of communication—the chance to talk, to respond, to read, to see pictures on the wall, to be called by one's name rather than "you" or no name at all—are ways in which millions of once useful but now obsolete human beings are detached from their selves long before they are lowered into the grave. (1963:393)

Applied studies that comment on the values and procedures in nursing homes in America have also been produced by Wilbur Watson and Robert Maxwell (1977). These investigators compared a home for blacks (174 patients) with one for Jewish elderly (328 patients) in regard to similarities and differences in health care and social interactions between patients and staff. Both homes had predominantly black staffs in the wards. In the home for blacks there was a joking relationship between staff and residents about institutional and other matters. No such relationship between patients and ward attendants was observed in the home for Jewish elderly; any joking that took place in this home was restricted to white staff members. Apparently, in America people carry the "color line" even into nursing homes, because in the Jewish home black LPNs reported that they were often the target of racially based hostility, while in the home for blacks none of the staff reported abuse or feelings of alienation with patients. On the basis of their findings, Watson and Maxwell conclude that positive interaction is more likely in nursing homes where caretakers and elderly share a common class and/or ethnic background.

While observing the operations of the home for Jewish elderly, Maxwell, Bader, and Watson (1972) turned their attention to spatial behavior, staff-patient interaction in terms of physical and psychological limitations of patients, and protective measures of staff members to promote their own self-interests. The study revealed that the most highly trained members of the nursing staff were the least involved in providing direct care and limited their attentions to the least disabled of the patients. The mentally and physically disabled were consequently left to the care of the lower-ranking, less-educated staff members.

The researchers also observed a pattern of segregating the most seriously ill from others, and they questioned whether this aggravated the condition and resulted in further deterioration. The study obviously raises serious questions about the need for extensive training for nurses who work with geriatric patients and it questions certain procedures concerning the relationship between the physically and mentally ill and the healthy residents.

Ethnicity has been shown to be an important consideration in nursing home operation and in the interaction between residents and staff. A study by Richard A. Eribes and Martha Bradley-Rawls (1978) has shown that knowledge of cultural differences is also important in explaining whether or not Mexican-Americans use nursing home facilities.

This study, carried out in Arizona, revealed a great under-use of nursing care facilities by older Mexican-Americans. Although other ethnic groups have a tendency to place their elderly in nursing homes as their income and standard of living rise, just the opposite is true of this population. Eribes and Bradley-Rawls write:

> Institutional residency rises with poverty rather than increased income . . . . The nursing home is a culturally defined alternative of last resort. As family income increases, families tend to provide alternatives to institutionalization, either within an existing family or through support towards independent living. (1978:370)

Whether the focus is on nursing home nutrition or agency-operated nutrition programs for aged living in an integrated community, the matter of cultural differences in food preferences is one that must be understood by both administrators and staff. Howell and Loeb warn that "although culture and ethnicity in the United States is not as precise a variable to define as in other parts of the world, certain characteristics of the dietary behavior of older persons can properly be considered 'culture bound.' It should be possible through strategic interviewing, group discussion, and observation, to identify quite specific dietary attitudes and habits of a cultural nature among subgroups of aged within the United States" (1969:36). Believing that field research on food preferences, aversions, and food-related health beliefs is needed, Howell and Loeb describe the range of nutritional problems that can be associated with differences in ethnicity, regional or urban-rural cultures, socioeconomic class, and age grades. They remind us that even the frequency of meals is more a matter of custom than physiological need and that food in some cultures has a kind of prestige seldom found in the majority culture in America. Food can be regarded as currency and as a means of fulfilling social and kinship obligations, and its preparation may be a means of acquiring creative satisfaction. Eating is often a pleasurable recreational activity, while for some food is often looked on as a medicine or as even a commodity of supernatural significance.

In "The Cultural Context of Aging" (1951), Margaret Mead examined a variety of foreign cultures where segregation of the aged is unknown. Mead suggests reducing the social and experiential distance between American generations by creating Grandparent-Teacher Associations (GPTAs), by encouraging occupational shifts in middle life to types of employment that offer some measure of recognition in later life, and by involving elders with younger people outside the family circle such as younger medical practitioners, lawyers, bankers, or stockbrokers. Mead continued this line of thought in another article, "A New Style of Aging," 1971, in which she suggested that not the young, but the old, have shunned their responsibilities to society. By withdrawing (or disengaging), they have deprived the young of a model through which they might learn what it is like to age, to be old, and to die. Grandparents today, insists Mead, have seen more change during their lifetimes than any generation that has ever lived, and they therefore have special knowledge that should be made available to younger generations. They need to reassure the young that change does not mean the end of the world but only the end of a particular kind of world. Very much an example herself of what she conceived a grandmother should be, Mead suggested that the aged can contribute to society in scores of ways and be rewarded in the process, but first they must give up the martyrdom of old-age loneliness that many find satisfying.

The force of values in the lives of old people has long been a focus in the work of Margaret Clark, whose study *Culture and Aging* (1967) documented the effects of the sociocultural environment on mental health among American aged. Clark believes that anthropologists can contribute effectively to the solution of the problem of today's aged by gaining a better understanding of life in societies where the values and behavior we impose on our elderly are already the core values and expected behavior of the culture. Such a society, she maintains, would be one that features a value orientation George Foster (1965) labeled the "Image of the Limited Good." In societies where this perspective prevails, any deliberate striving for goods or for prestige is seen as evil, because it is believed that such commodities are in short supply and to actively seek them is to attempt to deprive others. If our aged are to remain mentally healthy, they must, in Clark's opinion, be educated to accept the concept of the "Limited Good" and relinquish the Cinderella myth, the Colonel Sanders fable, and the Protestant ethic.

Adjustment in old age is also the topic of an article by Margaret Clark (1971) that discusses the problem of inner-city poor in regard to shelter, mobility, social interaction, and medical services. Although much has been written about the dangers and human misery associated with urban environments, Clark points out that such surroundings also have great potential for promoting human survival. Clark believes that when the aged urban poor are faced with basic physical and psychological problems of survival they seem to be able to develop remarkable informal structures for their solution. Stressing an *emic* approach to agency problem solving approaches, Clark suggests that "if planned programs can be constructed to emulate or develop these spontaneous arrangements among people, they are more likely to be acceptable and effective" (1971:65). In other words, she believes that urban programs must consider the cultural diversity that is an integral and characteristic feature of the city.

As many applied anthropologists have demonstrated in our own and other societies, the cultural system can be used to an advantage if there is sensitivity to its characteristics and dynamics. Solutions that are compatible with the values and behavioral tendencies of those who are faced with the problems are destined to be more satisfying and successful than programs planned without reference to the people, their unique needs, or their characteristic ways of approaching them.

SUMMARY

Retirement as we know it in America does not exist in preindustrial societies, but old age—however it is defined—often forces alterations in role behavior. In most of these societies, the role changes are much the same for both men and women. Neither is required to abandon productive roles altogether, although their activities may be quite different from those of their earlier years. The new roles are useful ones but probably involve less expenditure of energy, less stress, and less emphasis on quantity and quality of production. In the United States, on the other hand, there is a tendency to force men into idleness in their senior years but to allow women, at least those who are homemakers, to continue working at familiar domestic tasks as long as they are able.

Not only does retirement in America rob the individual of a most important source of status and identity—the work role—but according to Anderson (1972), retirement is a period of life when people are systematically forced to undergo *deculturation*. That is to say, they are required to relinquish cherished values and goals and accept a secondary social and economic role. Gerontologists Cumming and Henry (1961) suggest that there is a universal and natural tendency, which they label *disengagement*, for aged individuals to withdraw socially, economically, and politically. They see such behavior as "mutually advantageous" for both the elderly and for the society. Although they claim that this phenomenon is found in all societies, anthropological data prove that if the concept is valid at all, it is characteristically Western. Jacobs, however, observing the residents of Fun City, does not believe that disengagement is even particularly characteristic of middle-class America either. Simic, on the other hand, holds that Americans do not have to be urged to disengage because, in comparison with Yugoslavians, their culture never allows them to engage significantly in the first place. Americans' whole lives, he claims, are marked by isolation, individualism, and independence. Most anthropologists do not see disengagement as universal, natural, or beneficial to either people or societies.

Anthropology was at one time primarily interested in foreign and often exotic cultures, but considerable work is now being done at home. The United States is a pluralistic society, and the many ethnic subcultures represent highly divergent social and cultural environments within which the elderly function. The nature and effects of marginality, discrimination, and generational conflict are important issues that are only beginning to be understood. Cultural gerontologists are seeking to gain greater knowledge of the many adaptive strategies and familial structures that affect the status and maintenance of the old person of ethnic identity. Of particular interest to researchers in recent years has been the "roots" phenomenon and the effect it has had in establishing prestigious roles for elders as repositories of cultural heritages.

Some work has been initiated in studying the capacity of the elderly to grow intellectually and to engage in creative activity. Until recently, much of the research in this area has suggested that these capacities show consistent decline during senior years. It has been suggested, however, that longitudinal studies could do much to clarify this issue, and some investigators believe that there is already considerable evidence in the artistic and intellectual activities of scores of elderly artists and scholars that mental and creative capacities are normally unaffected by age. It is particularly important to note, however, that culture plays a vital role in encouraging or discouraging artistic and scholarly activity at advanced ages. The study of creativity might be considered one aspect of a greater effort to understand the relationship of culture to personality development. Researchers in this area, which is usually called Culture and Personality, or Psychological Anthropology, have focused on the influence on personality changes associated with old age, on the impact of age discrimination, and on the factors in our own and other cultures that contribute to mental health or mental illness.

Equally challenging are questions concerning normal and pathological physiological changes associated with age. Since physical anthropologists have traditionally specialized in research on skeletal materials, it is not surprising that studies of bone loss (osteoporosis), Paget's disease, and degenerative joint ailments (such as osteoarthritis) represent a major current of their research interests.

Still other cultural gerontologists are exploring the attitudes, anxieties, and perceptions concerning death and dying of elderly in a variety of cultures. Although death is by no means an event that takes place only in old age, it is the elderly who most directly and realistically must come to terms with this inevitability.

Anthropology, like most scholarly disciplines, has both theoretical and applied interests. Applied anthropologists draw on the facts and findings of their science and apply this knowledge in the solution of practical social, economic, political, or medical problems.

Those interested in gerontology have investigated nursing homes and retirement residences to discover (and try to improve) organizational principles and operational procedures. Others, like Mead and Clark, have assessed the philosophical and psychological climate in which the elderly in America must function and have suggested ways of improving senior participation and safeguarding the mental health and well-being of the elderly.

CHAPTER 4

Longevity

All organisms, from plants to human beings, have fixed, finite life spans. A mayfly can survive but a day, a dog 20 years, an elephant 85 years, a Galapagos turtle 150 years, and a human being 110 to 120 years. These figures should not be confused with how long the average of each of these organisms lives, however. Most representatives of the above-mentioned species die much earlier, since the term *life span* refers to the outside limit of survival. In other words, a person 120 years old is rarely found. In fact, it has been calculated that the chance of a human attaining that ripe old age is one in 2 billion. This means that there should be about two such remarkable individuals in the world today and about six in the history of mankind.

The proper term for the number of years actually lived is *performance,* and the term *life expectancy* is a projection applied to populations. Life expectancy is computed from life tables that predict the average number of years remaining for a hypothetical group of individuals based on the current set of age-specific rates of dying. Table 4.1 is an abridged life table for the United States for 1977. The table shows that, based on current mortality rates, a newborn could expect to live an average of 73.2 years. The age-specific death rate for that child in its first year of life is 1.4%. That is to say 1,421 of every 100,000 newborns will not survive until their first birthday. Of the ones who survive the average person can expect to live to be slightly over 73.

The *life span* (frequently designated maximum life-span potential or MLP) for human beings is approximately 120 years, but as Table 4.2 shows, *life-expectancy* figures for people in various parts of the world are lower.

Within the United States, there is considerable variation in life expectancy associated with differences in race, ethnicity, sex, and occupation (see Table 4.3).

As we have pointed out, the life-expectancy figure tells people how long (on the average) they can expect to live when they are born; the figure changes as they grow older. For example, although the average American man can expect to live to age 69,

Table 4.1. Life Table for the United States (1977)

Age Interval	Proportion Dying	of 100,000 Born Alive		Stationary Population		Average Remaining Lifetime (Life Expectancy)
Period of Life Between Two Exact Ages Stated In Years	Proportion of Persons Alive at Beginning of age Interval Dying During Interval	Number Living At Beginning of Age Interval	Number Dying During Age Interval	In The Age Interval	In This and All Subsequent Age Intervals	Average Number of Years of Life Remaining at Beginning of Age Interval
0–1	0.0142	100,000	1,421	98,751	7,316,270	73.2
1–5	.0027	98,579	268	393,693	7,217,519	73.2
5–10	.0017	98,311	167	491,106	6,823,826	69.4
10–15	.0018	98,144	173	490,355	6,332,720	64.5
15–20	.0051	97,971	499	488,723	5,842,365	59.6
20–25	.0067	97,472	650	485,756	5,353,642	54.9
25–30	.0066	96,822	637	482,517	4,867,886	50.3
30–35	.0070	96,185	677	479,306	4,385,369	45.6
35–40	.0097	95,508	928	475,369	3,906,063	40.9
40–45	.0151	94,580	1,428	469,565	3,430,694	36.3
45–50	.0239	93,152	2,222	460,552	2,961,129	31.8
50–55	.0372	90,930	3,379	446,727	2,500,577	27.5
55–60	.0555	87,551	4,861	426,258	2,053,850	23.5
60–65	.0858	82,690	7,095	396,531	1,627,592	19.7
65–70	.1173	75,595	8,868	356,669	1,231,061	16.3
70–75	.1764	66,727	11,768	305,147	874,392	13.1
75–80	.2647	54,959	14,550	238,929	569,245	10.4
80–85	.3612	40,409	14,596	164,964	330,316	8.2
85 AND OVER	1.0000	25,813	25,813	165,352	165,352	6.4

SOURCE: U.S. Public Health Service, *Vital Statistics of the United States, 1977*, Vol. 2, Section 5: *Life Tables* (Washington, D.C., 1977) Table 5-1.

Table 4.2. Life Expectancies in Various Parts of the World	
	Years
Sweden	76
United States	73
Japan	73
Greece	72
France, Germany, Switzerland	71
USSR	70
Portugal	67
Turkey	58
Indonesia	44
Ethiopia	35

Table 4.3. Life Expectancies in the United States	
	Years
White men	70
White women	79
Black men	60
Nonwhite women	67
Judges	78
Coal miners	65
Native American (Indians) men	44
Spanish-speaking men	57

Table 4.4. Metropolitan Life Insurance Life Expectancy Figure

| | Years Remaining ||
Age	Men	Women
55	20.4	25.8
60	16.8	21.8
65	13.7	18.0
70	10.9	14.4
75	8.6	11.2
80	6.8	8.7
84	5.6	6.9

once he acquires that age he can expect another 11.5 years of life. Table 4.4 shows the life-expectancy figures computed for people aged 55 through 84 by the Metropolitan Life Insurance Company.

Differences in life expectancy in various parts of the world or in various segments of our population can be accounted for in large part by differences in environmental hazards such as disease, diet deficiencies, radiation, chemical polution, accidents, rigors of the physical environment (climate), and mental and physical stress.

LIFE SPAN AND EVOLUTION

Life span (MLP) is not greatly affected by the hazards of the external environment. Life span is an inherent property of the species and is determined by the genetic make-up of the organism. Although an American man's life expectancy could perhaps be raised above the present figure of 70 if cures were found for cancer and heart disease, men would still not live longer than 120 years. This life-span potential was achieved hundreds of years ago by the human species and it appears to be relatively static. There has, however, been a dramatic rise in maximum life span throughout the history (or prehistory) of hominid evolution (see Table 4.5).

Table 4.5. Maximum Life Spans Throughout Hominid Evolution

Hominid	Antiquity (years)	Maximum Life Span (years)
Aegyptopithecus zeuxis	26,000,000	17.8
Ramapithecus punjabicus	14,000,000	42.0
Australopithecus africanus	3-4,000,000	51.0
Homo habilis	1.5,000,000	60.1
Homo erectus (Java man)	700,000	69.0
Homo erectus (Peking man)	250,000	76.9
Homo sapiens (Pre-Wurm)	100,000	88.5
Homo neanderthalensis	45,000	94.5
Homo sapiens sapiens (Wurm-Europe)	15,000	94.3

SOURCE: Cutler, 1975:4665.

Aegyptopithecus

Referred to by its discoverer, Elwyn Simons, as "the dawn ape," this hominid is believed to be the oldest common ancestor of apes and humans. It was a small primate weighing only approximately 12 pounds, but its brain, measuring 30 cc, was, relative to body size, larger than any animal living at that time. Anthropologists believe it was a social animal living in troops and interacting both cooperatively and competitively with fellow group members.

Ramapithecus

This animal is believed by most to be the first primate to be more human-like than ape-like. Its lack of large canine teeth (present in its primate contemporaries) suggests a behavior modification. It is assumed that the defense function of large canines was fulfilled by hand tools (weapons). Although no tool industry has ever been associated with hominids as ancient as this variety (9 to 14 million years), it may be that natural objects served as clubs or missiles for self- or group protection. Raymond Dart (1957) has pointed out that an antelope leg bone makes a good club; almost any stone makes an adequate missile; a length of wood can be used for striking or jabbing, and a wild pig tusk or even a broken pebble can function as an effective slashing weapon. It is also believed that the reduction in canine tooth size was associated with dietary changes and a trend toward bipedal locomotion, which, of course, would leave the hands free to use objects as tools or weapons.

Australopithecus africanus

By the time we arrive at what anthropologists believe was the first actual human being, *Australopithecus,* the maximum life-span potential had tripled over that of *Aegyptopithecus* (the earliest of primates to exhibit any human-like features). In *Australopithecus* we find all the criteria necessary for qualification as a human being. *Australopithecus africanus* and *Homo habilis* (also an australopithecine) apparently walked erect, ate meat, developed tool-using and tool-making traditions, and probably developed symbolic communication (language). At this stage in human history (1.5 to 4 million years ago), these creatures undoubtedly lived in permanent groups, cooperated in hunting activities, and lived a relatively nomadic life. At one site a semicircle of piled-up stones has been interpreted as a windbreak or temporary shelter. Considering the existence of their pebble tool tradition (Oldowan) and their capacity for providing themselves with shelter, it would not be unreasonable to credit australopithecines with possession of *culture*. With the arrival of culture, hominids became domesticated animals—self-domesticated to be sure, but still they were the recipients of the special security provided by an artificial (manmade) environment. In regard to the domestication of the human animal, Melville Herskovits has suggested:

> As one of the domesticated animals, man lives a life that is quite different from that he would have to live under natural conditions.... If there is any one word which summarizes the criteria of domestication and the conditions under which domesticated animals live, it is protection. (1949:629, 146)

While this artificial environment undoubtedly contributed to greater life expectancy because of reduced risks, the coming of *culture* also appears to have increased the life span of the species. *Culture* is defined as "the learned, shared behavior that people acquire as members of a society" (Holmes and Parris, 1981:176). The important consideration is that when we enter the sphere of culture we enter the sphere of learning and teaching. Cutler suggests "that the MLP of a mammal may be related to its ability to learn from experience, as compared to instinct abilities. To take full advantage of the ability to learn, and to teach what is learned, more time is necessary than in animals solely dependent upon instinctive behavior" (1978:332). The larger and more complex brains capable of learning also take longer to grow and mature.

The learning process associated with generation-to-generation transmission of culture is called *enculturation,* and as George Kneller observes, "the greater the knowledge and the more complex the skills required for cultural life, the longer education takes" (1965:79).

Margaret Mead also believes that postponement of sexual maturity (which is closely tied to life span) was an evolutionary development associated with human acquisition of culture. She writes:

> We also know that the postponement of the reproductive period in man has tremendous value for the development of human culture. Because of it, young children have enough time to learn before they become reproductive members of the society.
>
> We can only speculate about what happened in the very early stages of hominid development that gradually postponed reproduction until man acquired his present age of puberty. It is possible that what actually occurred was a shrinkage of the reproductive period at both ends. That is, puberty was postponed later and later and the menopause appeared—itself an exceedingly important biological change. Human groups with such genetic characteristics would have a superior chance of survival.... We can think of these as probably very significant biological innovations. (1967:33)

Mead goes on to suggest that the factor contributing to female longevity was the reduction of the dangers and stresses of childbearing because of a shorter period of fertility, but that the factors contributing to male longevity were not biological but social and cultural. Better cooperation in hunting, a new division of labor, better hunting tools that reduced fatal accidents, and ways of negotiating disagreements between groups (thereby reducing open conflict) permitted more men to live into middle and old age.

Societies that functioned in terms of learned traditional behavior had the advantage over the instinct-oriented, since their wisdom was cumulative and therefore unlimited. These early groups undoubtedly also developed food-sharing practices and food taboos so that those no longer active and agile could still survive. The survival of the aged was considered vital to the group, for they often carried in their heads the solutions to life-and-death situations. In regard to how the elderly might have contributed to the survival of the group during a time of famine, Mead conjectures:

> We have to assume a period in man's very early history when, in all probability, people could not describe the places where food could be found; they had to lead others there. Nor were there any ways of communicating information on distance or direction. But some old or older people (old probably meant 40-50 under these conditions) knew where food had been found 10 years ago, when there was a scarcity of food, and they could lead others there. This made such older people extremely valuable. (ibid.)

Homo erectus

Beginning with a maximum potential life span of approximately 52 years for the earliest of humans, it is possible to observe a steady improvement in MLP with greater refinements in human physique and with greater capacity for and development of human culture in such types as Java man and Peking man. These *Homo erectus* varieties are associated with an increase of nearly 25 years of life-span potential. In *Homo erectus* we find a more advanced hominid with a larger brain and a more advanced culture. Archaeological evidence indicates that they had better and more specialized tools, better shelter (camps on lake and stream banks and in caves), and the use of fire. Fire could keep dangerous beasts at bay, it could process and preserve food, it could help families survive cold climates, and it could be used in cooperative hunting operations to flush or control the flight of game.

Early *Homo sapiens* and Neanderthals

With the advent of early *Homo sapiens* and Neanderthals we encounter another increase of almost 20 years in maximum life span, and again this is associated with larger brains and with cultural refinements that insured greater protection from risk. Campsites and caves were warmed by fire, and there was great skill and cooperation in hunting, which was essential, because these early hunters took on game as large as cave bears (8 ft tall) and mammoths. Flake tools were used to prepare hides for tailored clothing, and there was leisure enough to develop religious rituals and special burial practices. Although the primitive, coarse facial features and skeletal specializations of

Neanderthal man led scientists at one time to assume that this hominid was a less-than-human dullard, it is now realized that Neanderthal man was completely modern in his capacity for culture. Subsequent varieties of *Homo sapiens* like Cro-Magnon in the Upper Paleolithic period of European prehistory did not expand the maximum life-span potential at all, nor has there been any great improvement over the last 10,000 to 15,000 years. Although life expectancy (average age of death) has increased with modern medicine and with reduced environmental hazards, MLP has changed very little. It remains at approximately 100 to 120 today, while Neanderthal and Cro-Magnon had a maximum life span of 95.

CALCULATING MAXIMUM LIFE-SPAN POTENTIAL

At this point the reader might question how scientists know what the maximum life-span potential was for hominids who lived millions of years ago. In some cases, analysis of skeletal material has allowed researchers to "observe" what the average age of death might have been and then calculate the life-span figure from that. For example, analysis of skeletal material (mostly teeth and jaw fragments) of 114 specimens of australopithecines by Mann in 1968 revealed[1] that the average age of death for *Australopithecus africanus* was 22.9 years. When a survivorship curve was constructed (i.e., a table showing percentage of population alive at various ages), it was found that no one would have survived past the 35- to 40-year bracket. Where a large amount of fossil material is not available for analysis, maximum life spans are calculated on the basis of body weight/brain size ratio, age of sexual maturation, maximum calorie consumption, and specific metabolic rate. The most important of these for our purposes is the body/brain weight ratio.

The maximum life span of an animal can be estimated with an accuracy of about 25% by using the ratio of brain weight and body weight; Table 4.6 shows the agreements between calculations and observations.

Table 4.6. Observed and Calculated Maximum Life Spans

Primate	Body Weight	Cranial Size (cc)	MLP Observed (years)	MLP Calculated (years)
Rhesus macaque	6,000	90	29	27
Gibbon	5,500	100	32	30
Gorilla	140,000	555	40	42
Chimpanzee	38,500	410	45	46
Human male	65,000	1,450	110	92
Human female	58,000	1,330	110	89

SOURCE: Cutler, 1975: 4665.

If we can assume that the natural world operated in much the same way a million years ago that it does today, we can make educated guesses as to the life span of early

---

[1] Based on development of teeth before and after eruption, as well as amount of wear.

hominids, since we do have fairly accurate knowledge of body and brain size for most of these early forms.

Another indicator of life-span potential is age of sexual maturation (Table 4.7). It has been found that there is a ratio of about 5 to 1 between life-span potential and the time required to reach full reproductive capacity. In humans, the sexual maturation age is between 18 and 20 years and the human MLP is slightly more than 100 years—roughly five times the sexual maturation period.

Other indices of MLP are metabolic rate and caloric intake, and these tend to relate to the overall size of the animal. Smaller animals (and early hominids were small) have a higher rate of metabolism in order to maintain their 37 °C body temperature. Metabolism used to generate heat is harmful to an animal, and the higher rates are associated with shorter life-spans. This rule, which was put forward by Max Rubner in the early 1900s, is not perfect, however. Some of the living fossil-like animals have unusually low metabolic capacities and so do human beings, a few other primates, and rodents.

Using these patterned and predictable relationships, paleodemographers and human evolution specialists have estimated the maximum potential lifetimes for early hominids beginning with *Aegyptopithecus* and ending with modern *Homo sapiens*. Table 4.8 is a compilation of those data.

It should be noted that some of the figures in the table for MLP of prehistoric human beings have been calculated from observations of contemporary preindustrial societies with cultures and environments similar to those of early hominids. For example, many Australian aboriginal populations in Victoria were found to subsist at a cultural level not greatly different from a number of prehistoric populations. They are hunting and gathering peoples with stone tools. A demographic study of these peoples during the years 1876 and 1912 revealed that 2% of the full-blood population survived into the 86- to 90-year age bracket. Infant mortality claimed approximately 25% of the population, but after the first two years of infancy chances for survival increased greatly. This type of evidence is considered of great value by paleodemographers seeking some perspective on performance and life-span potential of prehistoric populations. Thus, Acsadi and Nemeskeri write, "The biological rules of mortality of *Archanthropus* and *Palaeoanthropus* were not basically different from those of modern man. Putting it another way, this would mean that biological possibilities, realized in our day, were 'contained' in ancient man as well" (1972:173).

Table 4.7. Life Span and Sexual Maturation

Primate	Sexual Maturation Period (years)	MLP Observed (years)	MLP Calculated (years)
Rhesus macaque	4–5	29	20–25
Gibbon	7–8	32	35–40
Gorilla	8–9	40	40–45
Chimpanzee	8–9	45	40–45
Human	17–18	110	85–90

SOURCE: Cutler, 1975: 4665.

Table 4.8. Estimated Maximum Potential Lifetimes for Early Hominids

Hominids	Antiquity	Body Weight (g)	Cranial Capacity (cc)	Predicted Sexual Maturation (years)	MLP Calculated* (years)	MLP Predicted (years)
Aegyptopithecus	26 million	2,000	32	3–4	?	17.8
Ramapithecus	14 million	23,000	300	8–9	?	42.0
Australopithecus africanus	3–4 million	32,000	450	10–11	35–40	51.0
Homo habilis	1.5 million	43,000	656	12–13	?	60.1
Java man (Homo erectus)	700,000	53,000	857	13–14	40–60	69.0
Peking man	250,000	53,000	1043	15–16	40–60	76.9
Homo sapiens (pre-Wurm)	100,000	57,300p	1313	17–18	40–60	88.5
Neanderthal	45,000	58,000p	1460	18–19	40–60	94.5
Homo sapiens sapiens (Wurm-Europe)	15,000	58,400p	1460	18–19	?	94.3
Modern human male	20th century	65,000	1450	18–19	110	92.0

SOURCE: Cutler, 1975.
NOTE: p = predicted
? = not sufficient data available.
*Figures in this column were derived from fossil evidence and survival time in contemporary preindustrial societies with similar cultural development.

SENESCENCE

Before we explore the reasons for variation in maximum life-span potentials of the various species, let us first consider what *aging* represents. Aging, also known as *senescense,* is a natural loss of corporeal functions that begins in humans at about age 30. Alexander Leaf (1973a) tells us, for example, that by the age of 75 the level of functioning of the basic metabolism rate has diminished 16%, the cardiac output has been reduced by 30%, the maximum breathing capacity has dropped 57%, and the filtration efficiency of the kidneys has diminished by 31% from the level of the 30-year-old. Brain weight diminishes 8%, and nerve-conduction velocity is lowered approximately 10%.

Only in a few domesticated animals or ones in captivity, in animals at the top of the predatory pecking order, and in humans does this decline in organic functioning (senescence) take place. In the majority of animal species, death occurs shortly after the reproductive cycle has been completed. Each species of animal has different environmental hazards associated with its particular ecological niche. These environmental hazards are of two kinds: weather conditions and the balance of nature, or the complex food chain involving insect, plant, and animal predators and prey. The ability of animals to maintain maximum vigor varies greatly, and this ability is related to maximum life-span potential and to chances for survival in the wild. The European robin, whose annual mortality rate is 6%, has an MLP of 12 years, while the Royal albatross, with a 0.03% annual mortality, has an MLP of 45 years. Cutler maintains it does not make evolutionary sense for a mouse to have a 10-year MLP if 50% of the population in the wild does not survive past eight months and less than 5% reaches the age of 18 months (1978). However, it must be realized that if environmental conditions were equalized some animals would still live twice as long as others, because of genetic differences.

Aging rates are believed to be determined by relatively few genes. Considering the two-fold increase in maximum life span in the hominid evolutionary sequence over the last 3 million years, we can assume that this had to be accomplished by mutations in a small number of genes. In order to accomplish the increase in the MLP of 14 years per 100,000 years, chances are that the genetic mechanism involved is not overly complex. Roy Walford found that a small segment of the eighteenth chromosome of mice controls both the immune system and the level of DNA repairs. He concludes, "This ties together the life span, the rate of aging, the immune system and DNA repair efficiency into one package" (Kahn, 1979b:53).

Why We Age

There are two theoretical camps attempting to explain aging. Some researchers believe that aging is programmed in the genes, and others believe that aging results not from genetic plans but from the wear and tear of life.

An example of the first point of view is the cell division theory advanced by Leonard Hayflick. While doing cancer research in the early 1960s, Hayflick found that, although there is no division in muscle or brain cells, the fibroblast cells (a main component of body tissue) are programmed to divide 50 times and then die. He believes that this cell-doubling limit is closely related to the life span of an organism. Hayflick found, for example, that in a mouse, with a three-year life span, cells doubled 12 times and a chicken with a 30-year life span had cells that doubled about 25 times. He calculated that since the maximum doubling capacity in human cells is 50, then the maximum life span of people could not possibly be more than about 110 years (Cherry and Cherry, 1974:78).

Another theory stressing programming is the genetic master plan hypothesis proposed by P.B. Medawar and G.C. Williams. This theory suggests that a genetic master plan is built into the cells and this results in a kind of life-cycle clock that regulates childhood and adolescent growth and sexual maturation. Much like a computer tape, this master genetic plan triggers the appropriate developments at the proper times, but ultimately the tape runs out and the cells are left without instructions. This results in their rapid deterioration and eventual disintegration. In human beings, the tape begins to run out at about age 30, because from an evolutionary standpoint it has accomplished its task. It has brought the organism through the stage of reproduction, thereby allowing it to replace itself, but the tape takes no responsibility for its welfare thereafter.

Since everything known to mankind ultimately wears out, it is conceivable that the human animal itself should suffer the same fate. Those that take the "wear-and-tear" position believe that aging is a kind of degenerative disease resulting from genetic damage in the cells from things outside as well as inside the body such as natural and synthetic chemicals, ultraviolet rays, and radiation. Some researchers hold that aging results from an accumulation of "errors" or "mistakes" that develop in the cell's repair machinery. These could be production of extra chromosomes or imperfect DNA replication (producing mutations). These imperfections may affect the rate at which worn-out cells can replace themselves or recover from injury, and this cumulative effect, it is argued, eventually results in death.

Wear and tear is also seen as emanating from the body processes themselves. Such damage is often described as coming from the "internal environment" and is said to be of a *pleiotropic nature*. Pleiotropic factors that appear to be responsible for age are continuously acting processes and developmentally linked processes.

A continuously acting process is metabolism, and it is responsible for the production of toxic by-products such as free radicals. Free radicals are extremely reactive molecular fragments that collide with other molecules, particularly oxygen. These constant collisions result in damage that is responsible for age changes and age-related diseases. All living cells produce some free radicals as a result of energy production, but they can also be produced from forces outside the body such as x-rays, heat, drugs, and automobile exhaust-generated ozone. Free radicals can be counteracted, however, by substances known as radical scavengers. Vitamin C acquired from citrus fruit, or vitamin E acquired from whole-wheat bread or wheat-germ oil can quickly neutralize these ever-present free radicals.

An example of developmentally linked processes which are sources of harmful agents is the production of hormones that are important in regulating growth and sexual maturity but in the long run are toxic pollutants. Laboratory experiments have shown that removing the pituitary gland from animals reduced the rate of aging, and when salmon were prevented from maturing sexually they, too, had a longer life span.

The Immune System

If aging is indeed caused by pollutants and hazards either in the internal or external environment, we still cannot explain the variation in the MLP of various species. What seems to make the difference is the particular species' built-in capacity to handle damage, and the capacity of some species is greater than others. Some researchers see that the *repair* and *replacement* resources of the organism are all-important in determining life span. They claim that aging results because of the body's increasing inability to ward off disease. With the advent of senescence, they believe an individual's antibodies (produced by the white blood cells) have less and less proficiency in repairing or warding off cellular damage.

Some species have more highly developed immune systems than others and this allows them to operate at higher levels of efficiency. The fact that we live twice as long as chimpanzees is not because our bodies are constructed better but because of our greater ability to detoxify and ward off the chemical pollutants coming from both the external and internal environments and because of our innate capacity to repair the damage made by them. Cutler writes:

> Repair and protection act as antibiosenescent processes to reduce the rate of accumulation of cellular damage . . . . Only DNA can be repaired; other damaged constituents can only be replaced. (1978a:339)

Heredity and Environment

Much of our discussion up to this point has been directed at understanding the hereditary basis for longevity, but longevity is determined by both genetic and environmental factors. Although we do not know for sure, we might begin with the assumption that about 50% of how long we live relates to our heredity and about 50% relates to environmental characteristics such as climate, technology, emotional stress, and disease.

Without doubt the genetic background of an individual is important. Raymond Pearl discovered a positive correlation between the age of death of an individual and the age of death of that person's parents. He found that 45.8% of those who lived past the age of 70 also had parents who lived that long. On the other hand, only 13.4% of those over 70 had short-lived parents (Galston, 1975:14).

A study of Finnish and Swedish genealogies by Jalavisto (1951) established that both the longevity of the mother and the father tended to increase the average length of life of the offspring. He also found that the effect of maternal longevity is greater than that of paternal longevity, but that the paternal effect is greater in sons than in daughters.

One of the more fascinating studies on the role of heredity in aging was conducted by Franz Kallmann and Gerhard Sander (1948) on 933 pairs of twins. When they compared the life spans of same-sex twins, they found that the average intrapair difference in identical (monozygotic) twins was about half that of fraternal (dizygotic) twins. The total mean difference among the former was 36.9 months while the difference in the latter was 78.3 months. They found no examples of fraternal twins who died within less than three months of each other, but they did find one pair of identical twins who died the same day of the same causes at the age of 86. Two identical twin pairs died only 5 and 25 days apart at the ages of 85 and 69 respectively. One of these sets (sisters) developed similar senile psychoses, although their social and marital histories were quite different. One was married and raised a large family on a farm while the other remained single and worked as a dressmaker in the city. Both became totally deaf and blind in the same month and both were reported to have suffered massive cerebral hemorrhages on the same day.

Kallman and Sander report great similarities between aged identical twins in the "degree of general enfeeblement or its absence, the greying and thinning of the hair, the configuration of baldness and senile wrinkle formation, and the extent of eye, ear and tooth deficiencies" (1948:353).

In regard to one set of monozygotic twins 95 years old, Kallman and Sander write, "Born in Poland, they had lived in this country for over sixty years. One of them speaks English fluently, the other not at all. But if they do not indulge in conversation, hardly anybody can tell them apart" (ibid.).

One set of identical twins had lived in very different environments. One had married, produced a large family, and had practiced medicine in New York state for 50 years. His twin brother had never married and had lived on a ranch in the West where he had been a successful stock breeder. We are told that when the two brothers met after several decades of separation, they were found "to have resisted the development of complete baldness with practically the same residual amount of hair" (ibid:354).

Thus, we find that heredity plays an important part in establishing a species-specific life-span potential and also in controlling the rate of aging.

SUMMARY

All organisms have fixed, finite life spans, and the maximum potential for humans appears to be approximately 110 to 120 years. Most individuals will die much earlier, and life expectancy (a projected average figured at birth) varies from country to country and from occupation to occupation. It also varies according to race, sex, and class. While life expectancy has increased in modern times with better medicine, better diet, and fewer environmental hazards, the maximum life-span potential for human beings has not changed to any great degree since the time of Neanderthal, some 45,000 years ago. Length of life span is property of the species, but to understand the matter of human longevity it is necessary to understand the evolutionary history of the primates. From the first ape-like ancestors through modern *Homo sapiens* there has been a steady and progressive increase in life span with a noticeable gain with the advent of culture and a shift from instinctive to learned behavior.

Consideration of life span inevitably leads to the question of what aging is and why it takes place. Aging, known as senescence, is a natural loss of organic functions that begins in humans at about age 30, which is after the peak of the reproduction cycle. Human beings are one of the few species that experience senescence. Most animals die shortly after they have reproduced and guaranteed the continuation of the species. Much of this has to do with the natural hazards facing the animal. In the case of human beings, culture has provided a margin of safety, allowing longer life and therefore senescence. Although the security provided by culture is important, we must remember that the greater part of human longevity is determined by genetic endowment and is a product of the species' evolutionary history.

There are two schools of thought on how and why this phenomenon of aging takes place. One school believes that aging is programmed in the genes, and the other believes that aging is the result of the wear and tear of everyday living. In recent years, the greater share of investigators appear to be leaning toward the latter explanation, and considerable emphasis has been placed on the immune system, or the inherent ability of the species to cope with damage in the cells through repair or replacement.

As the volume of knowledge concerning longevity grows, we are struck more and more by the necessity for holistic analyses of the interaction between genetic and environmental components. Even though mankind is one species biologically, the fact that life-expectancy rates vary as much as 40 years among various cultures means that studies of the quality of the genetic endowment must always be linked with data concerning climate, diet, technology, disease, emotional stress, war, and genocide. Because of an awareness of the great importance of these environmental factors in longevity, scientists have sought to find cultures where the life-style is conducive to long life. Our next chapter discusses three such areas. Claims of extreme longevity in these Shangri-la enclaves will be presented and evaluated in terms of present scientific knowledge of the hereditary and environmental factors involved in determinations of length of life.

CHAPTER 5

Shangri-las

For many years the world has been intrigued by reports of little pockets of people who, apparently for genetic or environmental reasons, have managed to achieve surprisingly high longevity. Lewis Aiken writes, "Examples of very long life spans are found in sizable numbers among the Hunza people in the Karakoram Range of the Himalayas, the Abkhasia of the Republic of Georgia in the U.S.S.R., and the Andean 'Viejos' of the village of Vilcabamba in Ecuador. Nearly 50 out of every 100,000 people in the Caucasus region of the Soviet Union, compared to only 3 out of 100,000 (in the United States), live to be 100" (1978:8).

These societies not only claim high percentages of centenarians, but two areas have reported people living beyond what we have established as the maximum potential for human beings—120 years. For example, Sula Benet's informant among the Abkhasians of Georgia, Madame Khfaf Lasuria, was reported to be 140 years old, and in Vilcabamba, Ecuador, several investigators set the age of Miguel Carpio at 129. Claims for the Hunza of Pakistan have been a bit more conservative, with the oldest in this region reported to be 110. While investigators in each of these areas mention environmental factors, both physical and cultural, that might promote longevity, they generally assume that this unusual capacity for long life has a genetic base. Leaf writes of the Vilcabamba, "One leaves this Andean valley with the strong suspicion that genetic factors must be playing an important role in the longevity of this small enclave of elderly people of European stock." And of the Hunza he writes, "The impression that genetic factors are important in longevity was reinforced by what we saw in Hunza" (1973:293). But of the Abkhasians he writes, "The possible role of genetic factors in longevity seemed of less importance in the Caucasus.... The Caucasus is a land bride that has been traveled for centuries by conquerors from both the east and the west, and its population can scarcely have maintained any significant degree of genetic isolation. At the same time, when one speaks to the numerous centenarians in the area, one invariably discovers that each of them has parents or siblings who have similarly attained great age. The genetic aspect of longevity therefore cannot be entirely dismissed" (ibid:294-295).

In order to explore further the factors of heredity and environment in long life and in order to assess the reliability and validity of claims of extreme longevity, let us look at the three societies already mentioned, plus one other where claims of unusual longevity have been recorded.

THE ABKHASIANS

The Abkhasians live in the province of Georgia in the Soviet Union in a mountainous region bordered by the Black Sea on the west and the Caspian Sea on the east. The region is humid and subtropical in western Georgia but hillier and drier in the east. Neither climate nor altitude seems to make a great deal of difference in regard to longevity, however. Medvedev tells us that in Georgia "there are some places at sea level with a higher index of longevity than the nearest mountain regions, and the distribution of this index between mountain populations at equal altitudes is very wide" (1974:382).

As we have pointed out earlier, the people of Georgia have not been an isolated population. The Caucasus area, for example, is multinational, with some 20 different nationalities (each with its own language). In the past, the region was conquered by the Mongols, the Turks, the Persians, and, finally, the Russians. The population is so mixed that Berdyshev (1966) postulated that the high proportion of long-lived people can be explained by hybridization (heterosis).

Although life-styles vary, a number of behavior patterns are shared within the region and may have significance in explaining longevity. For example, evidence indicates that the diet of the Abkhasians is more likely to promote longevity than that consumed by Americans. For many years, yogurt was assumed to be the secret of Abkhasian long life. Although yogurt has high food value and therapeutic properties, particularly for intestinal disorders, and may promote good health, Abkhasian diet has other positive aspects. Sula Benet maintains that throughout all areas of the Caucasus there is a rhythmic regularity in meals and an aversion to overeating. Food is chewed slowly and well, and a calm atmosphere prevails at meals. The people insist that food be fresh, which means they do not keep leftovers. Everywhere in the Caucasus, people believe that health and food are closely related (1976:93).

Crawford and Oberdiech point out that "aged Abkhasians consume on the average 1900 calories per day in the form of 73 grams of carbohydrates.... By comparison, the U.S. Department of Agriculture reports that Americans consume 3300 daily calories with exceptionally high fat intake" (1978:39).

There is a good deal of debate in scientific circles about the relationship between calorie intake and longevity. Laboratory experiments with rats indicate that if they are reared on a diet extremely low in calories but with all the necessary nutrients they will outlive rats raised on a diet of more calories by 50%. It is reported that one rat outlived the others by three times. Restricting the protein diet in middle-age rats likewise increased their life span, but only by 25% or 30%.

A low calorie intake is also reported for the Vilcabamba and the Hunza. On the other hand, Rubin Andres, in a study of obesity and mortality rates in America, found that people 20% to 30% over the figure given on height-weight charts did not die any younger than those who had "normal" weight. Some studies even show that moderately obese individuals live longer (Kahn, 1979:24).

The people of the Caucasus eat little meat, eggs, or sweet foods but acquire great amounts of natural vitamins from fresh vegetables. Protein is derived from beans, nuts, and yogurt, and they get large amounts of vitamin C from wild apples and pears. (As mentioned before, vitamin C is known to be a "radical scavenger" counteracting the harmful effects of reactive molecular fragments whose collisions with other molecules are believed to be a cause of aging.) On the other hand, the consumption of wine is very high in the area (higher than France). Leaf also found an Abkhasian claiming to be over 130 years old who said he had smoked a pack of cigarettes daily for the last 62 years. And Khfaf Lasuria, believed by Sula Benet to be 140 years old, had a glass of vodka before breakfast every day.

The Georgian population is very active. The value of exercise, particularly in preventing coronary heart disease, is well established. J.N. Morris et al. (1953) showed that conductors on double-deck London buses who had to do a great deal of climbing have much lower incidence of heart attacks than the more sedentary drivers. A study that looked at records of Harvard University students attending at the turn of the century showed moderately active men (who lettered in minor sports or who engaged in intramural athletics) outlived both those who never went to the gym at all and those who participated in major sports such as football and basketball. Benet (1976) claims that there are six times as many heart attacks in the plains of the Daghestan region to the east of Abkhasia as there are in the mountains.

In the Caucasus everyone works hard, even the aged. Sichinava (1965) reports that almost three-fourths of the men and women over 80 years of age still do varied light tasks, and about 10% still work in the gardens and orchards. Approximately 5% still chop their own wood and carry their own water.

In Abkhasia, where the terrain is rugged, merely remaining a participating member of the community requires considerable exertion. People of all ages walk and climb a great deal, often on very rocky paths. Leaf writes of these Caucasus aged: "Forty-five percent of these elderly go for long strolls daily out to their gardens, twenty-four percent walk from one village to another, twenty-five percent walk only in the house or garden" (1975:12).

The remote mountain habitat also means that the air is pure and that the drinking water, which comes from melted snow, is unpolluted.

Finally, we must consider certain social and cultural factors that could contribute to a long life in the Caucasus. Most important among these are lack of stress, positive attitudes toward illness and old age, and the social system. Concerning the social system, Benet writes, "In the Caucasus, the old people remain involved in their family, their lineage, and their community. They are involved emotionally and physically. Their work provides them with physical exercise but also with the knowledge of their own meaningful contribution to their community" (1976:164). Because of this involvement and the absence of pressures and worries so often found in an industrialized society, Benet believes that stress is held to a minimum. Although the relationship of stress to aging is little understood, stress is believed to be a counterproductive force.

On the other hand, the sense of group-belonging enjoyed by Abkhasians, the interest in their surroundings, plus the proper attitude toward the illnesses in advanced years and a healthy attitude toward sex, provide optimum conditions for longevity. In regard to attitudes about illness and sex, Benet writes, "The Abkhasians expect to live long and healthy lives . . . . A continuation of sex life into old age is considered as natural as maintaining a healthy appetite or sound sleep" (1974:85-86). When the elderly in this society fall ill, they expect to recover regardless of their age or the nature of their illness. The terminal hip fracture, so characteristic of North American culture, is unknown in Abkhasia.

Over the last few years there has been a cloud of doubt over the Caucasus claims of extreme longevity. Gerontologists maintain that the 110- to 120-year life span maximum is valid for everyone, even the Russian citizens of the Caucasus. Michael Crawford writes, "There has been considerable skepticism concerning the actual ages of the 'dolgozhitili' " (1978:1). Some scientists, like Medvedev, have claimed that these so-called centenarians have "exaggerated their age to avoid the military draft" (ibid).

Medvedev's doubts are prompted by a great deal more than his assumption that ages were altered for draft evasion, however. He maintains that state documents about age distribution are not valid because all information was obtained verbally and without corroborating documents. He maintains that the 1970 census in the Caucasus showed a decrease in centenarians from 8,890 in 1960 to 4,925, although there is no reason to believe that any natural or man-made cause should bring this about. The answer is that the methods of collecting accurate information improved. The concentration of centenarians is highest in Moslem areas and here there is no practice of birth registration at all. Even in Christian areas it is difficult to find birth registrations, since about 90% of churches (and their records) were destroyed between 1922 and 1940.

Of the 500 people in the Caucasus claiming to be between 120 and 170, not a single one has been able to produce documents proving his age. Even if some of these people were correct in assessing the number of years they have survived, there is also the complicating fact that many in this group are Moslem and the Moslem year is only 10 months long.

Some researchers claim that the people are able to establish their correct age by associations with historical events. But many of these events concern only the village—such as the year of a famine or a plague—and cannot always be accurately placed in time. Also troubling is the fact that often more people are reported in the very old categories than in the younger ones. For example, in the Altay area of the Caucasus the 1959 census showed 15 people between the ages of 111 and 113, but 19 individuals between 114 and 116. In one area, statistics showed 72 persons between the ages of 100 and 104, 44 persons between 105 and 109 (a mortality rate of 39%) but then only a 12% mortality rate drop to 39 people in the 110- 114-age bracket. Theoretically, this pattern of attrition is not possible, and such statistics can be of little use in scientific research.

Although the average life span in the Caucasus is about the same as that for the rest of the Soviet Union, the reported number who reach 80 is 40% higher, the number

One of the "long-living" men, said to be in his nineties, at the village of Chlou, Abkhazia, U.S.S.R., and his wife, half his age, and their daughter. (Photo courtesy of Paul Lin.)

who reach 100 is 410% higher, and the number who reach 110 is 2,000% higher than the average for the whole country.

In addition to the problems connected with document validation, there is also the problem of correlating chronological with functional and biochemical evidence. In regard to the Abkhasian *dolgozhitili,* Frolkis writes that the "study of the health of longevous people usually results in an important paradox. The function and metabolism of longevous people of 100-110 years are on the same level as is usual for people 55-60 years" (1973). Although we do not have well-established criteria for what is physiologically normal for various periods of advanced age, most populations do not exhibit the kinds of discrepancies cited by Frolkis.

Berdyshev (1968) believes that social and political factors can explain the claims of high longevity in the Caucasus. He points out that in this area villagers seek out the elderly for advice and help in solutions of difficult problems, and the older the advisor the greater the respect and honor extended to him or her. This has a tendency to encourage age exaggeration.

Another factor is the great deal of attention that the international media has given in recent years to the phenomenal longevity of these people. This has resulted in considerable competition between villages to be able to claim the oldest individual or the greatest number of centenarians. A generation ago villages were claiming 115-year-old residents, but it is not unusual today to find claims of 160- or 170-year-old people.

Moreover, the Soviet Union as a whole enjoys the publicity and feels that a long life is a unique Soviet accomplishment. Many of the old people working on collective farms have been given special recognition by the state and applauded as national heroes. The fact that Stalin was from the Caucasus area is also significant. He encouraged the reports of longevity from his area of birth and did everything he could to establish the validity of such claims. Some suspect that few social scientists during Stalinist years would have had the courage to challenge the claims so much relished by their leader.

Even if the claims of long life could be safely rejected, today it would not be a good business, since the reputation of longevity has brought droves of foreign and domestic visitors to the region, and the residents are not only the recipients of material advantages but also a great deal of flattering attention.

THE HUNZA

At the northern apex of West Pakistan, between Afghanistan and China, the Hunza Valley lies within the Karakoram mountain range. This area, which is actually located in an extension of the Himalayas, has an altitude of between 5,000 and 7,000 feet. The climate is temperate with warm summers (often reaching 90 °F), but winter brings snow and cold temperatures. The land is arid, and although the Hunza Valley looks like a great formal garden, this is made possible only by using water from glaciers and springs high in the hills above in an ingenious irrigation system. The inhabitants of the valley, called Hunzakuts, subsist on grains, vegetables, and fruits (principally apricots).

Some 40,000 people live in the Hunza Valley. They are a non-Mongoloid people who appear Caucasian. Where they originally came from is unknown, although there are a number of theories, the most popular being that they derive from soldiers who deserted from the army of Alexander the Great. Their language, Burashaski, however, indicates that they have been isolated in these mountains since about 1500 B.C. There is no written language and therefore no birth records. The only event that can be used to establish any kind of time frame is the invasion of the British in 1892.

Although no census has ever been taken in the area, Hunza is believed to have a relatively high percentage of healthy and vigorous elderly people, some of them over 100. The oldest inhabitant of the valley was, according to Leaf (1975), Tulah Beg (aged 110) who Leaf found to have soft arteries, normal blood pressure (152/84) and a regular pulse of 90. His lungs were clear, his reflexes active, and his posture was erect. He was, however, somewhat feeble and had a large skin cancer on his forehead. He no longer worked but was aided in walking by his wooden staff and by his two vigorous sons, aged 70 and 74. Tulah Beg claims that he was 26 years old when the British invaded Hunza.

It is difficult to understand just why Hunza gained its reputation as a "Himalayan Shangri-la" (Taylor and Nobbs, 1962), although the area has long been considered a healthful environment. According to Leaf, "Dr. McCarrison (a highly regarded British authority on nutrition and public health), who spent seven years as a British army surgeon in India, noted the hardiness and good health of the Hunzakuts. He remarked on the rapidity with which they healed their wounds or infections, and this he attributed largely to their diet. Later in his career as an experimental nutritionist, he found that his white laboratory rats raised on a typical Hunzakut diet lived longer and were healthier than rats raised on the typical diets of other ethnic groups" (1975:27-28). When Leaf arrived in Hunza in 1971, he observed, "I was not able to confirm exact ages in Hunza. Yet I had the definite impression of an unusual number of very vigorous old folk clambering over the steep slopes that make up this mountainous land. It was the fitness of many of the elderly rather than their extreme ages that impressed me" (1973:96).

Earlier reports that Hunza were cancer-free were proved to be false, however. Sahoor Ahmed of the Pakistani ministry of health reported finding cancer (leukemic and rectal), and he did not believe that the Hunzakut as a group were exceptionally healthy.

If indeed Hunza has an "unusual number of very vigorous old folk," it might be assumed that the diet is basically responsible. The average daily caloric intake was found to be 1,923 calories (compared to 3,300 in the United States) with 50 g protein (100 in the U.S.), 35 g fat (157 in the U.S.), and 354 g carbohydrates (380 in the U.S.). Only 8% of Hunza calories are in the form of fat, and exactly half of American calories are so derived. Meat and dairy products constitute only 1.5% of the total Hunza intake. Oil obtained from the seeds of apricots is used for all cooking and virtually no animal fat is consumed. The people suffer from neither obesity nor malnutrition. There is no alcoholism, and elderly people do not smoke.

The isolation of Hunza may also be a factor in their longevity. Not only does their isolation insure protection from air and water pollution, but it may be responsible for the maintenance of a gene pool that promotes or is responsible for health and longevity. Not only have the Hunzakuts been isolated from the outside world for about 2,000 years, they have, for cultural reasons, avoided intermarriage with other groups in their area.

If reports of old age vigor and alertness are true, one might very well credit the social and political system that Leaf described:

> The old people are esteemed for the wisdom that is thought to derive from long experience and their word in the family group is generally the law .... The Mir (king) holds court daily at 10 a.m. with his council of elders. The latter is comprised of some twenty wise old men from each village in the kingdom. They sit in a circle on carpets spread at the foot of the Mir's wooden throne and listen to all disputes among the citizens .... Most continue their work until the age of 100. There is no fixed or forced retirement age, and the elderly are not dismissed when they reach a certain age as occurs in our industrialized societies. (1975:153-154)

VILCABAMBA

The village of Vilcabamba (meaning *Sacred Valley*) is 4,500 feet up in the Andes mountains in Ecuador. Paul Martin describes the Vilcabamba region as "an ecologist's dream with clear water provided by two rivers, pure air, and a temperate, even climate. Pollution is unknown" (1976:12). The inhabitants of this small rural agricultural community are of mixed ancestry—Spanish and Indian—but with a tendency toward European features. This farm community subsists mainly on corn, bananas, potatoes, wheat, barley, beans, peanuts, and grapes.

Vilcabamba is relatively isolated. The nearest town, Loja (25,000), is a long 25 miles away over an unpaved, rutted road full of switchbacks. Like other areas of purported high longevity, Vilcabamba has an interesting history of factual and ficticious reports on its health conditions. As early as 1825, Captain George Coggeshall, in his book *Voyages to Various Parts of the World,* reported that the area, with its pure air and healthful conditions, had many inhabitants of very great age. He described his visit to a couple, both of whom were supposedly over 100, and commented that they were physically active and mentally alert.

In 1954 Eugene Payne, a clinical investigator for a drug company, wrote of the Vilcabamba area, "Heart disease is almost unknown among the inhabitants .... Outsiders who come there with poor hearts often report within six months that they are well" (1954:12). This was the claim of Albert Kramer in 1959 who "cured" his heart disease by living there. Kramer also commented on the extreme longevity of his heart-disease-free neighbors. In 1969, a Peruvian doctor, Miguel Salvador, brought a medical team to Vilcabamba to investigate health and longevity claims. The team gave physical tests to 158 elderly men and 180 women out of the total population of 819. Salvador claimed that he found nine persons over the age of 100. If this is true, it would represent an index of 1,100 centenarians per 100,000. If the United States had such an index we would have 2 million centenarians. There are, however, only about 15,000 in the United States. Salvador concluded that he had found a natural island of immunity to the physical and psychological problems that shorten lives elsewhere.

Cultural factors in Vilcabamba might very well also contribute to longevity. For example, the constant physical exertion required to live in this mountainous terrain is believed to have kept the people's bones mineralized, dense, and strong and their hearts robust. Although hygienic and public health conditions are poor, the diet is seen by experts as conducive to good health and long life. The Vilcabamba's daily food intake totals only about 1,200 calories and this is derived from 35 to 38 g protein, 12 to 19 g fat, and 200 to 250 g carbohydrate. Their diet, which is composed mostly of fruits and vegetables and very little meat, is lower in fats than the diet of the Hunza or Abkhasians and only one-fifth that of citizens of the United States.

When Alexander Leaf left this Ecuadorian village he went with a number of unanswered questions. He wrote:

> I departed from Vilcabamba puzzled as to what was so different in this village from hundreds of other seemingly similar villages in the underdeveloped areas of South America. A subvigorous physical labor intensified by the mountainous terrain, and the respect of offspring for their parents were hardly unique in Vilcabamba. Because of the apparent family ties linking the elderly in this small enclave of isolated villages, I left with a strong suspicion that genetic factors were of prime importance. (1975:58)

Although Leaf suggests that genetic reasons account for 366 times more centenarians in Vilcabamba than in the United States, a recent study by Mazess and Forman (1979) revealed another explanation—*that they lie about their age.* These researchers claim to have found not a single centenarian in the lot. The oldest person in the village was, according to them, 96. Explaining that "age exaggeration appears to be a common finding in the extreme elderly throughout the world . . . associated with illiteracy and absence of actual documentation" (1979:94), they set about investigating claims of extreme longevity in this Ecuadorian village.

Mazess and Forman found some baptismal records, but many had been destroyed in a church fire. Those that did exist were difficult to read because of faded writing and the poor condition of the pages. Positive identification of individuals soon loomed as the major problem. They discovered "there were frequent duplications of given names and surnames. Misidentification and sloppiness of identification have characterized previous descriptions of this population. In Vilcabamba there are relatively few familial names in use, and several of these, such as Toledo and Carpio, are extremely common" (1979:94).

They also found that the same given names have been used again and again over many generations. When it was possible to compare birth records of individuals with their reported ages, it was found that there was a consistent and predictable pattern of age exaggeration. Mazess and Forman state:

> Systematic age exaggeration was found beginning at about 70 years; at a stated age of 100 the estimated actual age would be only 84 years . . . . We were able to demonstrate that nearly all cases of reported centenarians in Vilcabamba were in their 80s or 90s. (1979:98)

PAROS, GREECE

Although claims of extreme longevity in the Caucasus, Pakistan, and Ecuador cannot be substantiated because of inadequate proof of exact ages, one study of longevity

Many of the people of Paros are fishermen. This 90-year-old man goes out several times a week. (Photo courtesy of Jeff Beaubier.)

carried out on the island of Paros in 1970-1972 has not only documentary evidence of the ages of the five centenarians in the community of Paros but also has good enough demographic records to permit the construction of a life table (Table 5.1). A life table is a statistical life history of a group showing the number of persons in various age categories from birth to 100 and over, the expected years of remaining life for individuals in each age category, and the probability of surviving each age category. None of the earlier studies of areas of high longevity had sufficient or accurate enough data to compile such a table.

The remarkable fact about the people of Paros was that out of a population of 2,703 people five were 100 years old or older. That represents an index of 185 centenarians per 100,000. The prevalence of centenarians in Paros is therefore 70 times greater than what is found in the United States.

The records used to corroborate the age claims of centenarians as well as the rest of the community were birth registrations and baptism records, all complete with family members' and officials' signatures. Other substantiating evidence included records of taxation, property ownership, and military service.

Paros is described as "a society that requires physical work, and rewards and prizes mental activity. There is good nutrition, lack of pollution, excellent medical care, folk and preventative health, good family life, lack of crime and social strife" (Beaubier, 1980:41).

The people of Paros community fish, farm, and provide services to tourists. A few are merchant seamen. The standard of living is relatively high, and family life is

Table 5.1. The Life Table of Paros Community:
Mean Years of Remaining Life At Specified Age Categories for the Total Population

Age X	Probability of Survival from Birth to Exact Age X	Mean No. of Years Lived by an Individual in the Age Interval	No. of Person-Years Lived by a Cohort of 100,000 Persons	Expected Years of Remaining Life from Exact Age X
At birth	1.00	.98	-7,700,460	77.0
1	.96	8.62	7,602,290	78.9
10	.95	9.50	6,739,910	70.7
20	.95	9.46	5,789,600	61.1
30	.94	9.39	4,843,320	51.3
40	.93	9.22	3,904,300	41.8
50	.91	8.95	2,982,420	32.8
60	.88	4.32	2,087,010	23.7
65	.85	4.10	1,655,010	19.5
70	.79	3.73	1,244,970	15.7
75	.70	3.12	871,690	12.4
80	.55	2.34	559,220	10.1
85	.39	1.56	325,370	8.3
90	.24	.94	169,760	7.0
95	.14	.48	76,260	5.4
100	.06	.20	27,990	4.4
105+	.02	.08	8,480	3.9

SOURCE: Beaubier, J., *High life Expectancy on the Island of Paros, Greece*, New York: Philosophical Library, 1976.
NOTE: Generated by BIOS computer program TSL LIFTA written in Fortran by Dana Quade and Alexa Sorant.

satisfying, with great respect being shown to elders. The diet of the Paros people is much like that found in other areas of high longevity—large quantities of fresh fruits and vegetables and very little meat. Protein comes from fish and eggs, and yogurt and cheese are plentiful in all homes. The region has a moderate Mediterranean climate and is free of infectious disease. Major causes of death are heart disease, cancer, and stroke. The community has "extremely low or nonexistent rates of alcoholism, drug abuse, homicide, truancy, illiteracy, civil suits, felonies and misdemeanors, insanity, illegitimacy, venereal disease, bankruptcy, accidents, divorce or suicide" (Beaubier, 1976:131-132).

The people have strong marriages, relatively little stress, and an optimistic and positive attitude toward life. Although Paros is not paradise, the combination of excellent medical facilities (one doctor per 1,000 residents) and the wholesome physical and psychological environment help explain the extraordinary number of centenarians in this society.

CULTURAL FACTORS IN LONGEVITY

Although claims of extremely high longevity (above the human maximum life-span potential) appear to be highly questionable, there are without doubt, conditions that can prolong life and increase the percentage of elderly that survive to the century mark. Every society has its prescription for long life. The ideas of individuals in a society may vary somewhat on this issue, but there will be consistency within the society based on the group's concept of health, illness and important values.

Ideas of desirable physical and psychological environments also vary from culture to culture. Members of different societies may respond negatively or positively to the same stimuli. For example, in America stress is often cited as a factor detrimental to longevity, and noise pollution has often been cited as a major contributor to stress.

In Hong Kong, however, where there is tremendous crowding (20,000 persons per acre), noise does not contribute to stress. Anderson writes, "Noise, demonstrably a stressful problem in many crowded cities and households around the world, is not a problem here . . . . Noise in a household is the sign of life and action, and the household moves in a shimmering ambience of sound from waking to sleep . . . . I have never heard anyone complain about noise in a Chinese household. Noise is desirable or at worst ignored" (1972:145-146).

In spite of cultural differences in what is perceived as harmful or helpful factors in longevity, the similarity of the responses to what contributes to long life is remarkable. Generally, societies value work as a way of maintaining health and vigor, although few have as strong a work ethic as Americans. Moderation in eating, drinking, and smoking is often cited, as is the value of a proper diet. In a large number of societies, even preindustrial, people believe that one will live longer if one has had long-lived parents. The pleasures of sex and pleasant companions (spouses and friends) are often seen as advantageous, and in many societies, large, supportive, and respectful families contribute to longevity of elders. In most of the world, the general formula for a long life is to be happy, to be adequately (but not overly) fed, to be respected, to be moderate in one's vices, and to be active.

The following are a few formulas from elders around the world explaining why they have lived so long:

Ali Murad (Hunza, age 91) attributes long life to "normal work, no smoking, no suffering, adequate rest, and a moderate amount of wine; and one should eat a lot of green vegetables" (Leaf, 1975:39).

Four aged Abkhasians (ages 95-106) when asked the secret of their long life stated: "The clean Abkhasian air," "Good food and pure mountain water," "Constant exercise and exertion of farm life keeps you fit and helps strengthen the heart," and "Heredity. Long living individuals tend to marry other long lived, and longevity is concentrated in certain lineages (Rodi) in the community" (Crawford and Oberdieck, 1978:37).

Charlie Smith (former African slave claiming to be 130) recommends that the way to achieve very old age is to "eat raw sausages and crackers and drink 7-Up. I never drank green (raw) milk—only chocolate" (Weyl, 1977:167).

Sei (Samoan chief in his eighties) explains his longevity by the fact that "I work hard every day" (Holmes, 1972:75).

Belarmino Carpio (Vilcabamba, age 85) attributes longevity to "God and climate," and "We almost never eat meat" (Leaf, 1975:52).

"Satchel" Paige (former major league pitcher, age unknown but well over 65) maintains his formula for "stayin' young" is:

1. Avoid fried meats which angry up the blood.
2. If your stomach disputes you, lie down and pacify it with cool thoughts.
3. Keep the juices flowing by jangling around gently as you move.
4. Go very light on the vices, such as carrying on in society. The social ramble ain't restful.
5. Avoid running at all times.
6. Don't look back. Something might be gaining on you.

Democritus (Greek philosopher, age 100) volunteered the secret of his longevity: "Application of oil without, and honey within" (Bailey, 1857:16).

Ancient Hebrews believed that one must "Honor thy father and thy mother, that thy days may be long in the land . . ." (Exodus 20:12).

Hopi Indians maintained that "whoever is not mean will live long" (Stephen, 1936:11).

The *Palaung* of Burma attribute long life to virtuous behavior. Apparently, there are no "dirty old men" among these people.

Although these subjective opinions undoubtedly represent a great deal of worthwhile folk wisdom, and perhaps also scientific validity, it might be of interest in concluding this discussion to consider two very different examples of aging and their probable causes.

In his discussion of longevity Jeff Beaubier (1980) contrasts an American merchant seaman who appeared old, wrinkled, toothless, bald, and feeble, although only 42, with a vigorous, strong, well-preserved, and healthy Greek farmer of 105. The farmer, Beaubier tells us,

> works steadily every day on his small farm raising much of the food his family requires. He doesn't smoke or take any medications. His nutrition is excellent, mostly of fresh fruits and vegetables, light meats, fish, fresh baked bread, cheeses, yogurt, eggs, legumes, nuts, dried fruits, olive oil, onions and garlic, herbs, condiments and spices. He and his wife work side by side with harmony and affection. A brief catnap, or a glass of cool water on the shady veranda is a good rest break after completion of specific tasks. When work is done . . . they enjoy conversation with family and friends from the neighborhood. (1980:37-38).

The merchant seaman, on the other hand, had a very different life history and one that apparently was anything but conducive to successful aging. Beaubier writes:

> He had smoked heavily since he was a teenager and used drugs and strong stimulants. He had been mostly idle and without exercise, especially walking and running. His nutrition was poor and irregular. He had no lasting friends or relatives. He had no interests or healthy activities. He was insecure. There had been many conflicts in his life. He worried about the future, and regretted the past. (1980:40)

Although the human maximum lifetime potential will very likely remain unaltered in the modern world, our exposure to knowledge of societies where longevity is far greater than in our own society tells us a great deal about the role of culture in keeping people alive and well almost to the limits of their species-specific potential life span. It obviously takes more than advances in technology to achieve the record of longevity observed in Greece and possibly in locations in Russia, Ecuador, and Pakistan. Longevity is a matter of culture—diet, family organization, values, motivations—and this is where the cultural anthropologists can enlighten and propose ways for humans to achieve their life-span potential. The cross-cultural study of aging and life-style has much to offer.

SUMMARY

The possibility of extending the life span has intrigued mankind since the beginning of time. Most bodies of folklore contain myths about culture heroes seeking immortality, and many a modern short story or novel has featured a main character who sold his soul to the devil for the promise of a longer life. History even records that the purpose of Ponce de Leon's Spanish expedition in 1513 was to search the Caribbean for the fabled island of Bimini, which was supposed to have a Fountain of Youth. It is therefore understandable that people are attracted by the claims of travelers and a few scientists that Abkhasia, Hunza, and Vilcabamba are magic lands of longevity. We must remember, however, that when considering claims of extraordinary longevity, both the biological basis for life span as well as the ecological and cultural factors that govern length of life must be considered. Despite our great enthusiasm to believe that Shangri-las can exist, we must objectively collect and critically evaluate the data.

Chapter 5

This 105-year-old Paros Island farmer and his wife, 87, relax between chores in the courtyard of their farm. He still directs work on his land. (Photos courtesy of Jeff Beaubier.)

In each of the enclaves renowned for extreme longevity, nagging questions about reliability of data persist. Documents that could provide proof of age of the extraordinarily old are almost without exception nonexistent, and in Vilcabamba, evidence of a cultural pattern of institutionalized fabrication of age was discovered. Far more travelers than scientists have written about these pockets of longevity, and in the case of Abkhasia, evidence indicates that local and national political and economic interests may have led to the exaggerated claims of long life.

Data from the Greek island of Paros, however, do indicate that given the proper physical and cultural environment it would be possible to increase the average length of life of many of the world's populations (including that of the United States). While it is possible to document that one's chances of reaching 100 on Paros are 70 times greater than they are in the United States, there are no extraordinarily old people living there and there is nothing to indicate that the outer limits of the human life span (110 to 120) have been altered. Their people merely come closer to achieving the figure established by evolution for the species hundreds of years ago.

CHAPTER 6

Varieties of Aging Experience

In order to understand fully the rationale for the ways a society copes with the problems of aging and the aged, we must approach that society holistically—in terms of the physical environment, the economic or subsistence patterns that support it, the social structure that binds its citizens together, and the traditional values and procedures that have evolved throughout its cultural history.

This chapter presents three such analyses. These case studies in human aging present information on three very different societies in three very different physical environments with diverse subsistence patterns and distinctive traditions regarding the proper roles and status of old people.

The first group, the Eskimos of North America, represent a particular kind of hunting society—one located in a very rigorous climate where there are great environmental limitations in regard to natural resources and to the choice of ways of getting a living. These people are nomadic and this imposes hardships, particularly on the aged. But life is difficult for everyone in this society, and each and every family member is expected to contribute his or her share of effort and cooperation to the common welfare. The question of what happens when people are too old to make these contributions is an important consideration in this analysis.

The second society—the Samoan Islanders of the South Pacific—is one with a simple agricultural economy. These people live in sedentary seaside villages where nutritional requirements can be met with a minimum of physical exertion and where food-sharing practices ensure the well-being of the children, the handicapped, and the aged. A benign climate guarantees a reasonably comfortable and secure old age, and traditional societal values and extended family solicitude make old age a rather pleasant time of life.

The third society—the United States—is industrial, capitalistic, technologically complex, and essentially urban. It is a culture with great wealth and intellectual capacity, but it is an individualistic, youth-oriented society and as such is philosophically unable to honor its elders. The value system places great emphasis on independence, self-reliance, and freedom of choice, and the society confers status on the basis of production and achievement. Although this society has great sedentary cities, its citizens are highly nomadic, moving from city to city. Families are small and self-centered; there is neither room nor desire for extended family organization. Although this industrial society is the most capable economically of supporting the elderly, the old of this society are undoubtedly the most anxious and apprehensive of any of the three.

GROWING OLD IN A HUNTING SOCIETY: ESKIMOS

The Eskimo people occupy one of the largest culture areas in the western hemisphere. They share a common language and physical type and essentially a common culture within an arctic region stretching some 3,000 miles east and west and extending north and south from 60° to 72° north latitude. The word *Eskimo* was not found originally in the vocabularies of any of these people but is instead an Algonkian word meaning *raw meat eater*. In anthropology, this culture area is traditionally subdivided into a western and a central-eastern zone. The people of the western portion live in northwest Canada and Alaska, and the central-eastern people inhabit an area from Mackenzie Bay (Canada) to Greenland. The Eskimo population today numbers approximately 35,000 to 40,000—about half their precontact total. White men's diseases (measles, influenza, and tuberculosis) have seriously reduced their numbers.

The region the Eskimos occupy is essentially a harsh environment, with long winters and temperatures reaching as low as −65 °F and short, mosquito-plagued summers. The treeless landscape, called *tundra,* supports a minimum of plant and animal life, and this tends to impose restrictions on the cultural homogeneity throughout the entire culture area.

The major subsistence activities in most areas are sea-mammal hunting (mostly seals) in the winter, when the people camp near the sea, and caribou hunting in the summer, when they move inland. Alaskan Eskimos engage in whaling operations in spring and summer. Common traditional weapons include the harpoon and bow and arrow, with the rifle being added after the advent of the white man.

Although some Eskimos (particularly in the east) persist in fairly traditional subsistence activities, western Eskimos today are often engaged in trapping-trading operations, commercial fishing, and wage employment. Most Eskimos live in relatively permanent settlements in winter and then set up temporary hunting and fishing camps during the summer. Skin tents were traditional with all Eskimos during summer months but in winter Alaskan Eskimos lived in earth-covered homes and eastern groups lived in igloos. Much of this traditional housing has disappeared in modern times. James Van Stone described the settlement at Point Hope, Alaska (population 265), as follows: "The village consists of some fifty houses, all of which are of frame construction although there are a few that closely approximate old, semisubterranean type . . . . Many of the frame houses have a covering of sod around them so that they give the appearance of old-style houses" (1962:11). The village also contains two schools, an Episcopal church, a store, and a National Guard drill hall.

Certain objects of traditional material culture—kayaks, women's knives, bow drills, snow goggles, and dog sleds (fan hitch in the east and tandem hitch in Alaska)—are pan-Eskimo features. Men are dominant in subsistence activities, but women are essential to the household routine because they dress hides, make clothes, and prepare the food. It would be difficult for a man to survive on a hunting trip without a woman supporting his activities. Women were often loaned to single hunters who were about to embark on a hunting trip.

The Eskimo family is typically monogamous, but wife hospitality and wife lending are known. The immediate family is the significant social unit, and kinship, emphasizing ties to both male and female lines, is similar to that found in the modern American family. Formal political organization until very recently (when elected village councils have appeared) was nonexistent, and group activities involving leadership were confined to such events as whaling expeditions or communal seal hunts.

Eskimos believe that all animate and inaminate objects have souls, and they also believe in an impersonal supernatural force known as *sila* that somewhat resembles the *manitou* concept of American Indians or the *mana* concept of Pacific islanders. Mythology is not elaborate and centers on tales of Sedna, the goddess of whales, seals, walrus, and all that lives in the sea. Shamans (part-time religious practitioners) are prominent, but the only ritualistic ceremonies involving groups of people consist of yearly gatherings in which masked men impersonate the gods.

Although contact with the white man has brought many modernizing influences, we will turn to early accounts of the traditional system in investigating the role and status of the elderly in Eskimo culture.

Among the Eskimo, the aged were accorded great respect. They were treated with considerable deference and their words were regarded as final. Murdock reports that among the Eskimo of Point Barrow, "respect for the opinion of the elders is so great that the people may be said to be practically under what is called 'simple elder rule' " (1887-1888:427). Hughes records that among the St. Lawrence Island people informants maintained, "Oldest is boss for everything. Eskimos always ask first our oldest one, when we do something" (1960:265). Van Stone observes that "the transition to old age is not clear-cut. Parents whose children are grown, married, and have moved away from home are not necessarily old by Point Hope standards. Eskimo men seem to age early in terms of appearance, but remain active until relatively advanced years" (1962:93).

Within the Eskimo family the grandparent/grandchild relationship is one of extreme affection and support, with emphasis on mutual helpfulness and kindness. Eskimos believe that knowledge increases with age and teaching children is seen as an appropriate and valuable function of the aged. Instructing children in games, rituals, taboos, and other ancient lore is carried out by grandparents, who are considered repositories of songs, stories, and tribal history as well as monitors of proper behavior. The elderly are considered great storytellers, and stories are told for both education and entertainment. Rasmussen reports of the Polar Eskimo that almost every question was answered and every problem explained by a tale. His informants reported, "Our tales are men's experiences .... The experience of the older generations contains truth" (1908:97). Turner writes that Eskimos were extremely fond of these narrative sessions, and young people sat "with staring eyes and countenances which show their wondering interest in the narration" (1894:260-261). Old people also function as "village newspapers," making it their business to know and tell all of the recent happenings.

Family members always consult their elderly members about choice of marriage partners, division of material wealth, and settlement of family disputes. Elders are directly involved in the naming of children because of their involvement with name-souls. After death the soul associated with the name of the deceased is believed to hover around waiting to be reincarnated in a newborn child. Old people are believed to have special knowledge of the spiritual world, and they inform the child's father if a particular name-soul is agreeable to be given to the new infant.

The elderly play an important role in educating children and even adults in economic skills. Old men are often consulted by their sons as to the proper time to go hunting, how to care for a boat or other equipment, and how to apportion goods or game. Burch relates that "if some of these [elders] were wiser and more skillful than others, an ambitious young man might undertake to recruit these people to his own local group, or he might go to live with them. In return for food, shelter and protection, they could provide instruction and advice of a kind few of his same-generation kin could offer" (1975:219).

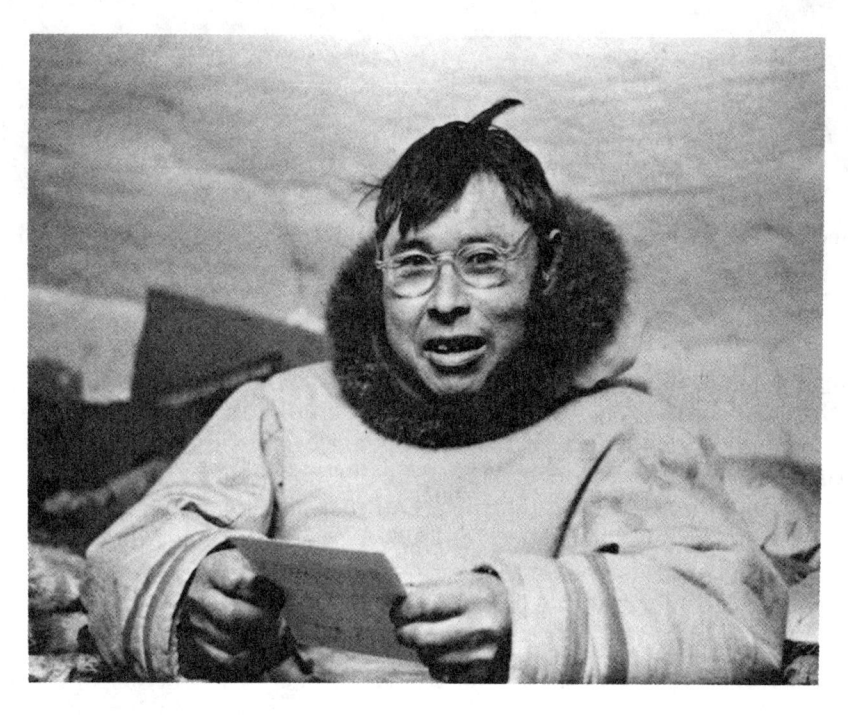

Among Belcher Island Eskimos, knowledge is believed to increase with age, and the teaching of children is a cherished function of the elderly. (Photo courtesy of Lee Geumple.)

Elderly members of the Eskimo family are always consulted on such issues as choice of marriage partner, division of material wealth, and alleviation of family discord. (Photo courtesy of Lee Guemple.)

Among most Eskimo groups, elders are seldom idle. If men can no longer hunt they fish or help snare birds. Ray (1885) writes that among the Point Barrow people old men made seal spears and nets and old women worked on clothing, boats, and the dressing of skins. Elderly and feeble Labrador Eskimo women plaited straw hats and baskets and cared for the family clothes. Old men in this group had special medical skills and old women were in charge of childbirth and the rituals following, which were performed to safeguard the newborn.

Of the Eskimos of northwest Alaska, Burch observes:

> Parents gradually gave over the heavier work to their sons and daughters as they began to age, busying themselves in the lighter activities of logistic support. Aging fathers tended to stay home and spend their days making and repairing tools, nets, and other equipment, while their sons hunted.

> Similarly, mothers increasingly limited themselves to watching over infant grandchildren for their daughters, and assisting them with lighter tasks, such as sewing. (1975:138-139).

Elderly Eskimos are believed to have considerable magical or spiritual power. Among the special supernatural capacities supposedly possessed by the elderly are: (1) the ability to foretell the future, (2) the ability to change one's future just by willing it, (3) the ability to interpret dreams and receive magical formulas in dreams, (4) the ability to "talk up" winds that will drive the ice offshore, and (5) the ability to ward off evil spirits. Supernatural power of all old people is believed to be considerable, and it was held that neglect of or offenses against an old person could cripple or sicken one's children. According to Burch, magical ability was not restricted to old people but they were believed to have more of it than others. In northwest Alaska, magical songs, charms, and techniques are passed on from grandparent to grandchild and not from parent to offspring (Burch, 1975:157).

Old age is not only glorified in the folklore of most Eskimo groups, but many of the gods, heroes, and demons found in the tales are elderly. For example, the Polar Eskimos believe the goddess Nerivik is an old woman who lives beneath the water and will not let seal hunters succeed until the village shamans visit her and groom her matted hair. Another myth tells of an old man who was transfigured into a luminous body and shot up into the sky, where he now exists as a bright star. Labrador Eskimos claim that an extremely old woman lives beneath the sea and controls the tides and the fortunes of fishermen. Another aged goddess lives inland and controls the caribou.

Although not always, the shamans are frequently elderly. Rasmussen describes the influence they exerted over the community:

> We believe our *angakut,* our magicians, . . . because we wish to live long, and because we do not wish to expose ourselves to the danger of famine and starvation . . . . If we do not follow their advice we shall fall ill and die. (1908:16)

The special functions shamans perform include drawing out dangerous foreign matter from the body and contacting the spirit world to counteract bad luck in hunting or to determine the cause of illness or barrenness. Public performances often include miraculous feats, such as drawing blood through a self-inflicted knife wound but then revealing later the lack of a wound. Spirits often possess the shaman and bring on hysterical behavior greatly resembling an epileptic seizure. The spirits often speak through the religious practitioner during these trance states.

Given the harshness of the arctic environment, the lot of the aged might be assumed to be a relatively difficult one. In some respects this is true, but Eskimo societies appear to be structured to provide as much support for the elderly as their precarious life-style would allow. As is often the case among hunting peoples, the Eskimo have developed food-sharing practices that ensure that widows, orphans, and the elderly are provided for. In some cases, the elderly men are in charge of food distribution and therefore they can make sure that young and old all receive adequate commissary. Graburn reports that in 1959 when "one band returned from a hunt near Charles Island with thirty-six large bearded seals some of the younger members did not want to share these with the other more than two-hundred Sallumiut, but the will of the older men prevailed and every household received considerable amounts of meat" (1969:176).

In traditional culture, the honor of being the successful hunter was only slightly greater than that associated with the generosity involved in sharing the kill. Graburn records that after a successful hunt there were often feasts where everyone was invited and "the male host basked in the prestige of being able to provide for so many *tujurngminat,* 'guests, invited strangers' " (1969:72).

Another custom required men to send special food gifts to the elderly women who acted as midwives at the end of their first successful hunt of the season.

One method that ensures the elderly ample food is to make certain kinds of food taboo for everyone except those who cannot hunt for themselves. Polar Eskimos reserve eggs, entrails, hearts, lungs, livers, and certain small animals and birds (hares and ptarmigans) for old men who in turn are permitted to share with women who have given birth to more than five children. Aged women among the Labrador Eskimos are guaranteed food for caring for men's boots. In spite of the fact that Eskimo societies are structured to be supportive, Graburn (1969) maintains that if the fall hunting had been poor resulting in a great shortage of food during the winter the patterns of food sharing often broke down.

A great deal has been said about the custom of gerontocide among Eskimo peoples, but it should be noted that not all groups resorted to such extreme measures. Van Stone (1962) reports that exposing the aged to die was never practiced at Point Hope, Alaska, and Burch writes of northwest Alaska:

> Aged parents were abandoned only under conditions of the most extreme hardships, and it was rare even then .... Abandonment occurred in situations in which old people had to be sacrificed or everyone would have starved to death. In the exceptional case, the individuals did abandon their parents; they came to be regarded as deviants as a consequence, and were subsequently treated as outcasts .... Old people were not left behind at all, it was so that the younger, more active members of the family could travel more quickly to where food could be procured, and *then return.* (1975:149)

The situation seems to be somewhat different for central-eastern Eskimos. Graburn reports that "often the old people would ask to be left behind or even killed if they felt they were useless, for those who died a violent death were thought to go to the highest of Eskimos' 'three heavens' " (1969:73). In paradise they would spend their time, with the spirits who died in the same way, playing football with a walrus head.

Most authorities agree that Eskimos show little concern for death, and Freuchen writes, "Fear of death is unknown to them, they know only love of life" (1961:145). There are undoubtedly more cases of suicide among the aged than there are of abandonment. This might occur, according to Freuchen, with

> old men and women who are burdened with the memories of their youth, and who can no longer meet the demands of their own reputation .... When an old man sees the young men go out hunting and cannot himself go along, he is sorry. When he has to ask other people for skins for his clothing, when he cannot ever again be

the one to invite the neighbors to eat his game, life is of no value to him. Rheumatism and other ills may plague him, and he wants to die. (1961:145).

Freuchen describes numerous cases of which he had personal knowledge, maintaining that in some tribes an eldest son or a favorite daughter was asked to put a skin rope around the elder's neck and hoist him to this death. This supposedly was done at the height of a party or feast when everyone (including the old person) was in high spirits. All the guests were supposed to assist in the hanging by pulling on the rope, for it was a great honor to be asked to help end the suffering of an old one who wanted the comfort and peace of the Eskimo hereafter. Old women, it is said, sometimes preferred to be stabbed in the heart with a dagger by a son or daughter. Particularly revealing of the attitude toward deliberately ending one's life is the following account by Freuchen:

> In the Hudson Bay area, I once arrived at a village at Wager Inlet in the midst of great commotion. Just before my arrival, an old man called Oomilialik had been found hanging from the ceiling of an igloo. He had climbed up on top of the snowhouse, drilled a hole in the roof, and lowered a rope down to serve his purpose. Fortunately, just after he had hanged himself, the eldest of his four sons returned home from the hunt and came in in time to cut him down. The old man was furious.
>
> All four sons assured me and their father that they did not consider him a nuisance or burden at all. They had plenty of meat and good game, and they wanted to see his face among them for a long time yet and take advantage of his renowned experience . . . . The old man said that he had been the greatest caribou hunter ever known, and now his knees were too weak to walk across the hills. So life had no more to offer him. Besides, he had no more tobacco, and without that he found it too hard to sit at home instead of accompanying his sons out hunting.
>
> The next year I passed by Wager Inlet again, and I went to visit Oomilialik's house. I found only his sons at home, and I asked them how their father was. They answered me that he was all right, doing well, because he was now dead. He had hanged himself again, and this time with greater success. (1961:153-154)

Cultural Change

With the coming of the white men and the trappings of their modern world, some things have improved for the Eskimo elderly but many things have worsened. Graburn (1969) reports for the Hudson Bay area that the elderly men are losing their influence and decision-making function in community affairs. Councils of elderly that once directed civic activities are now being replaced by elected community organizations in which young men have a great deal of authority. The old patterns of community food sharing are giving way to a commercial attitude toward hunting.

At Point Hope, the traditional functional definition of when old age begins (when men are too old to hunt) has been superseded by a chronological one (65—when old-age assistance checks begin). Old-age assistance and pension checks have, of course, provided a new source of value and recognition for the aged. Burch writes:

> After the advent of old age pensions, elderly Eskimos were able to make another major contribution to the welfare of the family. In the 1960s, for example, many a son obtained cash for ammunition and other items from the aged parents, supplying them with food in return. (1975:139)

This new source of status is, however, a poor substitute for the respect and admiration they once enjoyed. Education, once largely in the hands of the elderly, has since World War II been transferred more and more to the government-supported school. This has brought, among other things, significant changes in grandparent-grandchild relationships. Traditionally, grandchildren not only learn much of the culture from grandparents but also help the aging relatives in many ways. Burch reveals that when a grandchild was "five or six, it had begun to perform many chores for the grandparent, particularly if the latter was getting on in years or else was an invalid. Aged grandparents always had one grandchild more or less 'in tow,' following them around or playing in their immediate vicinity so as to be readily available should their assistance be required. This grandchild would help the grandparent check the net or snares, assist them over rough spots in the path, run errands for them or do innumerable other chores" (1975:156-157).

In many villages today, a language barrier has developed between the old (who speak Eskimo) and grandchildren (who are taught and urged to speak English in school). The result is very little intergenerational communication or learning. However, much of the knowledge the old people traditionally have imparted is now largely irrelevant anyhow, and both grandparents and grandchildren know it.

The elderly have also lost other traditional functions. Store-bought goods have eliminated the need for old people to make such things as weapons or clothing, and maintaining new mechanical and electrical gadgets requires skills they have never acquired. The elderly at one time performed magical services and taught young people magic songs, formulas, and magic techniques, but the coming of Christianity has done much to destroy belief in or use of such phenomena. In the larger communities, curing activities and midwife duties have been taken over by trained medical personnel.

LIFE IN A SIMPLE AGRICULTURAL SOCIETY: SAMOA

The islands of the Samoan archipelago lie in the southwest Pacific midway between Hawaii and New Zealand at 14° south latitude and between 168° and 173° west longitude. (Figure 6.1). Politically, its nine inhabited islands are divided into Western Samoa (an independent nation) and American Samoa (a territory of the United States), but culturally, racially, and linguistically, they are one. Ninety percent of the 190,000 people who inhabit the archipelago are classified as full-blooded Polynesians. It is a young population with 50% aged 0 to 14 years. Four and one-half percent are 60 and over.

The Samoan islands are located in the western part of the Polynesian culture area and share many traditional cultural traits with the Fiji and Tonga Island groups. Among them is a way of life which is based on simple slash-and-burn agriculture, supplemented by some deep-sea and reef fishing. Food plants consist of taro, breadfruit, coconuts, yams, bananas, papayas, and mangos. Domesticated animals are mainly chickens and pigs but a few horses and cattle have been raised in recent times. The land is rich and green, the climate warm and humid but pleasant, and with the exception of hurricanes or other disasters, it is a land of plenty, requiring only a moderate expenditure of energy to maintain an adequate if not abundant subsistence.

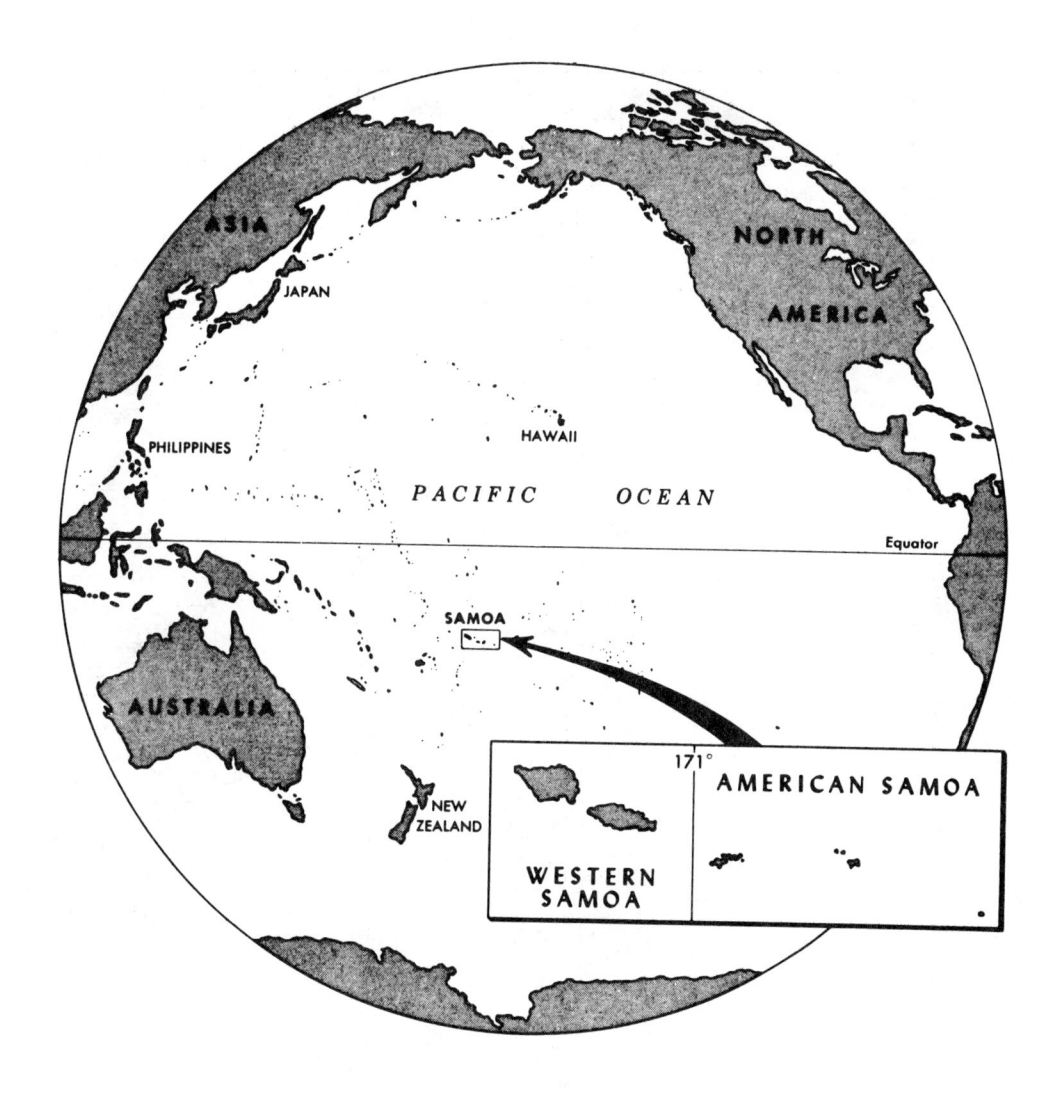

Figure 6.1. Samoan Archipelago.

Most Samoan communities, with the exception of Apia and Pago Pago (port towns), are seaside villages varying in population from 200 to 600 people. Villages consist of a series of houses strung along a sandy beach with a mixture of traditional *fales* (beehive shaped thatch-roof houses) and European-style houses (resembling summer or beach cottages). (See Figure 6.2) Every village has a school, a church (usually Congregational, formerly called London Missionary Society), and a *malae* (village green). Some have medical dispensaries, and most have general stores and copra sheds, where the kernel of the coconut is stored until marketed. All Samoan villages on the major islands of Tutuila and Upolu are connected by paved or graveled roads with the urban

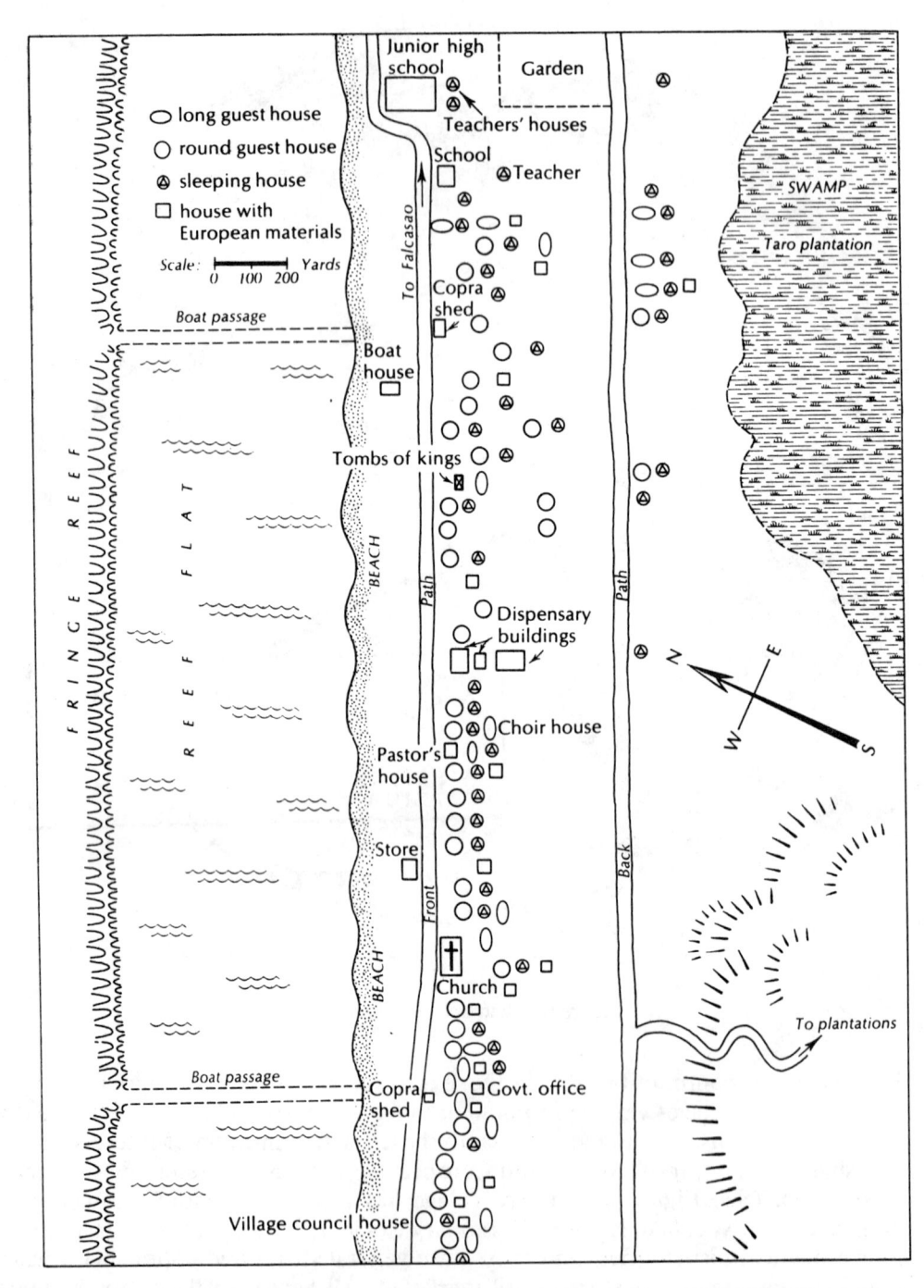

Figure 6.2. Ta'u village, a typical Samoan community. (Map by Lowell D. Holmes.)

centers which have shops, hotels, theaters, hospitals, and commercial houses and banks. Some villages on islands such as Manono in Western Samoa or Ta'u in American Samoa are relatively isolated and culture remains somewhat more traditional. Most Samoans are farmers, and they work lands that are relatively small in acreage and located on the mountainous slopes behind the seaside villages.

People in Samoa are said to be old when they are no longer able to do heavy agricultural work or the more strenuous domestic tasks. It is at this time that men are referred to as *toeaina* or *matuaali'i* and women are referred to as *lo'omatua* or *olomatua*. These labels are usually applied sometime between ages 50 and 60 but, of course, there is a good deal of variation, depending on the health and strength of given individuals. After occupying the status of "old" for several years the term *vaivai* (weak in the body) is often added, although in many cases it might not accurately describe the physical condition of the old person. Senility, as we know it in America, is extremely rare in Samoa.

Until very recently, most Samoans, young or old, have agreed that old age is "the finest time of life." The elders do not have to rise before dawn and go to the plantations high on the mountain slopes. They have the option of working or resting, depending on their inclination. During the day, they are free to sit for hours and chat with other elders of the village without feeling guilty about not carrying their full load of activities. When villagers pass by the *fale* (which is open on all sides), no one fails to wave and give the elderly a friendly greeting. Only the elders have time to observe fully the activities of the villagers, and they are often the most informed about the current events of the community.

Even though old people are excused from the heavier tasks, they all feel that it is important to be productive in some way. Most older Samoans explain their longevity by the fact that they keep busy every day. Generally, the young take care of the strenuous labor and the old account for the tedious labor—the kind you can do sitting down. Old men sew units of sugar-cane thatch for roofs and braid sennit, the coconut fiber twine so important in traditional house and canoe building. They weed the yard and help the women prepare pandanus leaf for mat weaving. In the afternoon when the tide is low and reef-flat exposed, old men often set their globe-shaped fish traps in shallow pools with hopes of snaring brightly colored reef fish. They also scavenge the reef for small eels and shellfish.

Elderly men are in many cases the titled heads of families and as such are referred to as *matai*. *Matai* are either *ali'i* (chiefs) or *tulafale* (talking chiefs), and they are elected to these positions relatively late in life by the members of their extended family. Whether one is a chief or a talking chief (orator) is a matter of family and village tradition. Various titles with various designations were created (or bestowed by indigenous rulers) for families at different times throughout Samoan history. Such titles have traditionally been awarded to men who are intelligent, knowledgeable of Samoan tradition and ceremonial life, and hardworking (on family enterprises). There are a few female *matai* but the majority are men. *Matai* are elected for life, although it is not uncommon for a very old family head to step down and request that the family select a younger man. They coordinate family work activities and control family expenditures. In some families, even people working at wage employment contribute heavily to family

In Samoa, old men sometimes "retire" to tasks that can be done sitting down. (Photo by Lowell D. Holmes.)

welfare by giving a portion of their income to the *matai*. At marriages, funerals, and title installations it is the *matai* who must collect money and gifts from his family; these will be used in the ceremonial property exchanges that take place on such occasions. Since generosity is a principal avenue to status, the *matai* is responsible for maintaining his family's prestige by collecting substantial sums of money and goods.

Although some chiefs are middle-aged, there is a tendency to equate being a chief with being old. The behavior expected of a chief is described by one of Margaret Mead's informants:

> I have been a chief only four years and look, my hair is grey, although in Samoa grey hair comes very slowly, not in youth, as it comes to the white man. But always, I must act as if I were old. I must walk gravely and with measured step . . . . Old men of sixty are my companions and watch my every word, lest I make a mistake. Thirty-one people live in my household. For them I must plan. I must find them food and clothing, settle their disputes, arrange their marriages. There is no one in

my whole family who dares to scold me or even to address me familiarly by my first name. It is hard to be so young and yet to be a chief. (1928:36)

The *matai* represent their families in the village council (known as the *fono*), which meets periodically to discuss village business. It is presided over by the village paramount chief, and to a large extent much of the business is controlled by the talking chiefs. Since all decisions must be unanimous, discussions are often long and drawn out. A role of considerable importance in the *fono* is that of *tu'ua,* or elder stateman.

Grattan describes the position as follows:

> As a mark of respect and dignity, the village may choose one of their orators to fill a position known as *tu'ua*. Not every village chooses a *tu'ua*. Such a person must enjoy high personal rank as an orator and have a degree of knowledge relating to the village and perhaps district affairs which fits him for the position. Considerable deference is paid to him and it is to him that the village looks thereafter for pronouncements on any disputed point. The *tu'ua* is the one entitled to sit in the middle post of the front of a house and if he should arrive late or unexpectedly at the village meeting and that post is already occupied, the place will be vacated at once and left open to him. (1948:19)

Two other honorific positions are reserved for elderly men in Samoan society. One is that of *tapuaiga* (the one who prays for the work) and the other, mentor at *fa'asausauga* (night assemblies for discussion of family and village traditions). A *tapuaiga* is considered to be an essential ingredient in any successful house-building venture. The old man who functions in this role does not actually pray but merely sits and serves as a conversationalist for the workers, many of whom are young men and enjoy the tales of old Samoa. The *tapuaiga* is not permitted to be critical of the quality of the work, but in carrying out his symbolic role of support, his very presence undoubtedly means that the workmen are somewhat more careful about their work. *Fa'asausauga,* on the other hand, provide the elderly chiefs with an opportunity to pass on important traditional and ceremonial knowledge. Although participation in these meetings is theoretically restricted to chiefs, they actually provide an excellent opportunity for young untitled men to come and sit outside the meeting house and listen and learn.

Older women also play ceremonial roles and are consulted on political issues. Every village has a Women's Committee, and this organization mirrors the village council in structure and family representation. It is often concerned with village welfare issues such as the adequacy of church or dispensary facilities, and they are responsible for providing hospitality to visiting parties (*malaga*) from other villages and support for the village council on village ceremonial occasions or at district political conferences.

Although men tend to be most visible politically and ceremonially, Women's Committees are very influential in determining village and inter-island social and political events. Elderly women often have important positions in these organizations, but the major contribution of old women in Samoa is economic. Women in this society produce a category of goods known as *toga*. This includes all varieties of weaving—floor and sleeping mats, baskets, fans, house blinds, fine mats, and barkcloth tapestries, known as *siapo*. Many of these articles are used in the home and all serve as wealth to be exchanged between families for *oloa*—pigs, food, and money—at weddings, *matai*

Elderly Samoan women weave floor and sleeping mats, baskets, fans, and fine mats. (Photo by Lowell D. Holmes.)

installations, funerals, or church dedications. All women produce *toga,* but the bulk of the production is in the hands of elderly women who can devote long hours to this tedious labor because they no longer are required to join their men in the cultivation of their agricultural plots. Much as elderly women in the United States engage in quilting or "fancy work," Samoan elders produce the heirlooms of the future while they tend the small children left behind by the mothers spending the day in the gardens.

They are often assisted in their work by teen-age girls or young women, and there is nothing of the segregation of age groups which is so characteristic of America. In Samoa, no old person ever complains of being "lonely," for it is difficult to be lonely or even alone in the average household, which numbers between 10 and 12 people and can include at least three and probably four generations who eat together, work together, and often sleep together in one large unpartitioned room.

Old men are often found assisting their wives or female relatives in some of the activities that might be considered woman's work, but in old age there is great freedom of choice. Young people who are siblings or cousins (the latter are referred to with the same kin terms as siblings) must observe a brother-sister taboo beginning at the time of puberty, but once they have attained old age there are no longer any social restrictions. Old people also have the privilege of violating many of the standards of decorum. They often perform bawdy songs and dances at *fiafia* (parties), and they are politely tolerated when they give long, tedious, and irrelevant speeches in the village council.

One job completely reserved for older women is burning candlenut and collecting its soot, which is used as a pigment in tattooing. At one time, every young man underwent the ordeal of tattooing, but then the practice fell off. In recent years, interest in this rite has revived. Although old women once delivered all the babies in the village, this function has now been taken over by Samoan medical practitioners and locally trained nurses. On rare occasions, elderly midwives are called on. Even today old women continue to be storehouses of knowledge concerning the medicinal properties of herbs and many of them are specialists in *fofo* and *lomilomi* (forms of massage).

GERONTOCIDE

Although abandonment or murder of the aged has been observed in hunting cultures in harsh environments, a custom such as live burial of the aged seems strangely out of place in a society of sedentary horticulturalists living in a hospitable environment. Yet such a custom did exist in earlier times in Samoa and has been reported by a number of European observers. In order to understand this rather bizarre custom, we need to consider three things: (1) the Samoan belief system, (2) the Samoan concept of honorable death, and (3) the importance of status and respect within the society.

Of the belief system, Leo Simmons writes, "Belief in a future life . . . has been generally so firm and matter-of-fact that it is difficult for modern man to appreciate it fully; and with the consequence that death has often been regarded as a welcome release from the fetters of age and a direct means of enhancing one's personal interests" (1945:224). In addition to this promise of a joyful afterlife, assured by the Samoan belief system, there was also the attraction that great honor and prestige could be acquired for oneself and family if one died a noble and courageous death. Before the colonial and territorial governments of white men did away with inter-island warfare and extended voyaging, it was considered desirable for elderly men whom fate had robbed of a glorious and honorific death in battle or on the sea to request being put to death by members of their own family. This was done through suffocation in a live burial following a normal ceremony of interment where large amounts of property were exchanged (the greater the amount the more important the deceased) and eulogies presented. Turner describes such an event:

> When an old man felt sick and infirm, and thought he was dying, he deliberately told his children and friends to get ready and bury him. They yielded to his wishes, dug a round, deep pit, wound a number of fine mats around his body, and lowered down the old man into his grave in a sitting position. Live pigs were then brought, and tied, each with a separate cord, the one end of the cord to the pig, and the other end to the arm of the old man. The cords were cut in the middle, leaving the one half hanging at the arm of the old man, and off the pigs were taken to be killed and baked for the burial feast. . . .
>
> The greater the chief the more numerous the pigs . . . . The poor old man thus wound up, furnished with his pig strings, and covered over with some more mats, was all ready. His grave was then filled up, and his dying groans drowned amid the weeping and the wailing of the living. (1884:335-336)

Thus, live burial was an honor and not an act of cruelty, allowing an old and ailing chief an honorable way out of life, amid the acclaim of his family and community. Although early accounts seem to indicate that this practice was a male prerogative and one that disappeared with the coming of colonial government, a 1965 Associated Press news release tells the story of a unique "funeral" ceremony in Samoa for an elderly woman that may represent something of a symbolic revival of live burial and conceivably may reveal something of the thinking of aged in old Samoa. The press release reads as follows:

> It was the jolliest funeral. There were 100 kegs of beer, 100 cases of canned fish and pisupo (corned beef), stacks upon stacks of *i'e tonga,* the treasured ceremonial mat of Samoa—and there wasn't a tear anywhere.
>
> Feasting on baked taro, fried bananas and the meat of five huge roast pigs, everybody had a whale of a good time. Most of all did white-haired Siatutoga, the 94-year-old grandmother whose funeral this was. She was dressed in a flowered, quilted nylon robe Friday for the ceremony. "This was a wonderful funeral, the happiest day of my life," she said. Gifts were sent by relatives in Hawaii and the mainland United States. Other members of her family saw to it that the guests seated in different *fales* according to rank, were properly fed and given gifts of mats, food and money in return for the presents they had brought.

It would appear that Siatutoga's "funeral" resembled those of old Samoa in every respect except that she was spared the live burial. In Samoa we find a custom that would normally be considered cruel and would normally be associated with quite different geographical and cultural circumstances. Matters of custom and their relationship to the valuation and treatment of the aged are complex and can easily be misunderstood by those who have a different value system.

Samoan families have always taken great pride in supporting their elderly, but today they have problems. Changing times, involving greater emphasis on a money economy and greater emphasis on educational needs of children (which every family has in abundance), have sometimes resulted in a shift of priorities from an emphasis on age to an emphasis on youth. Particularly in Western Samoa, where all children are charged tuition for their schooling and where incomes are low, there is often not enough money to guarantee generous support and proper medical attention for the elderly. Also, many Samoans have migrated to New Zealand and the United States, which means that some old people are left with only distant relatives to care for them because the bulk of their kinsmen have left the country. In American Samoa, the desire to earn money to buy modern goods has resulted in large numbers of family members being employed, which means that in many cases very old people are left with no one to care for them throughout the day but preschool children.

Although, inability to care for their own elderly is a source of some embarassment for families, the need in Samoa for institutional care for elderly is great enough that an old peoples' residence called *Mapuifagalele* (peaceful haven) was established in 1975 by the Catholic Church and is operated by the Little Sisters of the Poor. It houses about 80 to 90 Samoans, Protestant and Catholic, and provides them with comfortable rooms, food, and excellent medical care. The waiting list is always long.

Although modernization in the islands has often created conditions that make it more difficult for families to care for their elderly, it has brought new programs for the old, particularly in American Samoa, where its nationals are eligible for many of the federal programs enjoyed by elderly in the United States. The Territorial Administration of Aging with an office in Pago Pago has been surveying the needs of elderly since about 1975. There is a nutritional program (see Chapter I – "Cultural Relativism"), a Title II program that provides the elderly with eyeglasses and hearing aids at reduced cost, and a program that provides the aged with free transportation on inter-village buses, on inter-island motor vessels, and on airplanes flying between Tutuila and Ta'u village, Manu'a, and between Tutuila and Western Samoa. Transportation is a much-valued benefit in this society because of its traditional pattern of visiting relatives, often for extended periods.

One of the more valuable programs has been a craft project wherein Samoan senior citizens are brought into the Pago Pago Bay area and paid by the hour to work at traditional crafts. The products are sold to tourists in a special shop connected with the craft *fales,* and high school students are brought in throughout the day for classes in the indigenous weaving and carving skills.

In spite of numerous changes in Samoan life-style in recent years, there is still a strong emphasis on extended family living, and there is great concern and support for aged relatives. In a study conducted in American Samoa by Rhoads and Holmes (Rhoads, 1981) 71% of the aged interviewed maintained that they received better food and care than other family members; 98% believed that young people both respect and obey old people; and 97% spoke of special favors and kindnesses accorded them because of their age. Although 93% volunteered that they were still consulted about such matters as family problems, funerals, weddings, and titles, about 86% did not think that their words were heeded as much by the young as in the past. The remarkable thing about modern Samoan culture is the tenacity of the Samoan family both in the islands and in migrant communities in the United States and New Zealand. Approximately 88% of the elders interviewed by Rhoads and Holmes maintained that the extended family continues to be as important and influential in Samoan lives as it was 10 years ago, and this is seen by Rhoads as a prime factor in ensuring the welfare of the aged.

AGING IN AN INDUSTRIAL ECONOMY: THE UNITED STATES

According to the geographer J. H. G. Lebon, an Occidental industrial economy is one in which there is widespread use of mechanical power in mass production industry and extensive exploitation of oil, natural gas, minerals, water, and timber resources. Efficient production and management techniques in all facets of agriculture and industry create abundance and a high standard of living. Because of mechanization and advanced scientific knowledge of plant and animal production, a small percentage of agriculturalists can support large urban populations who engage in highly specialized occupations in industry, commerce, and the arts and sciences. Societies of this type have a highly mobile, achievement-oriented work force of individuals who are highly materialistic in their economic values and are peer oriented in their social affiliations.

The Cultural Setting

As a nation, the United States has long been thought of as a melting pot, but this is not entirely correct, because all the constituent national ingredients remain clearly recognizable. People of many nationalities have come to our portion of North America, and the social fabric of America is characterized by class, ethnic, racial, regional, and even occupational differences, all of which influence attitudes and behavioral patterns. But in spite of this heterogeneity, social scientists generally agree that Americans have a recognizable, predictable way of life. This is a life-style that by and large tends to be associated with middle-class America—a social category to which 82% of Americans claim they belong. The culture of this "establishment" dominates the educational curriculum and dictates the behavioral norms that most Americans, regardless of race or national origin, strive to emulate. This set of values and behavioral characteristics has been well documented by scores of skilled observers from Alexis de Tocqueville (in the 1830s) to Margaret Mead. Generally, the postulates of this American cultural system include the following:

1. An individual's most important concern is self-interest and this involves self-expression, self-development, self-gratification, and independence.
2. The privacy of the individual is an inalienable right; intrusion into it by others is permitted only by invitation.
3. All forms of authority, including government, are suspect; but the government and its symbols should be respected. Patriotism is good.
4. An individual's success in life depends on his acceptance among his peers.
5. Men and women are equal.

6. All human beings are equal.
7. Progress is good and inevitable. (Hsu, 1969:63)

How Old is Old

In the United States, old age is defined chronologically. One is old in America at age 65—an arbitrary figure that has been selected by representatives of government and industry as the time when it is appropriate for men and women to withdraw from productive labor and permit younger workers to take over. The figure 65 has very little to do with physical or mental capacity of Americans, but because it has been so universally accepted as the threshold of decrepitude few would challenge its validity. In the United States there is a tendency for age 65 to be considered the terminal point for all efficiency, creativity, and productivity. In most cases, people of this age are forced to retire and they have little opportunity for obtaining additional employment on either a part- or full-time basis. Some individuals have managed to establish successful postretirement businesses, but this is relatively rare. For some, retirement means increased time for travel or for pursuing neglected hobbies, but for many, it is a time of unwanted idleness, boredom, and stagnation.

The Aged Population

Twenty-three million men and women in America are over the age of 65. This group, which represents 10.5% of the total population is, contrary to popular belief, heterogeneous and it is rapidly increasing. In 1900, only slightly more than 3 million were elderly and they represented only 4% of the whole. This expansion in the proportion of the elderly is the result of two factors: a decline in birthrate and an increase in life expectancy from 48 years in 1900 to more than 73 years in 1980. The majority of aged in America are women. As is true of most countries, American women outlive their men by several years. By age 65 there are only 69 men to every 100 women, and by age 75 the number of men per 100 women shrinks to 58.

Residence Patterns

In recent decades many elderly Americans have moved to the sun-belt states of the South and West. The aged constitute 15% of Florida's population, while in California the elderly make up a little better than 13% of the whole. Distribution within states is erratic also. Inner-city areas have increased proportions of elderly because the young are moving away and leaving the old behind. For example, New York City's white population is growing progressively older and now constitutes 17% of the total. In some neighborhoods old people represent more than 20%.

Five percent (1,200,000) of our elderly are institutionalized. There are 16,000 nursing homes in America and these employ three-quarters of a million people. Institutions that serve the elderly are of various types. The skilled-nursing facility provides 24-hour nursing care for the chronically ill, whereas the intermediate-care facility has registered nurses in attendance only eight hours a day. They offer less quality nursing care, but do provide considerable personal assistance to patients. Residential-care facilities serve functional, independent old people, providing mainly recreational and nutritional services. There are also adult-care facilities that serve essentially as therapy centers for elderly who live at home but require some medical service.

Early History

In colonial and frontier America the aged were relatively scarce. In 1790, 50% of the population was under the age of 16, and people 65 and older made up a scant 2%. If people did survive to old age in those days, they received considerable respect and honor, although not necessarily a great deal of love and affection. Puritan belief, which dominated much of early social thought, held that old age was a sign of God's pleasure and that old people most closely resembled the image of God, who was usually thought of as grandfatherly and with a long white beard. Since so few people in colonial America were literate, respect for elders often stemmed from the fact that they were repositories and teachers of traditional knowledge and values. In the slowly changing society of eighteenth-century America, their experience and wisdom was ever relevant, and they were seen as important agents of communication. At public gatherings, such as New England town meetings, the places of honor were reserved for the elderly rather than the rich. Wealth made a difference, though, as far as respect was concerned; aged paupers were treated cruelly. Fischer records that "a New Jersey law of 1720 instructed justices of the peace to search arriving ships for 'old persons' as well as 'maimed, lunatic, or any vagabond and vagrant persons' and send them away in order to prevent the growth of pauperism in the colony" (1978:61). Widows are said to have fared badly since few were very well provided for by their husband's estate. Some were actually driven away by neighbors who were afraid that their presence would result in increased poor taxes.

The fact that there were a considerable number of poor and homeless old people in colonial America contradicts the commonly held belief that extended families were the rule in America before industrialization and urbanization. It is now believed, however, that nuclear families were the norm in Western Europe and America as far back as the Reformation. Certainly the emphasis on political and religious freedom that marked the social thought of colonial America would not have provided a very fertile environment for the existence of larger multigenerational extended families. Even in rural areas related nuclear families often lived close to one another and cooperated on agricultural projects, but the "Walton-style" family was probably a rarity. Fischer describes the pattern of family life before the twentieth century:

> The responsibilities of child-rearing normally continued to the end of life. Normally the first baby was born within a year of the marriage; the last came when the wife was thirty-eight and her husband was forty-two. As a rule, the youngest child did not marry until the parents were sixty-four and sixty. Men and women continued to live with their unmarried children nearly until the end of their lives. Very few old people lived alone; most remained in nuclear families with their own children still around them. Scarcely any of them lived in extended, three generational households. Those who did usually had taken a married daughter or son who had lost a spouse. When three generations lived together, it was more often the young who were in some way dependent upon the old than the old upon the young. (1978:56)

The only people who had a concept of retirement were New England ministers, but few of them voluntarily chose this option since they rarely received financial support. Some, however, were forced to retire by dissatisfied congregations. In early America, very few families were able to save a great deal for old age during their lifetime, and old age pensions were unknown until after the Civil War, when military pensions were awarded to nearly 1 million veterans. In regard to compulsory old-age pension plans for industry, Fischer writes that they "were denounced by clergymen as hostile to the morals of the Republic. They were condemned by economists as destructive to the spirit of enterprise. They were attacked by politicians as dangerous to American liberty. Capitalists called them a corrupt form of socialism. Labor leaders denounced them as 'deferred wages' " (1978:168).

Not until the twentieth century did private corporations establish pension plans. Railroads led the way; the Baltimore and Ohio Railroad initiated the practice in 1884. Various states—Ohio, Pennsylvania, Wisconsin, and Massachusetts—maintained pauper institutions for destitute elderly, but as late as 1922 no state in the union had enacted a satisfactory old-age pension system. Aged Americans had to wait until the Social Security legislation of 1935 for any form of government-sponsored plan of old-age assistance. While programs for elderly in America lag far behind those in other European countries, today elderly Americans can rely on Social Security, Supplemental Security Income (which ensures a reasonably adequate minimum monthly income, Medicare (a health insurance program that helps the aged meet the high cost of health care), Medicaid (a program for low income elderly that covers medical services not covered by Medicare), and many other local, state, and national programs.

Ceremonial Life

In America there are few ceremonies associated with aging. Aside from half-hearted recognition of the significance of sixteenth, twenty-first, and fortieth birthdays there is little observance of age milestones. The media tend to pay special attention to people who manage to celebrate their one-hundredth year of life, and there is some recognition of fiftieth, sixtieth, and seventieth wedding anniversaries, but there is nothing to match the excitement and prestige associated with completing the fifth 12-year cycle of life in Japan or Thailand. Retirement, which takes place for most at age 65, is sometimes marked by a special ceremony at which the retiree is given a gift (often a watch or a piece of hobby equipment), eulogized with humorous speeches from co-workers, and told to "drop by any time and see us."

Religion

The religious tradition observed in the United States has little effect on attitudes toward the aged. While the Bible urges believers to "Honor thy father and mother that thy days may be long," this commandment has never had the impact on behavior that the filial piety principle has had in oriental religions. It states an ideal but does not represent a guarantee of respect and responsibility. Like American society in general, American religion is youth oriented and for every congregation with a minister to the elderly there are 100 with youth ministers. Nearly every congregation has a young people's organization (e.g., Christian Endeavor, Canterbury Club, Christian Youth Fellowship, Catholic Youth Organization), but very few maintain special organizations for elderly. Some denominations do, however, operate residences or nursing homes for the aged, and the Catholic order, Little Sisters of the Poor, has established homes for old people in a variety of foreign cultures.

The Value Environment

America is a difficult society in which to grow old—probably more difficult than the societies of the Eskimo or the Samoan. It is a society where people anticipate old age with "sorrow or rebellion. It fills men with more aversion than does death itself" (de Beauvoir, 1972:539). To be old in the United States is to be a member of the country's least visible minority, and, in general, it involves being less healthy, less mobile, and less financially secure than most Americans. This dismal situation is the result of a combination of (1) a particular set of values, (2) a particular level of technological development, and (3) a particular form of social organization. Specifically, Americans' attitudes toward the aged and their own aging result from the fact that the United States as a culture ideally:

1. Places a high value on self-reliance, independence and success
2. Is characterized by social alienation
3. Is youth oriented
4. Associates physical beauty with youth
5. Is future oriented
6. Is precision and time oriented
7. Views the universe as mechanistic and conceives of man as its master
8. Is a wasteful, throw-away culture
9. Is democratic and egalitarian.

Self-Reliance and Success

Anthropologist Francis Hsu, a China-born analyst of American culture, maintains that

> the American core value is self-reliance .... Every individual is his own master, in control of his own destiny, and will advance and regress in society only according to his own efforts .... In American society the fear of dependency is so great that an individual who is not self-reliant is an object of hostility .... "Dependent character" is a highly derogatory term, and a person so described is thought to be in need of psychiatric help (1961:216-219)

Self-reliance is seen not only as the key to mental health but it is also the prerequisite to personal success. Having rejected nearly all forms of dependence on fellow human beings, the American finds that "security must come from personal success, personal superiority, and personal triumph. Those who are fortunate enough to achieve success, superiority, and triumph will, of course, bask in the sunshine" (Hsu, 1961:228). In America, the game is not played for the sake of playing; it is played to be won, and every activity of value represents an arena for competition. It is inconceivable in America that status-conferring tasks should be reserved for elderly people as they are in Samoa, for in America, winning is too important for rewards to be conferred without a struggle.

Most aged Americans are by definition, dependent—dependent on Social Security, on pensions, on family goodwill and interest, or on government health and welfare programs. Some are more dependent than others, but very few are productive members of the labor force. Furthermore, these elderly individuals have been ruled out of the personal achievement competition by societal laws that actually prohibit their participation. While economic achievement is ruled out by forced retirement, it is important for elders to hold their own. Not becoming a burden has become of ultimate importance. This has led to insistence on separate residences for elderly until physical or mental health problems necessitate institutionalization. This rather complete segregation of generations not only imposes problems on aged but on children as well. It deprives the aged of the companionship of grandchildren and other family members and separates them from young ideas and intergenerational perspectives. Young people, on the other hand, are robbed of a source through which they might better understand and prepare for their own old age.

Social Alienation

In the book *Man Alone,* Eric and Mary Josephson write that "alienation has been used by philosophers, psychologists, and sociologists to refer to an extraordinary variety of psychosocial disorders, including loss of self, anxiety states, anomie, despair, depersonalization, rootlessness, apathy, social disorganization, loneliness, atomization, powerlessness, meaninglessness, isolation, pessimism and the loss of beliefs or values" (1962:12-13). When societies become large, mechanized, secular, and bureaucratic, individuals tend to become alienated in the routinization and automation so necessary to maintaining a complex system. The United States is such a society; there is abundant evidence that it has become callous to personal needs and has found it convenient to treat individuals like faceless statistics. Most businesses, universities, and government agencies keep track of people through numbers rather than through names. Not to know one's Social Security number renders an individual beyond the help of most agencies.

The dehumanization and consequential loss of community that appears to be a by-product of our civilization in the closing decades of the twentieth century is a form of oppression affecting all human beings, but especially elderly ones. In a society characterized by anonymous beings, the aged are the most invisible, least valued of all. When asked "What is the relationship of fellow human beings to one another?" Erich Fromm answered that they are "two living machines who use each other" (1962:68). The employer uses his employees; the salesman uses his customers; everyone is to everyone else, a commodity. It is a marketing orientation, says Fromm. Modern humans in the United States see themselves as things to be employed successfully on the market; it is one's job to sell oneself effectively. It can readily be seen that the elderly do not fit into this scheme of things because they have nothing to sell. Retired men and women have been deprived of the one thing that gave them value—their world of work. The reason they are not saleable commodities is that the market is only buying new models. Simone de Beauvoir sums up the alienation dilemma:

> Old age exposes the failure of our entire civilization. It is the whole man that must be remade; it is the whole relationship between man and man that must be recast if we wish the old person's state to be acceptable. A man should not start his last years alone and empty-handed . . . . If he were not atomized from his childhood, shut away and isolated among other atoms, and if he shared in a collective life . . . . Then he would never experience banishment. (1972:264)

Youth, Beauty, and the Promise of the Future

In America, the emphasis is on what is young and what is new. To keep up with new trends and new ideas is to be young in spirit, and no one in America ever really looks forward to growing old. The American accent is on youth because the future belongs to the youth of the nation and America is future-oriented. In such a society, the people with the least value are those with the least future. Euphemisms such as *senior citizens, sunset years, golden age* attempt to hide the truth about growing old, and frequently "middle age" extends right up to senility or death. In America, most people will not reveal their age unless forced to, on the grounds that it might incriminate them. This is especially true for women, because aging is profoundly more painful for them than for men. Being physically attractive has traditionally counted more in a woman's life than in a man's in the United States. Men can age and still remain attractive and desirable but women cannot. Nora Scott Kinzer writes:

> Woman is a sexual object. Woman must use her sexual wiles to succeed in life. Success means having a man and keeping him. A body beautiful guarantees that the rent will be paid, the children will have shoes, there will be food on the table, and he won't walk out. (1974:4)

Although in reality there is an abundance of beautiful old people, the association of beauty with youth seems unshakable. On the other hand, the things that are often admired in men—competence, autonomy, and self-control—are not necessarily associated with age, and masculinity does not depend on youth or physical appearance. The fact that men can be considered attractive and desirable in spite of gray hair and wrinkles is well documented by the fact men of power and influence often have wives 30 or more years their junior. Witness the marriages of Bing and Kathryn Crosby (30 years' difference), Senator Strom and Nancy Thurmond (45 years' difference) and Supreme Court Justice William O. and Cathleen Douglas (45 years' difference). Of course, it is the men who make the proposals in American society, and these men in particular had considerable wealth, but undoubtedly other attractions led their wives to consent to marriage. When the situation is reversed and a very, wealthy woman marries a much younger man, the general public is less accepting. While the things that make a man masculine often are enhanced by the years, the things that have traditionally been associated with femininity—passivity, helplessness, dependence, noncompetitiveness—are not.

It would be ridiculous to assume that aging men have no anxiety at the prospect of aging, however. The middle-class Ameircan male's problems during the years of "middle age" are linked to the extreme pressure of having to be successful. It is terribly important in our society that men achieve the goals society has set for them and indeed, they have set for themselves. One's career accomplishments define one's membership in the middle class, and failure to meet societal and personal expectations is the root of the social and psychological pathology known as the "male menopause." This phenomenon, also related to the value of youth and the tyranny of time, is most common in men in their late forties and early fifties who suddenly realize that time is running out, that younger men are standing by to take their place, that retirement is in the offing, and that one's goals have not been realized.

In spite of the general fear of aging in America, most of its citizens are wishing their life away looking toward a rosier tomorrow. Americans seem to need something to look forward to.

Our whole credit system operates on a tomorrow concept. Buy today and pay later. The fact that elderly people often have trouble getting credit probably involves the perception that their future (when the payments will be made) is limited.

Compare these attitudes with those of groups that honor the past. In such societies, the worth of individuals is measured in terms of past experience and not future potential. The older, the wiser, and consequently the more respect due. In traditional China, offspring took pride in their parents' accomplishments and boasted about their ancestors, whereas in America, Christmas letters immodestly describe the triumphs of offspring, and Little League games and dance recitals are events where proud parents come to bask in their children's accomplishments. One of the most popular of special events at universities is Dad's Day at the football stadium. Here dozens of fathers line up on the field with their son's numbers on their backs and receive special recognition through identification with their sons. Although American culture gives young people few legal rights, they exert great control in families and are the recipients of great amounts of attention. Emphasis on the value of youth as opposed to old age is so great in America that the majority of citizens seldom question why parents are expected to support a child for as many as 22 to 25 years (if professional educations are involved) but have no guarantee that they will receive even a few years of financial support when they become old.

Precision and the Tyranny of Time

America is a nation whose industrial enterprise and commitment to science demand precision. Television and radio programs begin exactly on the hour and half hour and the accuracy of the nation's watches is monitored by Western Union. The society's artifacts—e.g., cars, planes, household appliances,—are produced on assembly lines and their parts are interchangeable because they are identical to the hundredth of a centimeter. Lives are lived on rigid schedules—8-to-5 work days, 7, 12, 6 o'clock mealtimes;

one soft-drink producer recommends drinking the product precisely at 10, 2 and 4.

In America, actuarial tables predict life expectancy with brutal accuracy. While some will live longer than the life-expectancy figure (which is an average) and some will live less long, all will be retired precisely at the age established by the employer—65 for most, in some cases, 70. While preindustrial societies judge old age functionally and therefore recognize that it comes to some earlier than others, in the United States old age comes to all precisely on their 65th birthday.

In a society that values precision as highly as America, people are constantly aware of the unrelenting movement of time. Old age and retirement come at 65 and death 14 (men) to 18 (women) years later. The aged retired American has no alternative but to sit idly at home observing his superbly accurate gold watch (which the company gave him on retirement) tick off the minutes and the days the life insurance company table tells him he has remaining. In contrast, people in preindustrial societies like those of the Eskimo and Samoan think of the life cycle not in terms of years but in terms of seasons or planting and harvest times. Few feel it is important to record or even recall how many such seasons they have lived. Ultimately they know they will grow too old to hunt or harvest and someday they will die, but they see no constructive purpose in accurately predicting and monitoring the eventuality. The American system guarantees that most people will spend about two-thirds of their lives worrying about getting old.

In the society of the United States where time is measured, spent, saved, squandered, budgeted, used to best advantage, and generally equated with money, temporal emphasis can be depressing for the elderly in still another way. Robert Smith suggests,

> An individual in his later years . . . used to being active, . . . may now find that an absence of scheduling poses problems for him. It no longer matters that he is on time for anything. He may, indeed, find that he is not required to arise at a certain hour or that he may eat at any time he chooses, in short, that his days are now stretches of time which an earlier discipline will not fill up. (1961:86)

A Mechanistic Universe with Man as Its Master

In describing one aspect of the American value system, Arensberg and Niehoff state:

> For many Americans the natural environment is something to overcome, to improve, or to tear down and rebuild in a better way . . . . This conquering attitude toward nature appears to rest on two assumptions: that the universe is mechanistic and man is its master. (1964:224)

This ability to control nature has become a major source of pride for Americans. American scientific know-how can accomplish almost anything. If Americans want a recreation lake, they have the U.S. Army Corps of Engineers dam a stream; if they need rain, they "seed" the clouds with silver iodide; if they need snow at a ski resort they merely bring in a snow-making machine; if a bone disintegrates or an organ ceases to function, medical science provides an artificial one. There is, however, one natural phenomenon that Americans seem powerless to do anything about, and that is the process of aging. In spite of a constant search for "fountains of youth," modern America has clearly failed to halt or reverse this dreaded natural process. Therefore, we consciously or unconsciously punish the messenger—the elderly population that is constantly before us telling us by way of their white hair and wrinkled faces that all of our science has failed. The elderly are reprehensible symbols of failure in our quest for mastery over nature. Old people are not only loathed for their dependency (forced on them by society), they are equally loathed for their failure to triumph over the physical degeneration of old age (forced on them by nature).

Democracy and Egalitarianism

The democratic, egalitarian nature of American society is, by and large, most laudable, but we must realize that elders do not fare as well in such societies as they do in authoritarian, collectivistic, totalitarian, and static ones. An examination of the cross-cultural data found in Leo Simmons's *The Role of the Aged in Primitive Society* (1945) reveals that those societies where old people have the highest prestige and the greatest security tend to be those governed by autocratic monarchs, despotic chiefs, or restrictive councils of oligarchs. These societies usually feature hereditary castes and classes, and important life decisions, such as choice of a mate or disposition of property, are made by the society or by the family and not by the individual.

Democracies permit individuals to operate free from traditional restraints, but they are societies impatient with the restrictions of convention. There is a hunger for new ideas and new ways of doing things. They are throw-away societies that would rather create than preserve. In a recent television series dealing with an interplanetary visitor, Mork from Ork, the principal character was perplexed by the fact that in America furniture becomes more valuable with time but people do not.

Democracies are societies on the move, and they have little time for ceremony or convention. Traditional lore, old families, and old people do not automatically command respect. It is probably no coincidence that our model of democratic government (Greece) was one where the prevailing attitude toward old age was contained in the proverb, "Whom the gods love die young."

CHAPTER 7

Universals in Human Aging

Universals are ideas, institutions, or forms of human behavior that are found in much the same form in a majority of societies around the world. The existence of these common denominators can be explained by the fact that cultures develop to satisfy human needs and that human beings are essentially the same (at least biologically) in all parts of the globe. People everywhere are of the same species, *Homo sapiens,* have common metabolism and thus common nutritional needs, come in two sexes, experience live birth, are nurtured by a kin group, learn a cultural system that largely determines their behavior, grow physically and mentally to maturity, reproduce, experience senescence, and eventually die. Human beings are introspective, empathetic, recognition-seeking, gregarious, culture-bearing creatures; in spite of many varieties of physical environments in which they must survive, and in spite of the many kinds of social structures that hold them together in families, clans, and communities, some basic requirements must be met for human beings to enjoy mental and physical health and life satisfaction.

Universals do not represent identical cultural forms in all cultures but tend to involve common denominators or constants of behavior. Although universals involve some behavior variations because they are products of the unique cultural histories of the various societal groups, there is a functional similarity. Universals should not be confused with absolutes, which are fixed forms of behavior that, as far as convention is concerned, do not vary from culture to culture or from epoch to epoch.

Discussions of human universals are enlightening, because they help explain what human beings as a species need and want out of life and therefore the major areas of concern to which cultural systems address themselves. When we discuss universal aspects of behavior involving old age, however, we are apt to encounter difficulties. As Myerhoff pointed out, this period of life is "less governed by well-known biological determinants and therefore may be more responsive to cultural conditioning than other periods of life" (1978:153). The fact that the old are past the childbearing and child-nurturing years means that they no longer have a role in the perpetuation of the species, and emphasis therefore shifts from the more prescribed biological roles to roles almost totally assigned by culture. Although we find basic similarities across cultures in the kinds of work performed by elderly, the place of the old in the family system, and societal attitudes about being old, we must remember that there are a "great variety of styles and forms of aging in different cultural settings. Here one is struck by diversity rather than uniformity, by variation rather than universality" (ibid.:152).

UNIVERSAL DESIRES OF AGED

One of the first works to attempt to enumerate cross-cultural universals of aging was that of Leo Simmons. His *Role of the Aged in Primitive Society* (1945) analyzed 71 "primitive cultures in order to discover uniformities and regularities in the aging process. The most notable of the generalizations derived from this study had to do with what Simmons regarded as "universal interests" of old people. These desires, which were presented as transcending cultural boundaries, are:

1. To live as long as possible, at least until life's satisfactions no longer compensate for its privations, or until the advantage of death seems to outweigh the burdens of life

2. To get more rest, release from the necessity of wearisome exertion at humdrum tasks and protection from too great exposure to physical hazards—opportunities, in other words, to safeguard and preserve the waning energies of physical existence

3. To remain active participants in personal and group affairs in either operational or supervisory roles—any participation, in fact, being preferable to complete idleness and indifference

4. To safeguard or even strengthen any prerogatives acquired in a long life (e.g., skills, possessions, rights, authority, and prestige)

5. To meet death, when necessity requires it, as honorably as possible, without too much suffering and with maximal prospects for an attractive hereafter. (1960:66).

The five universal interests expressed above—longer life, rest, prerogatives, participation, and honorable release—are basically desires for security, influence, and respect. Some cultures appear to meet these interests better than others, but security and influence in one's declining years are neither gifts of nature nor of the gods. Instead, they depend largely on how the society values the elderly and the prerogatives the elderly have managed to secure for themselves through property rights or through the respect and authority they have attained through their economic or social contributions to society. Societies do not instinctively honor or pity their elderly; whatever prestige and respect they receive is the product of social developments and custom. Custom or tradition grants the privilege of age, but just as easily as it is established originally, it can be taken away. Simone de Beauvoir writes:

> This happened frequently enough when there has been contact with whites. The aged Zande and Aranda no longer monopolize the women. Some young men—the African Lao, for example—leave the villages where they maintained their old parents and go to find jobs in town. The young Lele have thrown off the yoke of the aged by becoming Christian and working for Europeans. Where the authority of the old is still strong, the reason is that the community as a whole wishes to maintain its traditions by means of them. It is the community, according to its potentialities and its interests, that determines the fate of the old. (1972:86)

Attitudes toward the aged and the nature of their care are not totally independent of other sociocultural factors, however. Generally, the aged fare better in wealthy societies than in poor ones; they are more carefully attended in sedentary as opposed to nomadic societies; and the severity of the environment, a factor in both the extent to which the elderly can contribute economically and the degree to which they must be protected and aided in order to survive, undoubtedly shapes societal attitudes toward the old. However, as Gutmann points out, "A benign government does not guarantee the welfare of the weak and unproductive. Thus, the Thonga neglect their young and do away with useless aged. The dominant personality ideal in Thonga is the fat, strong and rich individual. There is little sympathy for any other" (1977:319).

On the other hand, a society with extreme poverty—the Siriono of the Bolivian tropical forest, for example—live from day to day, always knowing hunger, yet, although they sometimes leave elderly behind when they hinder tribal movements, the cultural system has ensured that there will always be enough for the elderly to eat. According to Priest:

> That many do survive after their usefulness has passed is due almost entirely to the Siriono system of food taboos, which do not apply, or apply only very loosely to the aged. Therefore the aged, even in a society not concerned with their welfare, are assured of certain foods that cannot be eaten by others. (1966:1,245)

The following are examples of taboos that provide "institutional" support for Siriono aged:

If you eat animal heads (especially brains), your hair will turn gray early.

If you eat the fat of the land turtle, you will be slow like the land turtle.

If you eat anything that you yourself shoot, your running will be impaired. (Good hunting requires good running.)

If you eat honey containing baby bees, your children will become crybabies.

If you eat the young of anything, your children's lips will turn white (anemic) and your children will be born foolish.

If young men eat bananas, they come home from the hunt empty handed.

Men and boys must give manioc and sweet potatoes that are damaged (when being dug from the ground) to the old people.

> Children must give their game and fish to the old people. They will get sick if they don't.
>
> Young women must not eat palm cabbage that they themselves have chopped out.
>
> You should not use new gourd drinking vessels. If you do, you will be sick. You should let the old people use them until they are no longer new; then you can use them.
>
> If you eat pacu fish, your children will be striped.
>
> If you eat striped agouti, your baby's hair will fall out.

Note that none of the consequences of eating the various foods would particularly trouble the elderly. When one is old, such developments as having gray hair, being slow in one's movements, having one's running impaired, or having one's children born foolish are hardly to be feared. Since women cease being reproductively active earlier than men, and since many of the taboos pertain to threats to small children, women come under the protection of the taboo several years before the men of this society.

In spite of the many curious variations in the treatment of the aged around the world, Simmons was able to state on the basis of data correlations that "old people generally gained in influence and security with the gradual establishment of permanent residence, the achievement of a stable food supply, the rise in herding, the cultivation of the sod, and the increase of closely knit family relationships" (1960:69).

Enlarging on Simmons's generalization that permanent residence, stable food supply, and closely knit family relationships[1] are conducive to the welfare of the old, Myerhoff suggested that lineage systems are more supportive of old people than kindred systems (1978:160). Lineage systems are those where descent is traced through one parent and involves the sum total of descendants from a common ancestor. This, of course, may go back many generations. The kindred, on the other hand, includes all those living individuals a person recognizes as being related to him or her through blood, marriage, or adoption. The kindred, therefore, has a horizontal dimension, while the lineage has a vertical one. The kindred places emphasis on collateral relatives (all those living at a given time), while the lineage principle emphasizes generations of relatives, many of whom may be dead. According to Myerhoff, "Kindreds are more often found in the changing, industrial, and Western societies that stress individuality, achievement and mobility. Where the lineage principle is used to generate the most important groups, the older members of the society accumulate great authority and status" (ibid.:160).

Lines from the radio dramatization *"Home Sweet Home"*[2] (spoken by a modern Chinese-American family head) are typical of the attitudes and thinking in the West,

---

[1] See also discussion of supportive nature of extended family systems in comparison to nuclear ones on page 172-173.

[2] *"Home Sweet Home"* is one of several dramatizations on anthropological subjects prepared under the direction of Walter Goldschmidt. These scripts were published under the title *Ways of Mankind* by Beacon Press, Boston, 1954.

where little or no honor is paid to ancestors and a minimum of deference is shown to living aged:

> Ancestors? Americans are a people on the move. They can't be bothered lugging their ancestors around with them. My father stuck to Chinatown in San Francisco. I am the half-way child. My children are real Americans. It has taken three generations; that is a long time to Americans. My children speak only English. They don't want to know anything about their ancestors. (Goldschmidt, 1954:97)

Varieties of subsistence, permanence of residence, and structure of the family have apparently all been variables that have had to do with the ease with which the elderly could be cared for or the extent to which the elderly could care for themselves. In many cases, certain conditions permitted the elderly to make substantial contributions to the welfare of their society and to their own welfare. In sedentary communities, the problem of age is basically maintenance, but in nomadic societies the problem of transport is added. If the environment is harsh, people live from day to day, sacrificing individuals for the good of the group, and often learning to stifle feelings and sentimentality when such measures are necessary to survive.

The matter of respect for aged appears to operate quite independently of any of the above considerations. Respect may mean authority, genuine love and affection, decision-making power, or merely being the recipient of honorific salutations and respectful addresses, being bowed to or allowed to go through doors first, or offered seats on crowded buses or subway trains. Simone de Beauvoir points out also that "theory and practice do not always agree; the old may be mocked in private and at the same time treated with outward respect. The contrary is also seen often—old age is honored in words and at the same time allowed to wither away in physical neglect" (1972:85).

COWGILL AND HOLMES: UNIVERSALS

Donald O. Cowgill and Lowell D. Holmes (1972) in their analysis of aging and modernization in 14 societies listed nine universals, some relating to demographic realities and some to common patterns of behavior of elderly or common features of social systems. The remainder of this chapter enlarges on these universals and presents others (in italics) that are suggested by the original nine. These are:

Proportion of Population

The aged always constitute a minority of the total population. Only in the artificially created age-homogeneous retirement communities of the Western world would this not be true. Simmons maintains that "the farther back we go into primitive and rudimentary forms of human association, the fewer old people are to be found" (1960:67). Percentages of people over 65 (our criterion of old age) constitute anywhere between 3% in such societies as Samoa and Thailand to as much as 13.6% in Austria. It should also be noted that our reference to "a minority" is to a numerical minority and not to a minority in the sense of an ethnic group or a subculture. Arnold Rose (1965) proposed that the aged might be thought of as a subculture, based on their patterns of interaction and common interests and problems, but other social scientists reject the idea on the grounds of great heterogeneity of life-styles, economic situations, social interaction patterns and family ties found in American society. Although some elderly who are in retirement residences interact mainly with other elderly and may indeed share common problems and interests, the percentage of individuals residing in such environments is relatively small when we consider the total aged population.

Sex Ratio

Older populations have more women than men. Nearly all societies that have not been unduly affected by immigration (men are always more mobile) have more women than men over the age of 65. Unless circumstances are unusual (like extreme childbirth mortality), women tend to outlive men. There have been societies, such as that of ancient China where Confucius taught that women were inferior to men, which led some parents to put girl babies to death. There have also been societies that believed the eldest offspring should be male, and they destroyed any female children whose birth preceded that of a male. These circumstances would, of course, alter the sex ratio, since they represent societal interference with natural trends.

Widowhood

Widows usually make up a high proportion of an aged population. Because women outlive men and because most adults in both preindustrial and industrial societies marry, widowhood is a universal phenomenon. In their studies of the 14 societies, Cowgill and Holmes found that widows made up between one-half to three-fourths of the elderly women, and the highest percentage of widows appears to be in industrial societies. Societies vary in the degree to which they encourage remarriage of women whose husbands have died, and the levirate is one institutional device that some societies use to ensure the rapid reentry of the woman into family life. The levirate, practiced by the ancient Hebrews and others, requires or permits a man to marry the widow of his brother or other close relative.

Life-Cycle Stages

All societies have some system of age grading. In all societies some people are considered "old."[3] How people are age graded varies from society to society. Most groups have some sort of system where the life cycle is divided up into such stages as childhood, adolescence, adulthood, and old age. In some societies, the onset of old age is reckoned according to physical appearance, strength, the capacity to carry out normal adult tasks, or changes in social roles. Still other societies assign the label *old* in terms of years lived since birth, how many generations of living progeny one can point to, or what formal age class or age grade their society has assigned people to.

The system of life stages used by a given culture reveals something of that society's concept of role and personality development. Some societies require very different

---

[3] See pages 23-25, 27-30 (Age Grades and Life-Cycle Analysis).

kinds of behavior and assign very different kinds of responsibilities to people at various stages of their life cycle while others require few alterations in behavior or personality throughout the course of the lifetime of its members. Compare, for example, the somewhat sexist life stages of William Shakespeare on the one hand and of the Nandi of East Africa on the other. (Tables 7.1 and 7.2).

Anthony P. Glascock and Susan L. Feinman (1980a) discovered that in 18 out of 57 societies drawn from the Probability Sample Files of the Human Relations Area Files two categories of elderly were recognized. They were (1) the intact, or young-old and (2) the decrepit, or old-old. Of these two categories Glascock and Feinman write:

> While an individual is considered young or intact by the rest of society, support for his/her existence is provided. However, once this individual passes over into the old or decrepit group of elderly, support is withdrawn; dramatically since the non-supportive behavior in all but one instance is death hastening. Societies therefore manage to have both types of behavior without internal strain because the two types of behavior are directed at different populations. (1980a:324)

Simone de Beauvoir also confirms this phenomenon and provides two examples. She writes, "Many societies respect the old so long as they are clear-minded and robust, but get rid of them when they become senile and infirm. This is the case with the Hottentots, who lead a semi-nomadic life in Africa" (1972:51). De Beauvoir also notes

Table 7.1 Shakespeare's Seven Ages

Age	Expected Behavior
1. Infant	Completely dependent period
2. School boy	Responsibility of being educated (often unwilling)
3. Lover	Courtship; little other responsibility
4. Soldier	Period of pursuit of honor through bravery
5. Justice	Establishment period; subject is secure, wise, and well fed
6. Pantaloon (old dotard)	Beginning of physical and mental deterioration
7. Senility	Complete dependency

Table 7.2 Nandi Age Grades

Grade	Expected Behavior
Males	
1. Boys	Cattle herding; servants to warriors
2. Warriors	Warfare and courtship
3. Elders	Marry, raise a family, and then serve as statesmen and tribal advisors
Females	
1. Girls	Household chores
2. Married women	Childbearing and rearing; homemaking

that although the northern Ojibway show infants great affection, do not wean them abruptly, and never punish them, the dependency of old age is handled very differently. "When very great age and decrepitude come upon a man there are striking differences in his treatment according to the families; but it often happens that the old are neglected and that the young steal the food meant for them . . . . The old preferred being solemnly put to death" (ibid:53).

Role Changes

There is a general tendency in old age to shift toward sedentary, more advisory and supervisory activities, to those directed toward group maintenance more than economic production.

As mentioned before (see Chapter 3), David Gutmann has postulated, on the basis of data from the lowland and highland Maya, the traditional or Western Navajo, whites in Kansas City, and the Druze of Israel, that as men age there is an inevitable shift in motives, attitudes, and actions. Men move from an "active, production-centered and competitive stance," labeled *active mastery* at ages 35 to 49, to one labeled *passive mastery* at ages 50 to 59, to one labeled *magical mastery* at ages 61 to 70. Gutmann writes:

> In the Druze case . . . the so-called passivity of the older men can be the central, necessary component of his engagement in age-appropriate controls . . . . He relinquishes his own productivity *per se*. Instead of being the center of the enterprise, he is now the bridge between the community and the productive, life-sustaining potencies of Allah. (1976:7)

In other words, the elderly Druze man abandons the role of active and productive farmer for one as keeper of the religious traditions.

Whether all elderly move toward more advisory and less active roles because of psychological or physiological considerations is a debatable question, but it should be noted that while not all societies have a category of labor known as "old people's work," the elderly tend to carry out similar social and economic functions in many societies. Barbara Myerhoff writes:

> Regardless of societal complexity, the division of labor awarded to the elderly has many similarities across cultures. Midwifery, entertainment, story-telling, beauty treatment, scarification, socialization, and ritual and religious specialization are often the business of the old men and women of the group. In preliterate societies, the acquisition and retention of knowledge and experience are directly related to living. Thus the old are the repositories of the wisdom accumulated and transmitted orally. (1978:163)

Value of Memory

The elderly often enjoy great respect and prestige because of their ability to remember. The memories of the aged are depended on to provide traditional solutions to survival problems, to instruct young people in the valuable subsistence or occupational skills, to maintain the mores, and to perpetuate the sacred tenets of the culture. Although the capacity to remember is perhaps a bit less important in societies with books and libraries, there is still a great demand even in modern societies for the personal reminiscences (oral history) that can only be supplied by old people. Given the recent interest on the part of American minorities in discovering their cultural roots, the information grandparents and great-grandparents can provide on now-extinct cultural ideas and ways of behaving has become eagerly sought by the young. Gerry Williams notes that among Oklahoma Indians

> the trend toward "Indianism" or a revitalization of the Indian cultural traditions may in part account for conflicting attitudes between generations. That is, we would expect an idealization of the aged for they are, chronologically at least, closer to an older form of social behavior which is now being stressed by the younger Indian. This stress upon the older Indians' knowledge of traditional behavior often times is an expectation which the aged Indian cannot fulfill. Individuals in their 60's and 70's today, except in a few instances, cannot begin to recall earlier forms of ceremonial behavior, past life-styles, and the movements and exploits of a hunting and gathering subsistence. (1980:109)

Similar demands are being made on the elderly in the People's Republic of China. In old China respect for the aged was maintained through the principles of filial piety enunciated by the Confucian tradition, but these concepts have largely been rejected under the Marx-Mao ideology that was established when the Chinese communists came to power in 1949. At that time, Mao believed that the skills of the elderly would be beneficial to his Revolution, and he called for including the elderly in a coalition of people of all ages, and he challenged them to continue the Revolution and to build a socialistic society. In present-day China, the basis for respect has changed from the Confucian-based ideology to one based on respect for the makers of the Revolution. Now the aged are valued because they have within their memories the facts about the Revolution that young Chinese want to know. They can tell of personal experiences involving the suffering, the struggle, and the hardships of the Revolution and the happiness associated with establishing the new order. The elderly are therefore valued for their memories not of traditional China but of the birth and growth struggles of the new China (Ganschow, 1978).

De Beauvoir comments that for the Miao who live in the high forest and bush country of China and Thailand:

> It is the old who hand on the traditions, and the respect in which they are held is chiefly based upon the ability to do so; their memory of the ancient myths can provide them with a very high standing. They are the community's guides and counsellors. (1972:71)

Among the Mende of West Africa the memories of the elders are even more important, for it is the aged who possess the traditions upon which Mende political organization is based. Mende society is constituted of two quite distinct classes. An upper class is made up of descendants of the hunters and warriors who first settled the territory, and this group consists of the chiefs and their families. The lower class, on the other hand, is made up of newcomers to Mende country and the descendants of slaves. The land is owned by the upper class and worked by lower-class tenants. The comprehension and perpetuation of the system depends in large part on the memories of the elderly.

> It is memory alone that makes it possible to state whether a person belongs to one class or the other. A man who aims at becoming a chief must know the country's history, the genealogies of the Mende, the lives of their first founders and of their descendants; and this knowledge is necessarily passed on to them by their ancestors. It is they, the old people, who possess the traditions, and the Mende's political organization is therefore based upon them. (de Beauvoir, 1972:72)

The fact that the elderly represent the repositories of traditional knowledge in pre-industrial societies has been widely recognized, and Maxwell and Silverman (1977) found that control and transmission of useful traditional knowledge by the elderly is a major factor associated with their good treatment and high status.

Ceremonial Knowledge

Societies rich in ceremonialism and religious ritual tend to honor the aged and accord them prestige seldom found in less formalistic societies. Because of their recollections of and involvement with the traditional, unchanging ritual phenomena of a society, the elderly man or woman is the appropriate person to be its caretaker. Old people are not only able to teach the details of the ceremonies but they represent in their remarkable long life a kind of liaison figure between the things of earth and the realm of the supernatural. Ritual is the celebration of the traditional and orthodox, and what is traditional is best known by those who have lived the longest. De Beauvoir expands on this point:

> As the custodian of the traditions, the intercessor, and the protector against the supernatural powers, the aged man ensures the cohesion of the community throughout time and in the present . . . .
>
> Generally speaking, the services, taken as a whole, that the old are enabled to render because of their knowledge of the traditions, mean that they have not only respect but also material prosperity. They are rewarded with presents. The gifts that they receive from those whom they initiate into their secrets are of particular importance—they are the surest source of private wealth, a source that exists only in societies that are sufficiently well-to-do to have an advanced culture. (1972:83)

Many of the ceremonial and ritual roles performed by the elderly are described by Simmons:

> They have served as guardians of temples, shrines, and sacred paraphernalia, as officers of the priesthood, and as leaders of the performance of rites associated with prayers, sacrifices, feast days, annual cycles, historic celebrations, and the initiation of important and hazardous enterprises. They also have been prominent in ceremonies associated with critical periods in the life cycle—such as birth, puberty, marriage, and death. (1945:164)

Ceremony and religious ritual have long been recognized as cultural foci of the Northwest Coast Indian tribes. Religion was extremely formalized and the complex ceremonies of religious societies made a great impression on the minds and emotions of their members. Membership in these societies conferred great status, and the ceremonies they conducted were seen as vital to the well-being of the society.

One tribe in this area, the Coast Salish of western Washington and British Columbia, has been described by Pamela Amoss (1981) as a society in which the aged, because of their knowledge of ritual and ceremonial detail, have continued to command considerable respect in spite of the influence of modernization. Amoss contends that "old men and women maintain prestige and high social rank through their control of scarce information about the old ritual practices and through the spiritual power people believe they possess. Far from losing ground as Coast Salish society has changed, they have actually improved their position in the last twenty years" (1981:227-228).

On the other hand, a society without a ceremonial tradition may provide little opportunity for prestige or participation for the elderly. In the western subarctic region of North America, ceremonials and religious ritual have never been a particularly important part of Indian life. Spencer and Jennings report, for example, that there was an absence of feasts and communalism in religion and that individualism and personal power were important elements in the belief system. They point out that although there was a modified guardian-spirit quest it could hardly be considered a ritual or dramatic happening, and while shamanism was present "it lacked the drama of either Eskimo shamanism or certainly that of the Northwest Coast. While there is some suggestion that shamans might sing at various occasions, such as before hunting, and sometimes in association with girls' rites, the practices associated with the complex appear essentially rudimentary and imperfectly developed and integrated" (1977:112).

Among the Chipewyan Indians of this subarctic region, elderly men who are no longer able to hunt command no respect and they are not able to gain it by telling myths or legends, as there is little interest in such things. This is not a society that engages in ritual behavior and therefore the elderly are left almost no opportunities for societal participation.

Political Leadership

Some old men continue to act as political and judicial leaders in modern as well as nonindustrial societies. Jack Goody has observed that "politics is an area, even in industrial societies, where old age is rarely an impediment to office. In the Western world, political leaders are often active after others have retired, and the same is true in nonindustrial societies" (1967:127). Shortly after Ronald Reagan was sworn into office as the fortieth president of the United States, he observed his seventieth birthday, an event which by law or precedent usually forces teachers, factory and office workers, captains of industry, and government employees into retirement. Many American workers are even forced to retire at age 65.

In 1981, six senators and 18 representatives in Congress were 70 or older, and of the nine Supreme Court judges (who are appointed for life), one (Brennen) was 75, two (Powell and Burger) were 74, two (Blackmun and Marshall) were 73, and Stewart was 66.

Turning to nonindustrial societies, Simmons informs us that "the office of chieftainship and/or membership in official council, regulative organizations, clubs and

In Samoa old age is a prerequisite for family and political leadership.
(Photo by Lowell D. Holmes.)

secret societies have afforded old people, especially men, positions of usefulness and prestige in which established prerogatives, ripe experience, and special knowledge often could more than compensate for physical handicaps or waning vitality" (1960:78).

The ongoing value of elders politically is confirmed by the existence in many parts of the world of gerontocracies, which, of course, are political systems where the political power rests in a council of old men, who by virtue of their purported wisdom, serve as community decision-makers, counsellors, and arbiters of disputes. Such societies, which often operate on an age-grade principle, are found in Africa, Australia, and Melanesia.

Generational Reciprocity

In all societies, the mores prescribe some mutual responsibility within the family between old people and their adult children. Leo Simmons has observed that

> social relationships have proved the strongest securities to the individual, especially in old age. With vitality declining, the aged person has had to rely more and more upon personal relations with others, and upon reciprocal rights and obligations envolved.... Throughout human history the family has been the safest haven for the aged. Its ties have been the most intimate and longlasting, and on them the aged have relied for greatest security. (1945:177)

Dependency is a reality of human life during both the beginning and the concluding years of the life cycle, and most societies think in terms of a kind of reciprocity where care received when one is young is paid back (with respect) when one's caretakers become old and need assistance and solicitude. Prevailing societal values can greatly affect this relationship, however. For example, in America (an extremely youth-oriented society) there tends to be an attitude that youth dependency (often extending as long as 25 years where offspring acquire professional education) does not carry a mandate for reciprocity when parents become elderly and in need of help. The more common pattern found around the world, however, is that there tends to be a balance between infant care and old age care. Furthermore, there is a tendency—so common that it might also be cited as a universal—that *the way the members of a society treat their aged is a reflection of the nature of child-rearing practices.* Societies with warm and loving relationships between parents and their small children appear to also promote warm and loving relationships between adult children and elderly parents. De Beauvoir suggests:

> If a child is kept short of food, protection, and loving kindness he will grow up full of resentment, fear and even hatred; as a grown man his relations with others will be aggressive—he will neglect his old parents when they are no longer able to look after themselves. (1972:80)

De Beauvoir also relates that after doing thorough research on this issue she found only one example where happy children grew into adults who were cruel to their fathers and mothers. That group was the Objibway. Numerous ethnographic examples support de Beauvoir's generalization, however. Marie Scott Brown tells us that the Kikuyu of Kenya are "noted for their warm and permissive child-rearing practices. There are particularly warm attachments between the grandparents and the grandchildren who symbolically belong to the same age group. There are, in fact, warm relationships between all the generations" (1980:89).

The Tiv of Nigeria also have extremely warm and supportive acculturation and socialization patterns, and, as a result, even grown children are very close emotionally to parents and grandparents, and the elderly are in general treated with respect. Similarly, de Beauvoir reports for the Yaghan of Tierra del Fuego:

> The boys and girls are very well treated, they are deeply attached to their parents, and when they are in camp they always want to live in their parents' hut. This love persists when the parents are very old, and all the aged people are respected. (1972:59)

In a number of societies where James W. Prescott found infants provided with a great deal of "tender loving care" (1975:67), it was established that attitudes toward old people were positive and supportive. Such societies are the Andamanese, the Chuckchee, the Maori, the Trobriand Islanders, the Jivaro, and the island people of Lesu. On the other hand, in societies where children are raised under austere enculturative situations, where there is little warmth, love, and affection displayed toward them, evidence indicates that the aged will also be treated badly. De Beauvoir writes: "The Yakut and the Ainu, who are badly treated as children, neglect the old most brutally" (1972:80). Trostchansky, who lived among the Yakut of Siberia for 20 years, reports that the aged were turned into slaves by their sons, who beat them and required very hard labor of them. Landor, in *Alone with the Hairy Ainu,* describes the fate of a neglected, starving, and physically ill elderly woman he encountered in an Ainu home. He reports that the woman was not "taken care of by the village or by her son, who lived in the same hut; but she was something that had been thrown away, and that was how they treated her. A fish was occasionally flung to her" (1893:55).

It is conceivable that this correlation between ill treatment of children and devaluation of the aged may serve as an explanation of the less than enthusiastic respect and support extended to the elderly in America. A 1953 study by John Whiting and Irving Child of child-rearing practices in a variety of cultures discovered that in regard to warmth and affection (measured in terms of nursing, timing and severity of toilet training, severity of aggression training and sexual training) Americans were among the least affectionate and warm parents investigated.

Savings and Property Control

Saving for old age appears to be a near universal desire and effort. Modern industrial societies have responded to this universal desire for security in senior years through the development of insurance plans, pension programs, and government legislative schemes such as Social Security and Supplemental Security Income (SSI), but in preindustrial societies security in old age is often ensured through control of property. De Beauvoir explains:

> Rarely do we find poor communities in which an old person has possessions that allow him to look after himself. Among hunters and collectors property does not exist: they do not even store food. Among the pastoral and agricultural societies property is often collective: the individual possesses no more than the product of his own or his wives' labour; if he outlives them or if they become infirm and he can no longer work himself—or if he is forbidden by custom to perform tasks reserved for women—then he is wholly destitute. (1972:80)

Where old people have been successful in acquiring property and where they have been able to retain the rights to that property in old age, they have enjoyed not only economic security but also power and prestige. By holding and controlling property, the elderly both maintain their own independence and control the opportunities of the young. Property owners in most groups provide work and make work assignments, and therefore the community's security depends on their decisions and knowledge. This maintains the authority of the aged long after their capacity to actually work the land has ended.

Leo Simmons suggests that the intergenerational process of property transfer that ensures old age security is like a game. The game involves progressively relinquishing just enough personal resources (land and other property) to make young people happy, while retaining enough to guarantee that family members will continue to render respect and personal care in exchange. He states, "Aging must be gamey up close to the end to remain good" (1962:50).

Let us look at how successfully this game is played in a variety of cultures. The prime example of how not to play the game is King Lear, who divided up his kingdom among his daughters and found himself without support or security for his old age. As Goody suggests, "No longer able to command their obedience, he is dependent upon their love; yet their gratitude is of far less value than he anticipated" (1976:119).

Something of the King Lear situation can be observed among the Fulani of West Africa. Here middle-aged household heads give portions of their livestock to each of their children when they marry and keep only those animals that they themselves can watch after. While the father gradually experiences the depletion of his herd, the mother in like manner gives away her decorated calabashes and other household property to her daughters as they marry. When the last daughter has left the household, the mother is, in effect, out of business as a mother, as a housewife, and as a dairywoman. D. J. Stenning tells us that the old man and woman even must abandon their own homestead and reside as dependents. The mother is considered of some use in caring for infants, but "an old man is regarded as of little use . . . . Old people in this situation spend their last days on the periphery of the household, on the male and female sides respectively. This is where men and women are buried. They sleep, as it were over their own graves, for they are already socially dead" (1958:98-99).

Although this arrangement appears callous or even cruel, incidents in our own society occasionally occur which are not too different. In June, 1981, the Wichita, Kansas, daily newspaper, the *Eagle-Beacon,* carried the story of a local elderly couple who were being evicted from their home by their son, who had acquired the deed to the house from his parents some six years earlier. Because of conflict over how the elderly couple should spend their Social Security income, the son was demanding their removal from his property.

The property game is played well in most cultures. For example, the Etalese of the Caroline Islands value land above all other property, and although most young men acquire some land from their parents, it is not until their parents are very old that they acquire full title. According to James Nason:

> Older people gain or lose respect in the community by the way they administer their property. It is thought foolish for an old person to dispose of all property—meaning here village and agricultural lands held with full title, individual trees, or important objects such as canoes—because it is almost an explicit statement of intent to withdraw from active social life in the community, an inappropriate form of behavior, and leaves one even more fully dependent on others than would otherwise be the case. The continued control of property is one way for an old person to remain somewhat independent and to exert some control over the way he or she is treated. An old person who has property need not fear neglect, since if kin fail, others will appear, hopeful of receiving the remaining property as their due reward. (1981:167-168 passim)

Nason found that people 45 and older controlled 60% of all individually owned land, and approximately half the canoes on the island were owned by men over 45. Property control is for them not only a strategy for maintaining authority and respect in one's family but it is necessary for the retention of respect within the entire community. Only foolish persons give away all their property, but on the other hand, attempting to hang onto all of one's property and thereby preventing adult offspring from acquiring some measure of prestige through property ownership is equally reprehensible.

Few play the property game better than the Kirghiz, a nomadic pastoral group in Afghanistan. In this society, household heads own the *yurt* (felt tent) and its contents, the herds, and all other material wealth associated with the family. However, the property is used to ensure the aging household head and his wife that there will always be someone present to care for them. The Kirghiz social system provides economic and psychological security by passing the responsibility for the parents down the line of sons. As each son marries and moves out of the natal household to establish his own, the next eldest son assumes the responsibility for the parents. When only one son remains in the household, he must stay within the household until the father dies, whereupon he inherits the yurt, the herds, and the household material goods. While he profits the most materially, the eldest son inherits the father's political influence and prestige. Throughout the parents' elder years all sons are expected to visit frequently and aid the parents in any way they can. This is especially true in regard to the eldest son, who must maintain a close relationship between his household and that of his father's.

In the Samoan islands, chiefs not only are the heads of large extended families but their titles also guarantee their right to control family lands. These titles are held for life, and succession to a chief's title comes not through inheritance but through election by kinsmen. Candidates are judged on the basis of their record of service, hard work, loyalty, and respect rendered to the family, particularly to its head. Thus, young men who wish to hold chiefly titles in the future are forced to show deference and obedience to their aging family leaders who not only control the family land but also the political future of the young men who work the land.

In 1979, Sonya Salamon and Vicki Lockhardt described research among Corn Belt farm families on the effect of control of land on the quality of intergenerational relations. They found that in the tightly knit German community of Heartland the elderly held a high position. What seems to have created this situation was a kind of "carrot on a stick" arrangement, where some land was turned over to an owner's children at their marriage and where there was a gradual increase in crop profit sharing and the actual transfer of land ownership tended to be reserved for some future time. Of this modern American farm community Salamon and Lockhardt write:

> An elder has prerogatives because she or he owns land which allows control of timing of retirement, use of land, sharing of management, and disposal of holdings. Those maintaining a future orientation and who planned for transfer of holdings tended to be well integrated with rich and respectful family relationships. (1979:21)

Not only were these parents successful in acquiring respect and establishing positive relations with their children, but they also managed to exert a good deal of control over their children's future activities. The community as a whole has been described as extremely successful at binding children to families and keeping them in farming.

It has been pointed out that hunters and gatherers have a minimum of property, and this normally puts elderly at a disadvantage. However, the !Kung Bushmen of the Kalahari have found a way to make the young dependent and responsive in spite of a lack of heritable property. According to Biesele and Howell,

> Economic accumulation as we know it is not a source of power for aging !Kung. This egalitarian society keeps individuals of all ages from hoarding goods, largely through the rules of generalized reciprocity and the *hxaro*, or gift-giving, system, which militate against accumulation of wealth. Older people do not generally own more goods than people in other age groups. (1981:92-93)

These hunting and gathering people are, of course, nomadic and claim little in the way of property in the form of land. Water holes and the food resources surrounding them are owned by kin groups by virtue of tenure of use. The elderly are, in effect, the stewards of the water holes and the resource areas because the "old *k'xausi* (owners) and their spouses provide genealogical stability over time to each water hole and resource area. Kin ties to these old people—as their siblings, offspring, or cousins—are the basis for young people's camp membership" (ibid:85).

Therefore, Bushmen elders do not have property that can be willed or turned over to heirs, for such ownership can only come through long-term use, but the elders do make possible the existence of community. While young people respect the wishes of the elders in regard to use of food and water resources, the old people never act without taking into consideration the wishes of the young.

Desire for Longevity

All societies value life and seek to prolong it even in old age. Although the statement is often made that "life is cheap" in non-Western societies this is an ethnocentric assumption with very little evidence to back it up. The truth is that most societies see life as extremely precious, and the bulk of cultural practices are dedicated to survival and maintenance of human life. This is not to say that life will be protected at all costs. When environmental conditions are extreme (as in the arctic), when life no longer seems worth the effort, or when people are suffering poor health, death is often chosen over life. Simmons found that abandonment of decrepit or elderly ill was practiced in 38 of the 71 tribes in his study, *The Role of the Aged in Primitive Society*, but a close scrutiny of the literature reveals that people are abandoned only as a last resort and often at the request of the elderly themselves, who are too sick or too tired to go on.

It is notable that all societies have a prescription for long life (see pages 79-80), and in many societies respect and prestige continue to increase with age. In such a situation only the foolish would not want to sustain life as long as possible and thereby bask in the admiration of their community. Few promises of a comfortable hereafter are comparable with rewards such as this. Few cultures have failed to look on long life as a positive goal, provided it could be lived in relative comfort. Weyl writes, "Man's quest for longevity outdates both Genesis and Greek mythology. It has roots as universal as man's consciousness of the inevitability of his own death" (1977:163).

Differences in Roles of Aged Men and Women

Before concluding this discussion on universals of aging it should be noted that a number of students of aging—Simic and Myerhoff (1978), de Beauvoir (1972), Gutmann (1977), and Simmons (1945)—have called attention to the fact that it is universally true that *old age does not have the same meaning or involve the same circumstances for men as for women.* Simone de Beauvoir (1972:84) points out, for example, that there is a great difference in the sexual potential of the two sexes. While men are capable of siring offspring when they are well into their seventies or eighties, after menopause a woman is no longer considered to be a person with a sex. In some respects, her status may be likened to that of a prepubescent girl in that in many societies she is free to ignore a number of repressive taboos and regulations. In Samoa, for example, the strong "brother-sister avoidance" patterns that begin at puberty no longer are in force with elderly women. They may sit and talk informally, make suggestive remarks, or even gossip about sexual matters with male siblings or cousins without shame or guilt.

Hamer writes concerning the Sidamo woman in Ethiopia that with senescence

> there is a noticeable change in her manner of approach to others. The essence of this change is relaxation and warmth in social interaction with old and young of both sexes. She is no longer subject to all the tensions surrounding the importance of her fecundity and labor in enhancing the prestige of her husband. Symbolic of this change is the fact that she no longer keeps her eyes focused on the ground when approaching other men, and may speak casually with them without first obtaining permission from her husband. An old woman may even be invited to eat and converse with the old men. (1972:23)

There are also striking differences in the extent to which men and women are able to acquire and control property, and this particularly affects the welfare of the elderly. Simmons (1945) found that although women have property rights in fewer preindustrial societies than do men, aged women seem to have had some advantage in this respect among collectors, hunters, and fishers. Among farmers and herders, however, men have had a great advantage over women, and their control of property seems to increase with cultural and technological complexity in general. Where elderly women control property, the situation tends to be greatly influenced by the prevailing form of social organization—for example, by matrilocal residence or by matrilineal descent, inheritance, and succession.

Role reversal often occurs in old age. While young and middle-aged adult men and women are, in most cultures, locked into certain kinds of roles and certain kinds of behavior that are thought of as "masculine" and "feminine," old age brings a blurring of these identifications. Quain reports that Fijian men invest increased amounts of time and affection in their wives and on household chores as they reach old age. They, in effect, become more "domesticated" as they age, and they find no stigma in spending a great deal of time gardening—normally a pastime of women. This kind of movement toward interests and activities that are not typically masculine is also found among old Hopi men. Simmons reports that when they were "unable to go to the fields any longer they sat in the house or kiva and spun, knitted, carded wool, or made sandals.... Corn shelling was woman's work but men would do it, especially in their dotage.... They

Although a "big man" in his village, this aged New Irelander encounters no stigma in his babysitting role with a grandchild. (Photo courtesy of Nicolas Peterson)

darned old clothes, cared for children, and guarded the house; and when there was nothing else to do, they would sit and watch the fruit drying in the sun" (1945:86).

Simic and Myerhoff point out, on the other hand, that in Yugoslavia and in parts of Mexico, women, required to be submissive in early adulthood, "become more assertive and independent with advancing years, and in old age participate to a far greater degree than men in both familial and nonkinship social areas" (1978:238).

Among the Chippewyan Indians of the Canadian Northwest Territories, performance and physical capacity are respected and are the basis for authority and prestige. Throughout much of their adult life men dominate their wives on this basis, but as a woman's children become adults there is a reversal in role dominance within the family. A father can continue to exercise his authority over his sons and command their respect as long as he remains competent and active, but as a man's strength begins to fail he begins to lose his ability to maintain this influence, and his position relative to his wife's suffers. In some cases, the wife actually dominates her husband. Sharp writes:

> In a real sense, the position of a man within his domestic unit is one of progressive diminution of influence throughout his life while a woman's position in her domestic unit is one of increasing influence until their respective statuses are virtually reversed. (1981:102)

Although this emphasis on competence among the Chippewyan has become less important recently because government agencies now compensate for the inability of elderly to provide for themselves, competence is still admired and the lack of it is a matter of great anxiety. Women can remain competent in this society longer than men, for men have but one important skill—hunting—and women have three—childbearing, handicrafts, and food processing. Although a woman's role as childbearer ceases at menopause, her role as child-rearer does not. Grandparents have the right in this society to adopt a child from each of their children's marriages, and through such adoption elderly women find not only satisfaction in an ongoing role of "mother" but also are assured the presence of young people to aid with such tasks as fetching water and firewood. Chippewyan women are also valued for their handicrafts—sewing and beadwork—and the preparation of hides. Most elderly women are capable of performing most of these activities, but even very decrepit ones can teach their skills to younger women and supervise their work. Finally, Chippewyan women continue to command respect well into old age through their skills as food processors. In addition to cooking, they cut dry meat and debone fish for drying. Much of this work is strenuous and takes place outside the comfort of the house, but most of this work is done by several women working together, and the very elderly ones invariably are able to get considerable help from the younger ones or they are merely permitted to supervise the work.

In most societies women seem to have a distinct advantage over men in adjusting to their senior years. Even in societies where there is no formal retirement, women seem better able to continue in a familiar, valued role—that of homemaker and nurturer. While a man may no longer be able to go to the fields to farm or to the bush to hunt, the elderly woman is usually able to carry on business as usual or at least some degree of it. The nurturing role also gives the elderly woman a special place in the hearts of her children that a husband can seldom compete with. Simic also found that elderly women may adjust to cultural change better than elderly men. They can migrate with their children to the city and perform a useful role—caring for and socializing children, preparing meals, and keeping the house in order—while the young people are off doing wage labor. Old men, however, have greater difficulty finding ways of contributing to family welfare.

An excellent example of the respect accorded to the mother because of her nurturing role is found among the Chinese of Taiwan. Here respect and responsibility for parents' welfare has been based on the time-honored concept of filial piety, but this standard, although it ensures security, does not necessarily guarantee love. In fact, in Chinese society filial piety is a culturally imposed imperative, and it often involves deep resentment toward parents because obedience is demanded and primarily based on a combination of fear and duty. This greatly influences how elderly men and women are treated. Harrell reveals:

> Growing old is quite different for Taiwanese men and women. Paradoxically enough, women, who are unquestionably treated as inferiors and even oppressed from childhood through middle age, are usually happier and less lonely in their final years than their once powerful husbands and brothers. (1981:199)

When no longer able to do physical work, the elderly father will turn over control of the family farm to his sons, but due to the harshness of the filial piety system, they will probably neither listen to his advice nor consider his wishes. In fact, they will probably ignore him. Their mother, on the other hand, will be the recipient of considerable affection, and sons will often seek her out and sit and talk for hours. At her advanced age she no longer can boss her sons' wives about, but she often is able to retain support and affection from them.

In some societies, however, men and women have been able, equally, to maintain a position of respect and areas for meaningful participation. One such society is the Kirghiz of Afghanistan. In Kirghiz society, there are important roles for both elderly men and women, and therefore the experiences of the two sexes do not greatly differ in prestige, although they do in kind. The Kirghiz believe that as one declines in strength one increases in wisdom, and consequently respect and authority should increase. Old age is viewed as a triumph for both men and women. Old men are considered to have extensive knowledge of oral history, local ecology, veterinary medicine, and curing rituals for humans. Old women are equally valuable because of their special knowledge of arts and crafts, of problems associated with both human and animal birth, and of curing diseases not associated with supernatural spirits. It is not remarkable, therefore, that among Kirghiz, old age is never referred to as the "declining years" nor does old age bring disengagement even among those handicapped by blindness or other forms of physical deterioration (Shahrani, 1981:190).

SUMMARY

Universals are common denominators of cultural behavior that develop in part from mankind's common biology and in part from the fact that human beings are empathetic, reasoning, gregarious, culture-bearing creatures. Universals are those practices that seem to turn up again and again, whether the society in question is preindustrial or modern, Western, or non-Western. Leo Simmons (1945) delineated a list of universal desires in his survey of primitive societies. He recorded that in nearly all of the societies investigated (1) old people want to live as long as possible (or until life's satisfactions cease), (2) in old age they want to get more rest and some release from the patterns of physical exertions of earlier years, (3) the elders want to remain active personally and socially, (4) old people want to safeguard their accrued prerogatives, and (5) they want to meet death with honor, dignity, and a minimum of suffering.

Simmons also noted a positive correlation between status of the aged and permanent residence, a stable food supply (as acquired through herding or agriculture), and an increase in closely knit kinship relationships (particularly those involving extended family). Cowgill and Holmes (1972) also found that certain demographic realities suggest universal features. They maintain, for example, that the aged always represent a minority, with women (in large part widows) outnumbering men. They observe also that all societies have some system of age-grading and that there is a general tendency for the elderly to shift from direct economic production to more sedentary, more advisory roles with advancing years.

Most cultures appear to have evolved some way of honoring the elderly for their special contributions. In some societies they are respected for their ability to remember important events of the past or kinship connections, or for their ceremonial knowledge. A large number of non-Western and Western societies also honor their elderly by permitting them to hold positions of political power or to serve in judicial positions.

A survey of the world's cultures reveals a pattern of mutual responsibility between parents and children and a correlation between the way members of a group treat their children and the way they will be treated in turn when they are old. Although societies develop traditions relating to how the aged should be properly treated (like the concept of filial piety), economic factors also appear to enter in. For example, control of property by the aged is everywhere an important element in the quality of their treatment, and Simmons has commented that to be respected and cared for adequately the aged must play the property game with skill up to the very end. All societies appear to value life, and most elders endeavor to prolong it if at all possible. There is, however, some variation in how rewarding long life is. Some societies value old age per se, while others withdraw respect and support when the elderly can no longer function normally. It is also a universal fact that old age does not have the same meaning or involve the same kinds of roles and satisfactions for both sexes, and this largely relates to differences in lifetime roles, the way work is assigned and valued in a society, and the availability of useful senior roles.

CHAPTER 8

Minority Aged in America

This book has been presented as an introduction to cultural gerontology rather than social gerontology. The reason is that it deals with aging from the perspective of anthropology rather than sociology, and culture has traditionally been the primary concept or orientation in anthropology while sociology has centered interests and theories in the concept of society. Growing out of the different approaches to the study of human beings by the two disciplines has been a tendency for sociology to concern itself with the ills of society (social problems), while anthropology has been more interested in cultural traditions—what they are, how they develop, how they are perpetuated, how they change, and what social, psychological, and biological needs they meet. True to the anthropological perspective, this chapter does not focus on negative aspects of life-style, or social problems such as poverty, racial discrimination, ill health, educational handicaps, or short life spans but rather on the roles, coping strategies, value orientations, and kinship affiliations and support systems that are characteristic of the ethnic tradition people participate in and identify with. Some minorities are so rich in family that they conceivably may not be fully aware of how poor they might be monetarily. Where tradition defines old age as a condition to be respected and where family support networks guarantee physical and emotional support, senior years can be a very different period of life than it is in social groups that value personal achievement, independence, and productive activity.

BLACK AMERICAN AGED

For many years, the influence of African roots on the behavior of American blacks has been controversial. Glazer and Moynihan staunchly maintain that "the Negro is only an American and nothing else. He has no values and culture to guard and protect" (1963:51). E. Franklin Frazier, in *The Negro Family in the United States,* argues that images of the African past are merely "forgotten memories" and that in regard to "the Negro family, there is no reliable evidence that African culture has had any influence on its development" (1939:12).

Opposing this point of view are a number of social scientists and historians (Herskovits, 1941; Hentoff, 1966; Billingsley, 1968; Wylie, 1971; and Pollard, 1978) who believe that American blacks represent an ethnic subculture with a unique cultural history involving the following circumstances: (1) blacks came from Africa and not Europe, (2) they came as slaves and therefore separated from their family systems and cultural orientations in which they had been enculturated, and (3) blacks have been excluded from meaningful participation in major institutions of the United States from slavery days until the present (Billingsley, 1968).

While these circumstances do not lead us to conclude that the value orientations and behavioral patterns of American blacks are markedly African, neither can we see justification for assuming that American blacks are carriers of the same cultural traditions as whites. One need only look to the literature on elderly black Americans to realize that life is quite different for them compared to their white counterparts. For example, Messer (1968), Wylie (1971), and others have established the following model differences between black and white life-styles of senior citizens. In comparison to whites, blacks

1. See old age more as a reward than a disaster
2. Have fewer anxieties about old age, and therefore higher morale
3. Are less likely to deny their actual age
4. Tend to remain part of their family structure to a greater degree, and consequently
5. Tend to be more respected and better treated
6. Are strongly supported by bonds of mutual assistance (with friends, neighbors, and family)
7. Are more likely to maintain useful and acceptable family functions
8. Are more likely to be tolerated by their families in spite of behavioral peculiarities
9. Are generally more religious but less involved in economic and political institutions
10. Feel less integrated into the society at large
11. Have a life expectancy of approximately six years less
12. Live longer once they reach the age of 69
13. Tend to be in better health
14. Rarely commit suicide.

While a case could possibly be made that blacks have had a different enough history of events in the United States to account for many of these differences, many believe that African patterns modified during slavery and post-slavery days account for the bulk of the variance.

Critics of the idea that African traditional influences can be discovered in New World family forms and various aspects of black social behavior often point to the immensity of the African continent and the multiplicity of cultural systems found there. Therefore, one questions how to narrow down this diversity to a single model of African behavior. However, Africans came to the United States as slaves, and the overwhelming majority came from a number of tribal societies located along the coastal area of West Africa between the Senegal and Congo rivers, with the bulk of the captives coming from regions known today as Nigeria, Ghana, Benin, Ivory Coast, and Sierra Leone. Although the cultural traditions of West African tribal societies varied considerably, Melville J. Herskovits (1967) has cited numerous common denominators that could conceivably represent a baseline for the New World black culture. Traits shared throughout the West or Guinea Coast of Africa are:

1. The people lived in large kingdoms with complex economic, social, and political institutions.

2. Societies were essentially agricultural, but were marked by a considerable degree of labor specialization (in trading, crafts, religion, and art), and cooperative labor and mutual self-help was the norm.

3. The extended family was well recognized, with kinship traced legally through one line (matrilineal or patrilineal).

4. Although monogamous marriage was most common, polygyny was sanctioned and in many cases preferred. In such marriages, the mother was the most important family influence in the children's lives, because a child had to share a father (who lived in a separate house) with many half-siblings, but lived with the mother who only had to be shared with a few siblings.

5. The fundamental sanction of the kinship system was the ancestral cult that tended to deify dead kinsmen. Elderly people were known as "almost ancestors."

6. In addition to ancestor veneration, the basic religious pattern featured a pantheon of gods, each with its own special groups of worshippers (cult) and its own elaborate rituals.

The attitudes and patterns of behavior that West African societies evolved in relating to their elderly are notable. In Dahomey, a popular proverb declared, "Respect the elders, for they are our fathers," and according to Herskovits, Dahomeans believed that

> with age comes considerable judgment, but more important, with age comes a closer affinity to the ancestral dead, and it is injudicious to act rashly with one who may any day have the opportunity to carry a grievance to the world of the dead (1938I:351)

In most groups, the elderly served as political leaders and counselors, and Burton (1864) describes the chief assistant to the king of Dahomey as being hollow cheeked and toothless, with a tendency to forget easily, an appearance of being half asleep, and a propensity toward childishness. Rattray (1923) maintains that among the Ashanti, elderly men and women were the ones who had accurate knowledge, and the people's respect for their wisdom was expressed in the proverb, "The words from the mouth of an old man are better than an amulet." Old men and women were, in fact, thought of as the coiners and keepers of proverbs.

In much of West Africa, elderly men and women were referred to as "grandfather" and "grandmother" as a mark of respect even by nonkin, and the word *grandfather* was reported in 1971 by Wylie to be a general term used by the Hausa of Nigeria to refer to the members of the village advisory groups. Among the Ashanti, "grandfather" and "grandmother" were terms used to address local deities (Ellis 1887:53-54).

The use of these kinship terms to convey respect gives some indication of what grandparents represented in the West African family systems. Herskovits relates that in Dahomey (today called Benin) "the relationship between grandparents and grandchildren is very close, and the young children often live with their grandparents by preference. There is, indeed, the saying that a man's grandchildren are his true children" (1938I:155). Not only were young people taught in the home to respect the elderly in general and their aged kin in particular, but secret societies such as the Beri and Sande among the Vai prepared youth for the duties of adulthood and trained them "to respect their parents and elders" (Ellis, 1914:126-127).

When the Africans (mostly young and mostly male) were taken from their homeland and shipped in overcrowded, squalid slave ships to ports in the Caribbean and the American South, the captives brought nothing except the clothes on their backs and the cultural traditions that they carried in their heads. While there were undoubtedly few if any slaves over 65 shipped out of Africa, there is evidence that age seniority was honored even if it involved only showing deference to fellow slaves just a few years senior.

Historians and social scientists who hold that slavery conditions were such that African heritages were soon forgotten in the New World are apparently not familiar with a wealth of evidence that indicates that certain aspects of culture can be tremendously tenacious even in the face of forced change. Felix Keesing (1953), for example, found that the area of "primary group relations," involving ascribed statuses of age and sex and intimate rights and responsibilities of household and immediate family kin groups, is extremely persistent. An equally conservative area of culture is found to be "status maintenance" (conserving established superior status and entrenched authority). It is also notable that those aspects of culture learned through conditioning as a child (as respect for elders was in Africa) tend to be more resistant to change than those learned as an adult.

It is not unreasonable to expect blacks to have retained various aspects of African family behavior, certain ideas about respect for the aged, and positive attitudes toward one's own aging. Importing slaves from Africa continued as late as 1808, and it is commonplace for particular values and culture patterns to persist among a people for periods much greater than 200 years, even in the face of adversity. An example is the

Jews, who in spite of a history of slavery, persecution, and even genocide have preserved many of their religious and cultural traditions for hundreds of years. Persistence of cultural values is also noted in Alexis de Tocqueville's *Democracy in America*. This book, written in 1835, describes a value system not greatly different from what is found in America today, in spite of the fact that since its writing we have moved from an agricultural society to an industrial one and from a rural society to an urban one.

Herskovits devotes two entire chapters of *Myth of the Negro Past* to Africanisms in contemporary American black culture, citing such aspects as motor behavior, religious fervor, etiquette, cooperative work patterns, folklore motifs, and musical styles, and most significant for our purpose, the importance of the extended family, a respect for age, and a special feeling for the mother and grandmother. Recalling that kin terms like *grandfather* and *grandmother* were often used as respect titles in West Africa, it is interesting to note that Frederick Douglass recorded in 1855 that slaves used terms of address such as "uncle" and "aunty" to show respect, even for people who were not relatives. Douglass also stated that "there is not to be found, among my people, a more rigid enforcement of the law of respect to elders, than they maintain" (1855:69). Equally interesting is the idea among slaves just before Emancipation that:

> It is considered bad luck to "sass" the old folks. This latter idea may have at one time had a real meaning, since the old folks were "almost ghosts," and hence worthy of good treatment lest their spirits avenge the disrespect and actually cause bad luck to the offender. (Douglass, 1855:23)

The fact that even in slavery the obligations that grew out of the quality of kinship ties were very strong and that the tendency to use kin-reliance as a coping method prevailed is documented by Mintz and Price. They write:

> The aggregate of newly arrived slaves, though they had been torn from their own local kinship networks, would have continued to view kinship as the normal idiom of social relations. Faced with the absence of real kinsmen, they nevertheless modeled their new social ties upon those of their masters to label their relationships with their contemporaries and with those older than themselves—"bro," "uncle," "auntie," "gran." (1976:34-35)

The role of "grandmother" was particularly important on the plantation. Elderly women were often placed in charge of the small children during the day, while their parents labored in the fields. The older woman's role as nurturer and educator of the young has been well documented. Within the actual family context (what little there was), the mother remained the most dependable and stabilizing element in children's lives. While the concept of fatherhood was of little importance to many slaveholders, and while fathers were often sold away, most masters kept mothers and children together at least until adolescence. The mother was devoted to her children, made tremendous sacrifices for them, and was generally considered the head of the family. In many respects, she functioned as mothers do in polygynous households in West Africa.

Conditions were little better for the black family during the Emancipation and Reconstruction periods. At this time, blacks had the freedom to die of starvation or illness. In some communities it is estimated that one out of four succumbed. The impact of this post-slavery era is described by Frazier:

> The disorder and confusion were the test of the strength and character of family ties. In many cases the family ties which were supported only by habit and custom were broken . . . . Through this chaotic situation, the Negro mother held the family group together and supported her children. This devotion was based partly upon her traditional role and partly upon the deep emotional attachment to her young that was evoked in the face of danger. (1959:72)

Even today it is possible to find features that generally set the black family apart. Frazier reports that 10% of black families in rural areas and 30% in urban areas have a woman as household head. In many cases, these heads are grandmothers whose authority is partly based on age and partly on the role of "granny" (midwife and repository of folk wisdom). Hortense Powdermaker comments on the grandmother role as she observed it in a small Mississippi town:

> Grandmothers are present in many households, and are likely to loom larger than mothers on the child's horizon, even when the real mother retains the chief authority . . . . When an elderly woman is head of a household including a married daughter, she carries authority with the children; and even where her position is less dominant, she is likely to take a share of responsibility for their welfare and behavior. (1936:200-201)

Life-Style Variation

Aged blacks are not "all just alike" in appearance, culture, or circumstances. There is probably greater life-style variation among aged blacks than aged whites. Although a 1976 Yankelovich survey discovered that 82% of the whites in the United States claimed middle-class status, Billingsley maintains that among American blacks 50% might be considered lower class, 40% middle class, and 10% upper class. In regard to family structure, always an important element in the welfare of the aged, Queen and Habenstein state:

> To cope with the vagaries of their social, political, and economic environment, black Americans through the years have developed a variety of forms of family organization. We have distinguished four types: (1) traditional matriarchal, (2) traditional small patriarchal, (3) acculturated middle majority and (4) adaptive urban matricentric. (1974:351)

Although the median educational level for elderly blacks is low—five to seven years—there are over 35,000 elderly black college graduates, and some hold PhDs or other advanced degrees. And although most aged blacks are plagued by deplorably low incomes (only 19% have incomes over $5,000 as compared with 49% for whites), and many are not even covered by Social Security, not all blacks live in poverty. There are even a few millionaires.

Although elderly blacks are more likely to live in large family groups than the aging population in general (Davis, 1971), the majority of black households with heads over 65 years of age contain only two persons, and one-fifth of aged black men and one-third of aged women live alone. However, Stanford notes that in order to receive aid from relatives, the elderly do not necessarily have to live in the same house. His San Diego study (1978) showed that 6% of the sample had brothers and sisters living in the immediate neighborhood, and 19% had siblings living in the same county. Mary L. Brooks Lambing's study of retired blacks in an urban setting (1971) revealed that blacks have closer relationships with siblings than white retired people. Joe Feagin's study of black families in Boston found that 84% of the sample had relatives in the city, and the majority claimed between 6 and 15 contacts with relatives every week. Hays and Mindel (1973) also found black extended family networks to be more effective than those of whites.

Without question, a greater proclivity toward family economic and emotional support of aged is a black ethnic characteristic, and this may be the main reason that less than half as many black as white elders are institutionalized. Stanford explains:

> At the time of life when emotional security is so greatly challenged, one's family and kin are expected to provide the necessary support for one's moral or well being. (1978:29)

AMERICAN INDIAN AGED

Describing *the* heritage of the American Indian is not possible, for there are some 266 officially recognized bands and tribal groups speaking approximately 149 separate languages (Voegelin, 1941) in the United States alone. While the average American tends to think of the American Indian as a buffalo hunter who excelled in horsemanship, wore a feathered war bonnet, and once fought U.S. cavalrymen, this image is hardly representative of Indians in general. In fact, the cultural variety in North America is so complex that anthropologists have been forced to use a classification device known as *culture areas* to conceptualize the mass of cultural data relating to Native Americans. A culture area is a region within which the inhabitants exhibit a greater similarity in cultural behavior with each other than they do with people in other regions. Various culture-area schemes have been used featuring anywhere between 7 (Kroeber, 1948) and 17 (Driver, 1969) regions of common culture in North America.

Within these areas, traditional Indian subsistence patterns include such ways of getting a living as caribou hunting in the subarctic regions, salmon fishing on the Northwest Coast, acorn and pine nut collecting in the Great Basin region of California, bison hunting on the Plains, and intensive agriculture in the Southwest and Southeast Woodlands. In the area of social organization, we find kinship to be traced through the mother's line (matrilineal) among many Southeast and Northeast Woodlands groups, through the father's line (patrilineal) among many Plains tribes, and through both lines (bilineal) among Plateau and subarctic region groups. Emphasis in some places is on the nuclear family (Chippewyan and other subarctic peoples), but on large households, extended families, and even clans in most other regions. Political units vary from bands (Plains and Western subarctic) to autonomous villages (Northwest Coast and Southwest) to tribes and tribal confederations (Southeast and Northeast Woodlands).

Just as variable as the economic and political traits of North American Indians were the attitudes toward the elderly. Simmons records that among the Pomo, decrepit aged were sometimes strangled, that among the Hopi the death of old people was often hastened by lack of care and "meanness" of daughters-in-laws, and that aged among the Chippewa might be killed by their sons or left to starve on a barren island. On the other hand, Simmons records that elderly Haida enjoyed great authority and respect and received exceptional care from their relatives. Aged Iroquois were often "rulers of the house" and Crow Indians were expected to provide their aged relatives with the best food—stripped tenderloin, dried, pounded, and mixed with bone marrow (1945:184).

With all this cultural diversity it is tremendously difficult to state just exactly how "Indianness" affects the aging process of this minority group. Most anthropologists are reluctant to generalize about what all these people hold in common and what could be used as a baseline to begin our discussion of what it means to grow old as an American Indian. However, J. Richard Connelly (1980), drawing heavily on the work of Alvin M. Josephy (1976), cautiously suggests that the following values and cultural tendencies tend (with qualifications) to be consistent among all American Indian groups:

1. *Appreciation for individuality.* Most tribes respect the individual and his freedom and autonomy. Tribal members are given freedom to assume responsibility for themselves and their actions. Individual decisions are highly valued.

2. *Group consensus.* The majority of tribes regard one another's opinion with respect. Many meetings, discussions, and powwows are lengthy, since Native Americans strive for group consensus, not majority rule, in their decision-making process. Among many tribes, councils decide on the course of action, with the feelings and opinions of each person considered too important to override.

3. *Respect for all living things.* Native Americans have reverent feelings for all living things. They believe that the growing things of the earth and all animals have spirits or souls and that they should be treated as humanely as possible, with respect and appreciation for the contributions made to Native American life-style.

4. *Respect and reverence for the land.* Native Americans believe that all things of this earth were given to them for their use. To exploit the resources of the earth is intolerable. A Native American should not be extravagant with any part of the earth's natural resources.

5. *Feelings of hospitality.* The majority of Native Americans greet friends, family, clansmen, tribesmen, and visitors with demonstrations of hospitality and regard. Historically, it was not necessary to either ask for food nor was an invitation required. Many long and friendly discussions were held with visitors who were shown real and honest hospitality.

6. *One should avoid bringing shame on oneself, family, clan, or tribe.* The expected behavioral customs of Native Americans are well understood by each group. Native Americans are taught to bring respect and honor to their families, clan, and tribe. Bringing dishonor is strongly negatively reinforced.

7. *A belief in a supreme being and life after death.* Most Native American groups have a strong belief in a supreme being. There is also a generalized belief in a guardian spirit that accompanies each Native American. A belief in life after death is also generic to most Native Americans (1980VI:18-19).

In addition, most Native Americans have always had great respect for the family. Most groups featured large extended-family interaction, and often single households were composed of an assortment of nuclear family members plus grandparents, aunts, uncles, and cousins. Within these family networks, the elders were responsible for preserving traditional cultural values and knowledge.

Though it has nothing to do with traditional culture, we must face still another common influence on the life-style of contemporary Indians: As a people they have for many generations experienced the worst poverty known to any other minority group in the United States. Block writes:

> For most, the poverty of old age is the result of a lifetime of deprivation. American Indians from the time of birth, have experienced substandard housing, limited education, inadequate income, poor health, malnutrition, a lack of urgently needed services, and the emotional problems inherent in a changing culture. With advancing age, the severity of these conditions is intensified. (1979:184)

As a result, elderly Native Americans are "eight times as likely as whites to die from tuberculosis, twice as likely to die of gastritis and cirrhosis of the liver and twice as likely to die of influenza and pneumonia" (Benedict, 1971:56), and much more prone to alcoholism, mental illness, and suicide. The average American Indian does not even reach old age, because life expectancy is only slightly more than 44 years.

In addition, Native Americans have also experienced racial and cultural discrimination and a subjugation by the white population under government policies which at successive periods were directed at (1) extermination, (2) expulsion, (3) exclusion, and (4) assimilation.

Extermination. The white man's desire to eliminate his competition began with devout Puritans in New England thanking God for sending smallpox epidemics to decimate local tribes and was perpetuated on the frontier with the "only good Indian is a dead Indian" sentiment. At one period, an actual bounty was placed on Indians, and payment came upon presentation of the victim's scalp; and during the Gold Rush days of California, miners, ranchers, and vigilante groups waged war on peaceful California Indians, often shooting them for sport (Kroeber, 1961).

Expulsion. During the years of America's western expansion, a series of treaties and laws removed Indians from their lands whenever a region became sufficiently populated by settlers. This pushed Indian territory farther and farther west until at last no more open land remained. At this point, Indians were rounded up and placed on reservations, which were generally undesirable parcels of land in places like Oklahoma, the Dakotas, Montana, and Minnesota.

Exclusion. With their placement on reservations, the Indians lost forever any hope of achieving equality with whites. Not only were they denied access to the white man's world but the white man came onto their reservations and tried to do away with anything that was Indian. Jeffries recalls:

> Many were sent away to Indian boarding schools. In their youth, then, many of our present senior citizens were separated forcibly from their families, were made to feel inferior and savage, and were ridiculed by white authorities if they spoke the Indian language or showed respect for their Indian heritage. They remember the government's outlawing their great potlatch festivals, their ancient secret societies, their religious ceremonies, their dances and songs, and their other bases of identity and culture. (1972:8)

Not only did Washington not want these people to be Indians, after World War I Congress decided that Indians were not really citizens and that they had no basis for equality with whites. Indians were not permitted to use their own land for whatever purpose they chose without securing a permit from the Bureau of Indian Affairs (BIA) and the Bureau even had the right to reverse terms of Indian wills if it disapproved.

Assimilation. From the very beginning, government policy toward American Indians has been to make them disappear as a recognizable ethnic group. Mission schools and then the BIA and public schools in Indian areas forbade use of native tongues because "real Indians must speak English." Cahn points out that "officials, including some Indian tribal officials, disapprove of efforts to preserve Indian languages by publishing textbooks and newspapers" (1969:133). The Bureau of Indian Affairs' relocation program encouraged Indians to leave the reservation by giving them a one-way bus or train ticket and a small adjustment allowance. Returning home was regarded as unforgivable and was referred to as going "back to the blanket." Cahn also maintains that "the Indian is rewarded for rejecting the approval or disapproval of his elders and his peers" and for rejecting "his people's standards of achievement, performance and contribution" (1969:136).

Given the diversity of Native American cultures and given the history of oppression and discrimination to which Indian peoples have been subjected, it is difficult indeed to make any general statements about the influence of Native American tradition on the status of Indian aged. Instead, let us look at a few examples of senior Native Americans on reservations and in urban settings.

The Reservation

The problems of American Indians are generally more critical on reservations than in urban areas. Economic, health, and education services are less adequate, the people are more isolated, and they have less freedom or opportunity to act independently in helping themselves. Their only source of help is a less-than-enthusiastic bureaucratic structure, the Bureau of Indian Affairs. Block writes of the reservation:

> Younger Indians are often forced to leave the reservation if they are to realize any sort of job opportunity. Wages are often minimal, barely covering basic needs. Unable to support additional family members, and equally unable to send money back to the reservation, the young Indian leaves his aging parents with no economic base. Older family members sometimes receive welfare grants, but these are usually inadequate to cover basic needs. The traditional kinship support system of the family

structure is unfeasible when the family has no resources, and the tribe is unable to assume the responsibility and care of the elderly because economically it is no better off. (1979:188)

The Navaho

The Navaho today (numbering approximately 110,000) live on the largest reservation in the United States, an area of New Mexico roughly equal in size to the state of West Virginia. Traditionally a hunting and agricultural people, they have been sheep raisers since 1680. The Navaho are both matrilineal and matrilocal, and women play a strong and influential role, partly because of their contribution to social and economic life and partly due to their control of a large share of family property.

The nuclear family is the basic social unit, and the household consists of husband and wife and their unmarried children. Extended families, consisting of a larger group of relatives linked matrilineally, live in the same locality and cooperate in farming, house-building, and herding tasks.

The elderly were traditionally held in high esteem, and the phrase "My Father" was a generic term of respect accorded an old man. The address "grandfather" was used in referring to deities. Much of the deference conferred on Navaho elderly was connected with their control of property, and Reichard tells us that aged Navaho owned large numbers of horses, sheep, cattle, and goats, as well as more intangible property such as songs, dances, medicine bundles, prayer sticks, formulas for increasing flocks, and knowledge of magic. The mother of the family also played a large role in the social and economic life. She possessed a number of sheep and goats—often more than her husband—and had complete control of them, but "knowledge wealth" was seen as more valuable than material wealth.

Responsibility for caring for elderly people fell on daughters or granddaughters, and it is said that they showed great kindness and patience. Old people, according to Reichard's 1928 accounts "usually have a large pile of sheepskins and blankets upon which to recline—the other members of the family have one or two—they occupy the warmest place in the hogan and they are patiently waited on" (1928:57).

The Navaho have been perhaps more fortunate than most Native American groups because they were able to continue their agricultural and herding activities with success until the 1930s, when overgrazing, erosion, and the decline of the wool and lamb markets resulted in government action to curtail these subsistence activities. Government agents began a stock reduction program and also put considerable pressure on the older owners of stock to give substantial numbers of animals to their heirs for support of the younger generation's large families. This not only undermined a traditional source of prestige for elders—the massing of large flocks—but it also brought early transfer of property, a situation that universally resulted in declining prestige for the elderly. With these new conditions, "knowledge wealth," particularly information about how to care for and increase flocks, had no value, since the government would not permit flocks to grow in size. Other traditional sources of prestige for aged were threatened as well. According to Reichard, in former times young men trained in the use of magic were required to give their aged teachers large gifts, and "certain old men could make a good living by the performance of healing rites" (1928:90-91). Now, since young men cannot increase their flocks, it is impossible for them to pay for years of apprenticeship to a ceremonial healer, and anyway, free medical services on the reservation are competing with the expensive and time-consuming traditional healing rituals.

Young people are now encouraged to shift from traditional economic pursuits to wage work, and old people are a burden in this cash-oriented economy. The traditional domestic skills of the aged are of less importance in the more modern homes that the young people prefer, and young people who have managed to become educated do not always appreciate the old way of doing things. Levy writes, "Young mothers complain that their parents do not care for the infant grandchildren properly. They are said to be unsanitary, careless and do not 'discipline' the children" (1967:232-233).

More and more Navaho families today are finding it a burden to care for their aged, and there has been increasing discussion about the possibility of building a nursing home on the reservation. This is a far cry from the days when Reichard reported that the elderly received the best the family could offer—good food, a warm place by the fire, and most importantly, great respect.

The Rio Grande Pueblo

Like the Navaho, the Rio Grand Pueblo peoples[1] of New Mexico have always shown great respect for their aged and for traditional ways. A 1977 study by Rogers and Gallion discovered that 65% of the elderly among these people live in extended families, the pattern being that the elderly share their home with children and grandchildren even after the death of the spouse. The housing today is a blend of terraced adobe apartment buildings and modern ranch-style adobe houses. The more traditional houses are without running water, indoor plumbing, electricity, or telephone, although some of the newer ones have some conveniences.

One of the major problems for the elderly is transportation. The pueblos are all located in rural areas with few shopping facilities. At least one-third of the elderly have no dependable source of transportation, and this, plus their English language difficulties, means that they maintain little touch with the outside world.

Both elderly men and women seem to find important tasks to occupy their time, and there is no concept of retirement. Men continue to work family lands, although physical limitations may decrease their effectiveness, and women care for children and grandchildren much as they have done most of their lives. Old people continue to be thought of as "keepers of the culture" and a good number of them function as storytellers and teachers of traditions and legends.

Although age-old traditions are important to these people, their commitment to older ways often stands in the way of human service delivery from the few agencies that could help them. For example, eligibility for various kinds of government assistance is often based on the number of people in the household, and since government programs often favor elderly couples or widows living alone, the fact that Rio Grande Pueblo people live in extended families rules them ineligible. Income guidelines

---

[1] Rio Grande Pueblos include Acoma, Isleta, Jemez, San Juan, Santa Ana, Taos, Tesuque, and Zuni peoples.

are also difficult to meet here because of their different concept of property ownership. Rogers and Gallion write:

> Their culture is based upon the notion of community property and their individual assets can be viewed as either all the tribal resources, or nothing. The notion of dividing assets to determine individual wealth is foreign to their cultural traditions. (1978:487)

The government winterization and utility bill assistance programs are an example of legislation that helps these Native Americans very little. Since the pueblos are heated with firewood and have no indoor plumbing or electricity, assistance with utility bills is meaningless. Yet, there is no provision for buying firewood (or helping them gather it), and there is no provision for aiding them with the transport of water to their homes.

On many of these reservations and on the Salt River Pima reservation investigated by Marvin Munsell (1972), a substantial number of households might be labeled matrifocal or matricentric. This is a phenomenon that seems to be related to extreme poverty combined with the disorganizing conditions of cultural change. Men, and often couples, leave the reservation to seek wage employment, and children remain behind to be cared for in many cases by elderly women who maintain the household with welfare income. Among the Salt River Pima, half the households are headed by aged, and a large number are women. This development has in many cases enhanced the status of the elderly and at the same time has given them an important and satisfying role in the nurturing and personality development of the grandchildren and other youthful relatives.

The Urban Aged

The Relocation Act of 1952 was designed to force assimilation of Native Americans by moving them off the reservations with promises of occupational training and jobs. By 1968, nearly 68,000 Indians had moved to town, and today more American Indians live in urban areas than on reservations (550,000 to 214,000). Native Americans have not really migrated to the city voluntarily, even though the Relocation program was first called the "Voluntary Relocation Program." Indians have come to cities because of lack of employment opportunities and because of overwhelming educational, social, and health problems on reservations. The Indians who migrate come from a great variety of backgrounds, but they share the fact that they have all come from a small, rural community with a cultural heritage very different from white America and from a situation of dependency and often a distasteful association with the Bureau of Indian Affairs. They arrive carrying many of the problems that plagued them on the reservation (e.g., lack of education, often drinking problems, poor health) and are often confronted with a whole set of new ones growing out of their unfamiliarity with the white manners, the anonymity of the urban area, their darker skin which may invite discrimination, their lack of occupational skills, and, in some cases, their inadequate use of the English language.

They may find some encouragement and assistance. Many are able to live with relatives until they can find work and a place to live permanently. Ablon writes:

> In general all Indians . . . tend to feel the responsibility of helping their kinsmen or tribesmen when asked, and will give money, food or lodging to a needy family. The flexibility of the Indian household often seems to be infinite and most Indian families assume that there is always room for five or six additional persons at their table or for lodging, no matter how small the actual living quarters may be. (1964:298)

Elderly Native Americans tend to remain on the reservation when their children migrate to the city, but when they do move, their economic situation is seldom improved. Where all food must be purchased and where high rents must be paid, any funds available for support of old people do not go as far as they did on the reservation. Some of these aged Native Americans get small amounts of "land claim money" (for land leased to cattle ranchers or oil companies), but these checks are often not enough to live on and in addition, may render the recipients ineligible for public welfare.

The plight of the urban-dwelling Native American is a depressing one. A National Indian Conference on Aging report summarizes the condition of many of these individuals:

> They suffer from arthritis, tuberculosis, alcoholism, heart attacks and strokes, loneliness and depression. They do not receive a broad range of medical and dental care; most medical care is of an emergency nature only. Their depressed state goes untreated. Many drink to mask their loneliness and fear. (1978:133)

Considering the problems Indians of all ages encounter in the city, it is not surprising that the matrifocal family also is found with some frequency in this setting. Moore tells us that "as tribal life has eroded, and husbands and fathers have fallen in battle or have died of accidents, suicides, tuberculosis or alcoholism, Indian mothers and grandmothers have assumed the major family-care role" (1979:458). Some have found that elderly people in general have been very important in holding the urban Indian family together. A number of studies have shown that the commitment of elders to the family is so strong that they pass up meals at nutrition sites because of their babysitting responsibilities to grandchildren or other young relatives at home. This sense of obligation has generally been rewarded with respect, but in some cases this pattern is eroding. Although some researchers have reported a rise in elderly Indian status brought on by a desire on the part of some young people to recover their cultural heritage, the forces of acculturation to Anglo standards have been great. Federal programs tend to emphasize assisting younger Indians and the pressure on these young people to adapt to a materialistic ethic has been highly detrimental to traditional Indian ideas about the importance of kin reliance and obligations to family members, particularly elderly ones.

MEXICAN AMERICAN AGED

Of all the ethnic groups in the United States the Mexican Americans have been among the most successful in retaining their culture and language. In part this is due to patterns of segregation. Most urban communities in the southwest contain barrios where Mexican Americans speak their own language, read Spanish language newspapers, hear Latin music, buy ethnic food, and attend Catholic churches almost exclusively made up of Spanish-speaking worshippers. Life-style retention can also be explained by the fact that Mexican Americans are constantly being reinforced culturally by people arriving from Mexico. An estimated 58% of the Mexican American population were born in Mexico and 42% are second- and third-generation descendants, most of whom were born in one of the southwestern states. A good share of the foreign born arrived as children between 1910 and 1930, a period marked by the Mexican Revolution and also by labor shortages in the United States. The remainder arrived as adults to find wage work after 1953, when there was a great increase in Mexican migration.

In order to understand the role and status of Mexican American elderly, we must trace their cultural roots to Mexico and investigate how the family and its members function in relation to one another and in relation to the community. Although the village of Santo Tomas Mazaltepec in Oaxaco cannot represent all Mexico, it does give us some idea of familial patterns and value orientations in a small agricultural Indian community. It is from villages such as this that many of our Mexican Americans have come.

The people of Santo Tomas Mazaltepec are corn farmers who live primarily in three-generational family households. Household heads are usually elderly men who live with their spouse and their sons' families, or in lieu of sons, the families of their daughters and sons-in-law. The isolated nuclear family is almost unknown here, and even when elderly couples live apart from other relatives visitation by the latter takes place every day. Elderly make up a fairly small percentage of the population (4%) and this is generally a young population. Old people do not retire but instead continue to work at the same kinds of tasks as younger men and women as long as they are able. In time, the older men are not able to handle the heavy agricultural work and must settle for lighter chores, often indistinguishable from those of children. Adams maintains that "deference to old people includes, in theory, not only respectful behavior toward them but also absolute obedience to their commands" (1972:108). Old people also enjoy greater freedom of action than the average individual, and greater tolerance of idiosyncratic behavior. Although the family pattern is definitely one of male dominance, women tend to become more outgoing and domineering as they get older, often to the point that they lord it over their husbands. The society, however, does not think this is proper behavior. Both old men and women function in the role of teachers, delineating proper conduct, relating historical events, and explaining the origin of things. While both sexes remain influential within the decision-making process of the household, a kind of public disengagement pattern is forced on elderly men.

After the age of 60 men are referred to as *afuera de la ley* (outside the law). They no longer vote or pay taxes, and they cease their involvement in community politics. Their opinions may influence the action their young relatives take politically, but they are expected to retire from political action themselves. The community has a kind of advisory board made up of past mayors of the village. This group of aging men are collectively known as the *representantes,* and while their opinions are solicited, they have no veto power.

A good deal of the Mexican pattern has been carried over in Mexican American families today, although about 80% of these families live in cities. In order to understand the Mexican American system and its impact on aging, we shall draw upon the insights of David Maldonado, Jr., a Chicano professor of social work. He writes:

> Most students of Chicano life tend to agree that the family holds the key to Chicano culture . . . . In spite of variations in interpretation, there is considerable concensus that the following are key characteristics of the Chicano family: (1) familism, (2) age hierarchy, (3) male leadership, and (4) mutual aid and support. (1979:178)

Familism. This is a term that refers to the centrality of family. Self-identity cannot be separated from family identity, and social status is derived from family status. Family welfare is usually considered more important than individual welfare. Kin networks figure greatly in daily living. Valle and Mendoza (1978) found that in San Diego 88% of their sample had family in the immediate neighborhood and reported frequent contact.

Age Hierarchy. On this point Maldonado comments:

> As an individual matures, he/she increases in status. The younger children must respect and obey the older siblings, who at times play parental roles. Adults are always to be respected, especially the elderly. To a large extent respect was associated with the authority that rested in the older person, but was also related to the continuing functional role that the elders played in the extended family. (1979:179)

Male Leadership. Although the *machismo* concept has been overemphasized, Mexican American culture does support the role of male family head as one who directs its activities, controls its behavior, arbitrates its disputes, and represents the family in the community and in the society. Ideally, the woman's role is one of subordination, but the woman who is too submissive is thought to be a fool. Actually, she has a good deal of decision-making authority on domestic issues.

Mutual Aid and Support. Not only is there a strong pattern of reciprocity and cooperation within the family but this willingness to help others extends also to friends and neighbors. Offspring are expected to provide support in their parents' old age, and traditional Mexican American parents have been secure in their anticipation that in old age they will be respected and wanted by their children. The elderly consider themselves vital members of the family because they perform important enculturative functions and because they view themselves as important links to the past. Therefore, they do not feel useless or burdensome and are not embarrassed by support from their children or other family members. Although more than 70% of respondents in a San Diego study (Valle and Mendoza) stated that when in difficulty they would turn first to family for help, a number of investigators (Leonard, 1967; Valle and Mendoza, 1978; and Cuellar, 1978) have reported that most Mexican Americans believe that the responsibility for meeting health, housing, transportation, and economic needs growing out of retirement belongs to the government (primarily federal). Leonard explains:

> Spanish tradition and custom impose rigid class differences that include a set of rights and duties concerning the needy. Aging rural people expect their landlords and other employers to provide them with a minimum level of subsistence in old age. This is not considered charity but rather a type of deferred payment for services. Obviously, it is not a major transfer to shift this attitude to the state. (1967:247-248)

The Mexican American community also has a strong pattern of mutual aid which is known as the *servidor* system. Valle and Mendoza found that in San Diego, 74% of their sample of aged were providing neighborhood assistance to needy elderly. This included assisting neighbors with day-to-day needs such as food, temporary housing, and transportation.

Ideally, the Mexican American family is devoted to its elderly. They are seldom left alone, they are given the best of the family's food, the most comfortable of its chairs, and great affection. Maldonado writes:

> It is common to see a very old man bedridden at home, but surrounded daily by his children and grandchildren. And it is equally common to see a very old woman in such a situation. In a way, that bedridden person even becomes the center of the family's life. (1975:214)

Mexican Americans rarely institutionalize their elderly, and the poorer families who are least able to support ailing old people are often the most insistent on keeping them at home.

Grandparents are revered by their children and grandchildren alike, but the father remains the prime decision maker. Grandchildren often go to grandparents with questions they are afraid to ask their fathers, but any important decisions regarding the children have to be referred to the father. Grandmothers seem to command greater attention than grandfathers, and Murillo maintains that "the mother continues to be close and warm, serving and nurturing even when her children are grown, married and have children of their own" (1971:104).

The Changing Scene

As noted earlier, 80% of Mexican Americans live in urban areas where they tend to occupy ghetto-like enclaves known as *barrios.* This movement from farms and small towns in the southwest or directly to cities from Mexico has taken place since World War II and has been associated with the growth of industry in the West, particularly California.

The extended-family concept traditionally associated with Mexican Americans is showing signs of being replaced by nuclear family structures. If this is true, then we might expect major changes in the role and status of the aged. While extended families usually confer high status and ensure maximum security for the elderly, this form of family tends to be incompatible with urban life. Researchers at San Diego State University in 1978 found that 75% of Hispanics (mostly Mexican) were living alone or with one other person. The Hispanics were in sharp contrast with Samoans in their area (who tend to retain extended family living even in cities) who had only 16% of elderly living alone or with one other person.

The Mexican American family, like that of many other ethnic groups, is succumbing to pressure to conform to the dominant American norms. As young people have migrated from rural to urban areas, they have often brought their aged with them. Extended family living in rural areas allows elderly to perform useful, productive roles, but city life usually leaves them with little to do except menial domestic tasks and babysitting. Out of their element and surpassed in education by younger generations, the elderly find little that they can contribute in the way of knowledge or skill that is meaningful in the urban environment. The dilemma of the urban-dwelling elderly Mexican American is described by the Reverend Lawrence Matula:

> In addition to the economic difficulties which are encountered by the aged Mexican American, they find themselves in a world apart. They are for the most part a lonesome group. They get sick rather easily, they lack good neighbor relationships, and their thinking is very different. They have difficulty getting their food and medical care because of distance and ambulatory problems. They feel themselves an imposition upon relatives and friends if they ask for help. (Senate Hearing, 1969)

Young and old alike feel the tension and anxiety of a life-style in the process of transition. Although Mexican Americans cling to the ideal of extended-family living, urban circumstances make it impossible. The young continue to respect and cherish the elderly of their families, but their inability to care for them in traditional ways has produced guilt and a tendency to conceal their problems. Human-service delivery people often continue to labor under the misconception that the extended family cares for its own and therefore move on to the needs of other minorities, content with the belief that the Mexican American aged are being well attended by their families.

ORIENTAL AMERICAN AGED

The term *Oriental Americans* technically includes Chinese, Japanese, Koreans, Vietnamese, Laotians, and Thais. This discussion, however, deals only with two major groups, the Chinese and Japanese, who have the longest history of migration and settlement in the United States, a history that began at least as early as 1850 for Chinese and 1880 for Japanese. The people of Korea and southeast Asia are, by comparison, relative newcomers. Although Chinese and Japanese are quite different in traditions, language, and religion, they have a number of things in common that set them apart from white Americans. Both peoples come from countries with very old and very highly developed civilizations. They followed one another in successive waves of migration to the United States and Canada, where they occupied a low occupational status as farm workers or common laborers. They settled in Hawaii and in West Coast states, and the bulk of them remain in these parts of the country today. Both groups are racially distinct from other Americans, and both have encountered considerable racial discrimination. Theirs has been a common experience that has resulted in a tendency to take pride in the achievements of Asian peoples and a shared resentment at their treatment in America. The fact that both identify strongly with their lands of origin and the fact that human-service delivery personnel and scientists alike often lump them under a common category should not suggest that all Asian elderly are homogeneous. Let us instead review their separate histories and separate contemporary circumstances.

Chinese Americans

The Chinese began their migration to America in the 1850s, when they came as coolie labor to work in California gold mines, at railroad building, and in domestic service.

Later they became laundrymen, cooks, busboys, kitchen helpers, and porters. The high point in their population growth occurred about 1890, but then the population steadily declined until the 1930s when immigration restrictions were enacted. At this time, a considerable number of Chinese returned to their homeland.

Most Chinese live on the Pacific coast, and about 95% live in cities. The largest population of Chinese lives in San Francisco, of which approximately 10,000 are elderly. These elderly constitute approximately 7% of the population, with the sex ratio being heavily weighted toward men (3:1). Only 27% of elderly Chinese Americans live with a spouse, compared with 43% in the general population. Ninety percent of these San Francisco elderly were born abroad and the greater share of them have problems with the English language. These old Chinese have spent most of their lives living in a culture they do not understand and one they have not been able to influence. The culture in which they spent the early years of their life had the following cultural characteristics:

Traditional China was an age-centered culture. The average Chinese genuinely believed that old age marked the beginning of a higher and more respected status. Old age, which was thought to begin at about age 55, was perceived as a blessing and as a period of life when one could sit back and enjoy the fruits of his or her labors. As is true of many non-Western cultures, the elderly were considered the repositories of wisdom.

Respect and responsibility for the aged in China was based on the Confucian teaching of *The Hsiao Ching,* which outlines the concept of filial piety. Within this tradition, support of aged parents is not presented as a matter of choice but as a moral duty. According to Francis Hsu:

> The son owes his father absolute obedience, support during his lifetime, mourning when he passes away, burial according to social station and financial ability, provision for the soul's needs in the other world, and glory for the father by doing well or even better than he. (1971:68)

Although filial piety directly relates to father-son relationships, the status of the aged in China is also tied to the nature of the total kinship system. The Chinese family places emphasis on paternal kin through five degrees of kinship and a select number of close relatives on the mother's and wife's side. The extended-family emphasis involves mutual obligations and privileges, and households, often three-generational, include parents, their several sons, and their families. Unless a couple has been unfortunate enough not to have had children, aged Chinese have little to worry about in their declining years.

The close father-son tie involves authority on the part of the parent and filial piety on the part of the son, but the mother also feels maximum security. By the time she reaches 50 or 60 she has several daughters-in-law whom she can dominate in the operation of the household. At this age, she is relatively free from male domination, although she may depend on her sons for support. If a male is the eldest son, he can anticipate heading his family, but if he is not the eldest he can still look forward to being responsible for the education and upbringing of his grandchildren. This is a role of disciplinarian and moral leader.

The relationship between grandparents and grandchildren is very close, and since they tend to have more leisure time than the children's parents, the very old have great influence on the very young. It is said that the liberty grandparents are permitted to take with their grandchildren would cause the breakup of most American families. Hsu maintains that they can do "almost anything they see fit in regard to the children, even if it means going over the parents' head" (1953:78).

This close and warm relationship provides the children with an ever-present model for future roles, and the aims of education are to mold the younger generation after the pattern of their parents, grandparents, and ancestors. Children are praised for behaving like adults.

In the United States, Chinese American elderly live in urban neighborhoods, and because of the many cultural anomalies many experience great insecurity and isolation. If they had remained in China, they would now be enjoying leisure, much attention, and great respect. The elderly who were reared in China were enculturated in a system in which children were expected to be subservient and dependent, and it must be difficult for them to understand the ways of American-educated youth. Most of their own children (now middle-aged) were able to acquire a better education, more saleable skills, and therefore greater earning power than their parents, and this must be seen as very abnormal for traditionally minded Chinese who had never experienced such upward mobility in their Chinese homeland.

Much of the isolation that elderly Chinese feel is associated with their inability to communicate with Anglo Americans. A San Diego study (Cheng, 1978) found that 80% of the sample indicated that Chinese was their first language preference and 30% maintained that they could speak no English at all. Only 32% could read and understand printed matter well enough to avail themselves of health services. Because of their lack of communication with Anglos and their different cultural orientation, 24% of these old people distrusted Western medical practices, and 38% claimed that they did not receive any medical care because of the cost. Many, however, were taking Chinese herbal remedies and seeking help from Chinese medical practitioners.

Most Chinese American elderly expect help and support to come from family, friends, and community. But in San Francisco, a high percentage of unattached men lives alone, and in Los Angeles, Wu (1975) found that two-thirds of the elderly Chinese were living independently. Cheng found that in San Diego, only 28% of Chinese American elderly live with children. This study revealed, however, that 70% belonged to a friendship club made up solely of Chinese, and other communities have reported the existence of benevolent-aid societies and ethnic clubs. These supplied help and a sense of identity.

Since the American experience has been one of exclusion from community participation and government benefits and less than marginal political influence, elderly Chinese Americans tend to refrain from seeking legal advice, health care, or financial assistance from governmental sources until their difficulties become critical. In New York City, Cattell (1962) found that one-third of the elderly unattached men in the Community Service Society case-load files had never had any previous contact with either a public or a private welfare agency.

Both problems and life-styles vary according to whether elders live with their children or live independently, but regardless of the variety of circumstances encountered by old Chinese Americans, Wu believes that their adjustment as senior citizens in this country has been remarkable. He explains:

> First of all, endurance, another Chinese virtue, seems to be at work. The Chinese have been trained to accept reality . . . . Second, Old Age Assistance has enabled many of them to live independently without becoming a burden to their children. Their frugality, another Chinese virtue, further helps them live on Old Age Assistance income without undue hardship. Third, and above all, their faith in God gives them strength to cope with many of the problems. (1975:274)

Japanese Americans

The sixtieth year of life has traditionally been observed as the beginning of old age among Japanese. This is the time that it takes the signs of the East Asian zodiac to complete one full cycle. In old Japan this was the occasion when samurai retired from office and peasants were no longer required to perform a full day's labor on collective village enterprises.

Japanese culture has long involved a concept of respect for seniors and elders, and in old Japan communities hold annual ceremonies honoring the elderly. This tradition has been revived in recent years into a national holiday known as Respect-the-Aged Day (September 15). Most writers on traditional Japan stress the fact that the relationship with elderly in the family grew out of the Confucian concept of filial piety and respect for hierarchy. Masako Osako, however, points out that adherence to Confucian ideals varied a great deal, depending on class status. While samurai families rigidly followed the dictates of filial piety, within peasant families (the kind that made up the bulk of emigrants to North America) the emphasis was on corporateness. Osako explains that "the family as a corporate entity owns and manages property to insure the survival of its members and to perpetuate the family occupation" (1979:451). Within this context, Osako suggests that as elderly family members' contributions declined so did their status and influence. David Plath and other scholars support this idea, although they believe that by and large, the premodern ethic called for sacrifice for one's parents, support for them in their declining years, and respect for elders in general. The *Encyclopedia of Japan* records:

> Old people who were hale or judicious, those who were wise or who could act as guardians of life's mysteries, probably could command respect or attention. This may not have been true for the frail, the senile, the incapacitated, or those with no living kin. There long have been traditions about "sudden death temples" (*pokkuri ōjō*) in which old, feeble, or desperately ill can pray for a quick and painless demise. Many tales and dramas have recounted the story of *obasute* in which useless old people are taken to a mountain (*yama*) and left to die. (A mountain in Nagano bears the name *obasuteyama* today.) There is no evidence that the senile ever have been routinely abandoned in Japan. But the lesson is that even elders might not merit unconditional support when they ceased to be an asset to community or family. (1982)

The pattern of family in traditional Japan was the patrilineal, patrilocal, extended family based on the principle of primogeniture. The ideal was that old people would live in the same household with their eldest son and his family. Aging women were expected to dominate their daughters-in-law with the sanction of their sons. Men held the position of head of household until the age of 60, but even after that they expected to be relied upon for guidance. Kiefer maintains that "old people were ideally indulged by their juniors. They were allowed greater freedom in dress, speech, and comportment, and were encouraged to enjoy themselves within their means.... Among humbler folk, they were rewarded with gratitude for such tasks as babysitting, caring for animals, tending fires and floodgates, mending tools, sewing, cooking, providing home medicine, and dispensing their store of knowledge concerning nature and human events" (1974:171).

To understand the role and status of Japanese Americans it is important to review the relationship of Issei and Nisei generations with each other and with the majority culture of the United States. The term *Issei* means first generation and is used to identify the original migrants to the United States. This group, which began arriving in this country in the late 1880s through early 1900s, is described by Osako as having been "born and raised in Japan, emigrated to the U.S. in their youth, worked hard, and raised their families in a climate of racial discrimination. Any Issei can recollect the dire hardships they experienced in pre-World War II days. Working twelve hours a day for seven days a week was not unusual. Farmers, in particular, toiled in the face of insecurity generated by anti-Japanese legislation and a boycott of their products" (1974:449). The Issei were barred from citizenship, property ownership, and intermarriage. The intermarriage prohibition gave rise to the practice of importing "picture brides." These young women, often only teenagers, were selected on the basis of snapshots sent from Japan. Although this arrangement left much to be desired by American standards, it probably was no less personal than traditional family-arranged marriages, and it did allow the migrants to establish permanent families in this country.

Racial attitudes toward Japanese Americans resulted in the Immigration Exclusion Act of 1924, which ended all immigration until 1965. Fear and prejudice also resulted in the executive order during World War II that Japanese Americans be rounded up and placed in concentration camps (euphemistically called relocation camps) where they remained imprisoned for the duration of the hostilities. For middle-aged men, enculturated in a culture that honored age, the relocation camp experience was undoubtedly emotionally crippling for a number of reasons. Kiefer writes:

> The authority of the men was largely replaced by that of the War Relocation Authority, who favored the American-born children of the Issei in their dealings with the prisoners. The men lost their jobs and their businesses, and with these the economic basis of their authority within the family. Even the communal rituals which had functioned to dramatize the values and authority patterns of the prewar communities became all but impossible in the camps. (1974:175)

Upon their release, these middle-aged Japanese Americans found employment again on farms, in factories, or in stores, but many felt themselves too old to try to reestablish the businesses that they had lost because of the internment. Most of their children were still too young to support them, and they could not return to the country of origin because it now was a vanquished nation.

The Nisei (second generation) were all born and educated in America. Although they had experienced the destructive effects of prejudice and discrimination themselves and had seen the struggle that the Issei had undergone in America, they had been protected from many of the economic hardships by their parents. They were urged by their parents to educate themselves and often the Issei made great economic sacrifices to make it possible for their offspring to manage the tuition. As a result, the Nisei group is highly educated, with at least one-third of them engaged in professional or highly skilled occupations (Kitano 1969). The Nisei are truly bicultural and bilingual and are familiar with most facets of American culture. Of their relations with Issei, Kiefer writes:

> Most Nisei have felt a certain embarrassment about their parents' "Japaneseyness" even though they took their responsibilities toward those parents seriously. While they do not openly oppose many of the Issei's ideas and customs, they are prone to ignore them when it is expedient to do so. (1974:177)

Partly because of the loyalty and sense of responsibility of their children, the Issei have fewer problems than most minority elderly. Only 19% of them (mostly women) have incomes below the poverty level, and the median annual income for males in 1976 was $2,842. A survey in San Diego found that Japanese American elderly were relatively better off than the majority of ethnic groups in regard to health level, quality of housing, and transportation.

Japanese Americans, in spite of their educational level and degree of acculturation to Americal life-style, remain physically and emotionally close to their aged. A Chicago study (Osako, 1979) reported that the majority of the Issei sample lived very close to their children. Thirty-five percent shared the same household, 17% lived within the same flat or apartment, and 10% had children living in the immediate neighborhood. A San Francisco study (Kiefer, 1974) found much the same. Out of a group of 21 Issei (many of whom were widows), only 2 reported living alone; 3 lived with a spouse, and 16 said that they were living with relatives.

Although Nisei are strongly supportive of their elders, when the two generations live together, minor frictions are not uncommon, and relationships are never quite what traditional Japanese culture holds up as the ideal. Osako maintains that the "most often mentioned sources of disagreement are differences in opinion about the rearing of the third generation (Sansei) grandchildren. The Sansei's clothing styles, dating, and school performance may turn into a focus of brief, but heated argument. Minor frictions come and go, often without leaving permanent traces. Yet, the parents realize sooner or later that they can no longer interfere with their offspring's business without creating animosity" (1979:450).

In some respects, the relationship between the Issei and the Sansei (their grandchildren) is very good. The latter often look to their grandparents as models of traditional culture and "attribute to the old folks the Japanese equivalent of 'soul' " (Kiefer, 1974:178). But there are also problems. In many cases, the grandchildren cannot communicate with their grandparents since few Sansei speak Japanese and many Issei speak very little English. They therefore have no way of acquiring an understanding of the way their elderly relatives view the world even though traditions have recently become an object of intellectual curiosity in a search for cultural identity. In regard to Japanese culture, Osako maintains that "Issei cling to the tradition, the Nisei shy away from it, and the Sansei, despite their extensive acculturation, rediscover it" (1979:454).

While undoubtedly there are strains between the several Japanese American generations, Osako (1979) believes that a basic compatibility between traditional Japanese and middle-class American values (in regard to diligence, thrift, and politeness) has aided the Issei in their adjustment to American culture. He writes:

> The continuity in the filial norms between the two cultures assists the Issei elderly in their adjustment to advanced age. But the contribution of cultural similarities stops here; the emphasis on group goal orientation and acceptance of dependence, which are not shared by American culture, also help the Issei to cope with their children's upward mobility." (1979:453-454)

PACIFIC AMERICAN AGED

Within the last 70 to 80 years the United States has become home to a new and somewhat unfamiliar variety of ethnic population—Pacific Islanders. The majority of these—Pilipinos[1], Samoans, and Guamanians—have been able to migrate because of the particular political relationship of their home islands to the United States. The Phillippines, for example came under the control of the United States (and her citizens became nationals) after a defeat by this nation in a war in 1902. American Samoa was ceded to the United States by the local chiefs in Pago Pago in 1900, and Guam came under American control in 1898 after the Spanish-American War. This meant that immigration barriers did not apply to these people, and in the case of Pilipinos, they were much in demand as cheap labor when Japanese and Chinese workers were no longer permitted to enter the United States between the years 1910 and 1930. Migration from American Samoa began in the 1950s after the U.S. Navy turned over control of the island group to the Department of Interior, and Guamanian emigration accelerated after the Organic Act of Guam made these north Pacific Islanders United States citizens in 1950. In terms of numbers, Pilipino elderly are most numerous, with Samoans and Guamanians second and third. However, precise numbers of Pacific Islanders in this country are not known because until 1980 the census included such people under the category of "others." At the time of publication of this book, 1980 figures were not available.

One other Pacific Island population, the Hawaiians, should also be noted. Because they live within the United States (in our 50th state), Hawaiians are considered Native Americans, although their status is quite different from that of others within that category, such as American Indians and Eskimos.

Very little research has been done on the aged of any of these Pacific people but the author has personal knowledge of the aged Samoan population in America and will therefore focus on this group.

---

[1] Pilipino is the more acceptable spelling of the term for inhabitants of the Philippines since there is no "f" or "ph" sound in the native language.

Samoans

Most Samoans in the United States are from American Samoa, an unincorporated territory consisting of five small islands midway between Hawaii and New Zealand. This island group in the southwest Pacific is inhabited by approximately 30,000 pure Polynesians who still retain their native language and much of their traditional culture. Significant migration to this country began in 1951 (although there was some in the 1930s) when the U.S. Navy turned over control of the islands to the Department of the Interior and members of a home guard unit called the FitaFita were permitted to transfer to the regular Navy. A Navy transport took these men and their families to Naval installations in Hawaii and on the West Coast. Some were even assigned to the Brooklyn Navy Yard and Norfolk. Today, the bulk of Samoans live in Hawaii, California, and Washington, but there are Samoans living in all 50 states. Independence, Missouri, for example, has a Samoan population (mostly Mormons) of approximately 400. The author's research on Samoan elderly has been carried out primarily in the San Francisco Bay area but the conclusions compare favorably with research by W. H. Ishikawa (1978) in San Diego.

Migration to the United States has generally been undertaken by young people (mostly men) seeking jobs and/or educational opportunities. Some have come as members of the armed forces, all of which recruit heavily in the islands. Most immigrants have relatives with whom they can stay until they establish themselves and are able to send for wives and other family members. Most families have considerable financial difficulty surviving in the city because of lack of technical skills; several household members must be employed to make ends meet. The need to have someone at home during the day to care for small children and to maintain the home for working members has resulted in many Samoan couples sending for elderly parents or other aged relatives to fulfill these functions. In most cases, this arrangement is assumed to be temporary, but economic hardships often make the roles permanent. The percentage of aged to be found among the Samoan migrant population, however, is relatively small, making up somewhere between 3% and 5% (probably about 3,000 total in America).

The Samoan community in the San Francisco Bay area is widely dispersed, but there is a concentration near Daly City and South San Francisco. There are no Samoan ghettos, but Samoans, who tend to be poor, are often found in neighborhoods populated by underprivileged minorities. A fair number of middle-income Samoans, however, own their own homes in middle-class neighborhoods. Samoans are so inconspicuous that most San Franciscans are amazed when told that several thousand of these South Sea people live in their midst.

Samoan households vary in size from 6 to 14 individuals, with the average being 8. Family heads tend to be young to middle aged. There is a high percentage of children, and in many cases these include nieces, nephews, grandchildren, and other collateral relatives. In many respects, life is less eventful for Samoan old people in San Francisco than in Samoa, since they rarely venture outside the house. Fewer demands are made on them, since stateside households of extended families are smaller, more dispersed, and less in communication with each other than is the case in the islands. There are, however, new problems.

Obesity is frequently a problem for older people since they are now eating three meals a day instead of the traditional two, engaging in less physical activity, and eating a diet heavier in fats than they did in their homeland. There are also intergenerational conflicts concerning the importance of Samoan ways, particularly with teenage and young adult males. In the new urban setting, these young people are free from the traditional controls of family and village discipline and have difficulty handling their new freedom and independence. A considerable amount of evidence indicates that Samoans are prone to stress-related diseases such as peptic ulcers and hypertension (Baker and Lieberman, 1976), and problems of culture shock and value ambiguity must surely aggravate these conditions.

When asked to identify "serious problems" associated with life in San Francisco, elderly informants cited "poor health" (89%), "poor housing" (86%), "not enough medical care" (81%), "not enough education" (81%), and "fear of being robbed or hurt by a criminal" (80%). On the other hand, only 3% complained of loneliness, whereas a Harris poll found 36% of the general elderly American population citing this as a serious problem. A comparison of an island sample population (Holmes 1978) to the San Francisco sample shows the anxiety associated with being old and culturally different in a major metropolis. In Samoa, for example, only 4% complained that "too few friends" was a serious problem, but this increased to 25% in the San Francisco population. "Too few clothes" was a problem for only 21% of islanders but was a predicament for 50% of the stateside sample. While only 31% in American Samoa complained of not enough medical care, this worried 81% of elderly in San Francisco.

When Samoan elders in the Bay area were asked to comment on where life was better (in Samoa or in the United States), the California sample split evenly. A variety of reasons were offered to defend their choices, but attitudes about returning to Samoa seemed to be related to where the old person's children and other close relatives were located. Some stated that since all their children lived in California they now thought of the state as their home. Most expressed a desire to return to Samoa for a visit, however.

We will not comment at this point on the traditional ways of Samoans since that subject is dealt with at some length in Chapter 7, but it should be noted that a number of cultural factors represent real barriers to human-service delivery for the elderly Samoan population. For example, when Samoans encounter difficulties they immediately turn to the extended family for help. They not only have a predilection to kin reliance but such action is undertaken as a matter of pride. When discussing the needs of their elderly, Samoans vehemently insist that the family takes care of its own and that they have no need for government aid or nursing homes or other residences exclusively reserved for aged. Families may even oppose efforts of human-service agencies to aid their elderly on the grounds that such assistance might be interpreted by other Samoans as a failure on the part of the family to meet its filial obligations. Of course, Samoans who are eligible for Social Security (60%) welcome the checks and some 72% of the San Francisco sample have at one time or another taken advantage of Medicare. Many government programs that were available in the islands are not available to San Francisco elderly since they are not citizens (they are nationals) and they do not qualify as Native Americans. Nonvoting populations also do not get much attention from local or federal politicians.

Samoans have no national organizations like Urban League or N.A.A.C.P. to promote causes. A few of the better educated and more acculturated Samoans have formed associations such as the Office of Samoan Affairs for California, Inc., or Samoans for Samoans of California, which helps their people seek out local or federal aid and human-service assistance, but these organizations are staffed by volunteer workers and they have little in the way of operating budgets. Samoan churches (17 in the Bay area) offer some sense of security and identity to Samoans of all ages, and 97% of the elderly claimed church membership and regular attendance. Churches, however, are mainly evangelical in function and have little in the way of social-action programs. Church activities do, however, facilitate communication and therefore are important in marshalling assistance for elderly in need.

When Samoans deal with white Americans, they tend to be extremely formal and reserved. In some cases, when difficulties are encountered and when a Samoan believes he cannot win in a confrontation with the dominant group, he withdraws. Attempts by whites to be friendly and informal often produce even greater withdrawal tendencies. Samoans believe that relationships between themselves and those in positions of authority should be properly characterized by formality.

Although Samoans in the Pacific and in San Francisco understand the value of modern medicine and often take advantage of it, they are also extremely fatalistic about serious illness and death. They greatly rely on God's will to provide for their recovery. It is not a bit unusual for elderly Samoans to refuse to go to the hospital when seriously ill, and as a result, die from what might have been fairly easily remedied by proper medical attention. Samoans also believe, particularly the older, more traditional Samoans, that one should die at home or a troubled spirit will result.

For many elderly Samoans living in the United States such barriers as red tape, inadequate transportation, their own reticence to involve themselves in unfamiliar situations, their tendency to withdraw when difficulties with non-Samoans develop, problems of cross-cultural communication, and general differences in perception of needs between themselves and human-service agency personnel mean that much of the aid for the elderly comes from their families. Considering the present economic and social problems of most stateside Samoan families, however, senior Samoans are not likely to receive the same level of benefits enjoyed by most elderly white Americans. Most aged Samoans, however, are so rich in family goodwill and affection that they may not realize how deprived they are. It is reasonable that many white Americans might even envy the Samoan system detailed by Ishikawa from his observations of San Diego families:

> Respect and deference in demeanor toward the elderly were not only values imbedded in history, but structural in the social roles of family members, lived out in member relationships and sanctioned by the community. (1978:28)

Guamanians

One of the few studies, if not the only one, of Guamanian elderly in the United States was also conducted by W. H. Ishikawa in San Diego (1978a). Ishikawa maintains that most of the Guamanians in the San Diego sample migrated to California between 1935 and 1954. Of the 23 respondents, 19 lived in their own homes (with a household size of 3.4) and 4 (all widows) lived in the home of their daughter's family (with an average household size of 6). This pattern of residence of elderly Guamanian widows with daughters' families is believed to be unique among Pacific people.

Ishikawa found all of the Guamanian elderly to be bilingual, but the majority preferred to speak Chamorro; approximately one-fourth of them claimed to have difficulty communicating in English. Many maintained that they belonged to a Guamanian community club, Sons and Daughters of Guam, which provided them with a measure of ethnic identity and common cultural participation; all but one also belonged to a church which had recently dedicated a Guamanian community patron saint.

Guamanians resemble Samoans in that

> the family member is the key person in problem solving in that the elderly would in all probability, turn to him first when difficulty arises. The family member by virtue of this responsibility, is in the position to provide the help depending on his skill and resources he commands, or make a referral to public, or private resources. The study concludes that the needful, the first helper and the household constitute the persons and site of the initial stage of problem solving for the elderly Guamanian. (Ishikawa, 1978a:27)

Pilipinos

Pilipinos migrated to this country in substantial numbers between 1910 and 1930 when the Philippines were a trusteeship of the United States and when there was a demand for cheap labor as seamen, farmhands, and cannery workers. In America they encountered much of the same kinds of discrimination as Chinese and Japanese had before them—repressive laws and practices in the areas of land ownership, citizenship rights, housing, and travel (Levkoff and others, 1979). Hostility toward Pilipinos increased to the point that by 1934 immigration quotas permitted only 50 individuals a year to enter the United States. In 1965, however, immigrations quotas were repealed and there was a great flood of Pilipinos into this country. As a result of this migration history, Pilipino aged in America can be divided into two distinct groups: (1) a group of elderly single men who live in urban areas in boarding houses and hotels with no family ties, and (2) migrants who have come after 1965 to be with their children. These more recent immigrants, primarily women, live in suburban areas in single-family homes where they care for grandchildren and help maintain the home for the families of their adult children. Peterson maintains that

> when a Pilipino is old he/she expects to be respected and cared for, not only by family members, but by the rest of the community as well. Respondents indicate this by their recommendations to youngsters to help and respect elders and to carry on traditions which are identified as helpfulness and caring. (1978:28)

Traditionally, Pilipino culture stressed reciprocal physical and financial aid. Gift exchanges were associated with births, housewarmings, weddings, and funerals, and much shame came to those who would not contribute financially when the family was having difficulty. Levkoff writes that

> the Pilipino American elder commanded the authority and respect of their family and community. Their age status granted special privileges and responsibilities.... For today's elderly Pilipino, these values are still strong. However, their ability to fulfill these values has been influenced by a history of discrimination and the assimilation of dominant culture values and life-styles by younger generations. (1979:18)

For those elderly who have family (81%), this is their primary source of assistance. More recent arrivals to the United States have a greater tendency to seek agency help. Language difficulties (81% of a San Diego sample preferred a language other than English), lack of knowledge of services available, and pride and feelings of shame about being in need represent major barriers to human-service delivery. The pattern of reciprocity is so strong in these people that they may also not turn to neighbors or friends if they feel that they will not be able to repay them. Traditional patterns of mutual aid were once strong, but they are breaking down today. Peterson maintains that

> although 25.7 percent indicated that Pilipinos help each other today, 20.3 percent said the Pilipinos are now more "on their own" or more independent. A common comment was that Pilipinos are no longer "close in relationship." These statements indicated a breakdown of helping networks, for, although 75 percent of the respondents indicated they help others, they do not offer assistance in the traditional manner. (1978:16)

Hawaiians

Although there are undoubtedly elderly Hawaiians living on the mainland, we shall reserve our comments for those living within the state of Hawaii and discuss the role of *kūpuna* (elders) within what remains today of the Hawaiian way of life. This cultural system is difficult to isolate, but has been described by Benjamin Young as "Hawaiian ways which have come about through the intricate and delicate mixture and synthesis of many factors and forces, including intermarriage, acculturation, introduction of new concepts, preservation of old concepts, and the tenacious clinging to roots and ties of the past. Given the diverse backgrounds of today's Hawaiians, one must look at a cultural system and lifestyle that varies from locale to locale and from community to community" (1980:11).

There are, however, some universals of value and behavior among those who identify with the Hawaiian tradition. First of all, the *'ohana* (extended family) is the center of all human relationships, and it is from this institution that all values and coping strategies emanate. Unlike Anglo families, Hawaiians stress that as children grow up there should be continuing dependence on family and increased contribution to its welfare. Enculturation patterns do not stress independence but rather mutual assistance and collective welfare. Gillimore, Boggs, and Jordan maintain that in Hawaiian families "youth depend on parents; parents depend on youth" (1974:65). Dependence, however, goes hand in hand with reciprocity, and therefore there is no shame associated with dependence since being helped necessitates returning the favor at some future date. "Achievement and maturity are marked by generosity, helpfulness, reliable contributions and commitment—these are the rules" (ibid.). For elderly Hawaiians this undoubtedly represents a secure social environment.

In the Hawaiian system, *kūpuna* and *kūkū* (grandparents) are objects of love and respect. In old Hawaii respect for grandparents was so great that the *hiapo* (firstborn) was given to them to raise. A boy was given to the paternal grandparents, a girl to the maternal grandparents. It was believed that through this *hānai* (adoption) system the child did not lose its parents but rather gained a more intimate relationship with its grandparents. Within this relationship the child was taught the family genealogy and other skills important to family welfare. The *hānai* system no longer functions but the feelings of love and affection between grandchildren and grandparents are still there and indeed, many children spend a great deal of time with their *kūkū*.

Kūpuna today also play an important part in the community. The Hawaiian school system has secured the services of many elderly Hawaiians to teach public school classes on traditional subjects. The voyage of the Hokule'a (a traditional Hawaiian catamaran) in 1976 to Tahiti revived interest and pride in Hawaii. *Kūpuna*, along with anthropologists, conducted workshops for young people in the rudiments of Polynesian navigation, food preservation, feather lei making, quilt making, Hawaiian language, and traditional sports. All this emphasis on traditional culture reinforces the feeling of respect the young have for the old.

There is a disproportionate number of poor among the Hawaiians, with considerable numbers of them on welfare, but most elderly can depend on family for support in periods of financial need or disability. However, this dependence on family and the tendency to avoid outside help unless the source is trusted or has ties with the Hawaiian community (as in the case of the Lunalilo Home for the Aged in Honolulu) means that elderly are often deprived of services that legally should be theirs. Young writes:

> Communication with the Hawaiian community is perhaps more complex than with any other group. It must be a subtle and delicate blending of concern and intimacy tempered with reserve and observation. Nonetheless, a discussion of the problems, especially those of coping mechanisms, is meaningful, because a large majority of Hawaiians still cling to Hawaiian values and have not been able to traverse the bridge of acculturation into twentieth-century society. (1980:16)

SUMMARY

Throughout its history the United States has been home to a variety of ethnic populations. Some, like the blacks, were brought against their will; some, like the Native Americans, were here long before our founding fathers; and others, like the Spanish-speaking peoples, the Chinese, the Japanese, and the Pacific Islanders came as immigrants for economic or political reasons. Some of these people have been assimilated in the American cultural mainstream, but for most, significant cultural differences in regard to world view, family structure, language, and national character set them apart from the general public and have an impact on the way they value and care for their aged. Anyone who is charged with providing human services for the elderly of these ethnic populations must be aware of these values and must learn to work in accordance with them.

Black Americans, by virtue of their West African cultural origins, their devastating history of American slavery, Emancipation and Reconstruction, and modern racial discrimination, see the world, the family, and their aged in a very different light than do representatives of white America. The elderly also have a different self-concept; they are more comfortable with old age than whites, they remain more a part of the family structure, they tend to be in better health, but their life expectancy is roughly six years less.

Native Americans, on the other hand, are difficult to characterize as a group. Officially, there are 266 recognized bands and tribes, and there are some 149 Indian languages still in use. In spite of all of the cultural variability, however, some general similarities have been noted. These include a high value on individuality and freedom, a reverence for all living things (and especially the land), and a respect for family and clan. Native Americans have also experienced defeat and discrimination and today face the worst deprivation of any ethnic group in America. As a result, the life expectancy of Native Americans is slightly more than 44 years. The most critical problems (particularly for the aged) are found on reservations, which tend to be isolated, have inadequate economic, health, and education services, and are run by less-than-enthusiastic bureaucrats. In many cases, the elderly serve as household heads on reservations and also in urban areas because they often have small pensions or other forms of income, which means they are often able to keep families together by providing economic and social stability. Elders have also acquired status in recent years as bearers of a cultural tradition that young Indians want to learn about and participate in.

The Mexican American tradition, of course, has its cultural roots in rural Mexico and has been carried by migrants into the agricultural areas of the Southwest and into the city barrios of a variety of midwestern and southwestern states. This cultural heritage is one that stresses familism, age hierarchy, male leadership, and mutual aid. Ideally, the Mexican American family is devoted to its senior members, but the problems of urban living and the intrusion of dominant American norms often mean that there sometimes is an inability or a lack of desire to relate to and care for the elderly in the traditional way.

The people of the Orient—China, Japan, Korea, Indochina—have come to the United States to seek economic opportunity or to escape political oppression. Although the cultural traditions of all of these peoples vary a great deal, these groups also have some things in common—ideas like respect for family, filial peity, mutual obligations and privileges among generations, and a sense of cultural distinctness that has often resulted in isolation. In America these people from the Far East have often encountered discrimination and oppression, even imprisonment (the Japanese in World War II) merely because of their cultural identity. Chinese and Japanese migrants began arriving in the United States as early as 1850 and 1880, respectively, and it is not surprising that there are a considerable number of elderly American-born Orientals in many of our West Coast cities. As is the case with many other immigrant groups, a clash of ideas between the various generations has been a dilemma for oriental aged. The most notable example of this involves the different attitudes and life-styles of Issei, Nisei, and Sansei Japanese.

In some respects the history of Pilipino migrants in America parallels that of Orientals, since many of them came to the United States as coolie laborers and have also suffered significantly from racial prejudice and discrimination. The case of Samoans and Guamanians has been somewhat different. Political circumstances made it possible for these island people to migrate freely to obtain better jobs and better education. As American nationals, these people have been somewhat more acceptable than Pilipinos or Orientals, and considerable numbers of these people now live in Hawaii, California, and Washington. While Samoan and Guamanian migration has not been going on long enough for the migrants to have attained old age in America, many of these Pacific people have sent for their parents or elderly relatives to maintain the home and tend children while both parents work. Although it is ordinarily difficult to perpetuate extended family structures in urban areas, Samoans have done remarkably well in maintaining extended kin relationships and this has tended to be a supportive factor in maintaining status and authority for the aged.

While the Hawaiians who inhabit our 50th state certainly cannot in any sense be considered immigrants, a substantial proportion of them practice a culture that can be considered ethnically different. In their respect for the extended family, their veneration of the elderly, and their patterns of reciprocity between generations, the Hawaiians greatly resemble Samoans. Although a disproportionate number of elderly Hawaiians are poor and on welfare, this ethnic group's pride in Hawaiian traditions and their general feeling that age is in itself a thing to be valued mean that elderly Hawaiians enjoy a secure social and psychological environment.

CHAPTER 9

The Aged and Cultural Change

The study of social and cultural change has always been an important interest of anthropologists, and it is therefore understandable that it has been a primary focus of investigation for anthropologists concerned with cultural gerontology. Change, which can influence the status and treatment of aged, may come from within the culture or from outside. Internally generated change may be caused by "technical inventions, individual struggles for land and power, reformulations of ideas by specially gifted inquiring minds, . . . pressure of population on the means of subsistence, and perhaps climatic changes" (Firth, 1958:148). All these factors can conceivably affect the care, status, and opportunity for participation enjoyed by the aged in our own as well as other cultures. This chapter singles out one internal factor in particular for special scrutiny: population composition. For many years America has been characterized as a youth-dominated and youth-oriented society, but recent developments in health technology and in attitudes toward family size have resulted in an altered population age profile that is characterized by an ever-increasing percentage of middle-aged and elderly citizens and a progressively rising average age. This change in age composition is called by some writers "the graying of America."

Cultural systems are also affected by external change. Change that comes from outside the society involves borrowing ideas, and it has been estimated that few societies in the world have themselves invented more than about 10% of their cultural content. When borrowing results from ongoing contact between representatives of societies with different cultures, the situation is referred to as one of *acculturation*. Examples of this are white frontier settlers and American Indians or southern white masters and their African slaves. In such situations, borrowing seems to be two-way, regardless of whether or not one society is more technologically advanced than the other. Sometimes change takes place as the result of ideas or traits of one culture being borrowed by another but without day-to-day interaction of peoples. An example of this is the introduction of noodles and gunpowder into Italy in the 13th century, when Marco Polo returned with these items on one of his trading trips to China. This kind of spread of ideas from one society to another is called *diffusion.*

Regardless of the source or variety of change, it must be recognized that change is constantly taking place in all societies be they folk or modern, Western or non-Western, provincial or cosmopolitan. Some societies, however, welcome change more than others, and therefore change is more rapid and pervasive. Arensberg and Niehoff maintain that change is ever-present for the "single reason that people of different cultures are always in competition with one another . . . . This competition between peoples of different cultures is the basis of the drive toward modernization by the underdeveloped countries" (1964:57-58).

This particular kind of change, *modernization,* has dominated the interest of anthropologists in recent years, particularly those who are interested in what happens to old people when societies become subject to rapid and profound transformations of their life-style through contact with the West. It characteristically involves changes in culture in the direction of the urbanization, industrialization, scientific development, and the establishment of mass education and higher levels of communication through mass-media exposure.

Contacts between Western countries and hunting and peasant societies have in some cases only added a few new ideas to these preindustrial cultures, which by and large retain their traditional form. In other cases, however, life-styles have been revolutionized and there has been a wholesale imposition of new legal, economic, political, and religious values and behavior. Modernizing influences have often shattered customs and institutions that preindustrial peoples have built up with painstaking effort over long periods of time. In these situations, modernization represents a form of external change, since the source of the transforming culture items is outside the culture. It is, however, possible to talk about modernization as an internal force for change as we look at the history of technological development, industrialization, and urbanization in America.

In 1972 Donald O. Cowgill and Lowell D. Holmes investigated the influence of modernization on the status of the aged in 14 societies, each representing different positions along a continuum running from preliterate (sometimes called "primitive"), to peasant (agricultural and herding), to modern societies. Based on evidence from an earlier cross-cultural work by Simmons (1945) and a variety of reports by other cultural gerontologists, the two investigators hypothesized that *as societies become increasingly modern there is a concomitant drop in status of the elderly.* Although the study was cross-cultural rather than longitudinal (with different societies representing the various gradations of modernization), the study demonstrated a general fall in status accompanying increased modernization with only two exceptions, and these the authors believed could be explained and should have been predicted in terms of unique cultural circumstances. The study, however, was admittedly not methodologically perfect, and the researchers recognized that variations in values and social structure among the societies could greatly influence how each of them reacted to the forces of modernization. For example, Holmes cautioned:

How a society develops under the impact of modernizing forces depends to a great extent upon the values it held previously. A society whose major religion is Buddhism may be quite differently affected by industrialization and urbanization than one operating under a Judeo-Christian tradition. The same is true for traditional differences in political or economic philosophy. In Japan, with its traditional ideas concerning family loyalty and filial piety, modernization has brought about drastic social changes in family organization and familial ethics but it is still possible for Norbeck to write concerning the aged that they have "found a way to live with peace of mind" and a sense of security seldom found among aged in the United States. (1972:87)

The "Machine Age" Maya, described by Manning Nash (1967), are an example of a people who, although exposed to the pressures of disrupting influences of industrialization, have shown little inclination to alter their attitudes or behavior patterns toward their aged. Industrialization came to the settlement of Pasac in Cantel, Guatemala, in 1876 by way of a textile mill. Thirty-four percent of the 1,823 inhabitants of the community over 15 years of age are employed in this plant. Because of the wage labor from the mill, sons are usually richer and more economically secure than their parents. Where parents are supported by offspring, the child is likely to be a mill worker. Support of parents by children represents a reversal of the traditional dependency relationship, and it violates cultural expectations. Although this vital social change emanates from modernization it has not to any extent broken down emotional relationships or altered patterns of respect for elderly. There is little difference in this regard between families of factory workers and those of nonfactory workers.

Various theorists have hypothesized that the way the aged are treated in a society and the way they feel about their own status is related to such things as rate of change, family emphasis (extended or nuclear), nature of the economy, amount of physical mobility, or the percentage of aged in the population. However, long-term value orientations can conceivably overshadow any or all of these variables. An analysis of 13 preindustrial societies described by Margaret Mead in *Cooperation and Competition Among Primitive Peoples* revealed a strong correlation between low valuation of the aged and a value orientation marked by emphasis on personal achievement, private property, and security based on individual activity. On the other hand, she observed that societies that accord the aged high status and ensure their physical welfare are those that tend to submerge the individual in the group and provide people of all ages with an unthreatened sense of security. While sedentary agriculturalists generally are deferential to elders, variations in value orientations seem to explain why for some peoples in Mead's sample (e.g., the Zuni) status increases with age, whereas among the Ifugao (also sedentary agriculturalists) the aged experience a decline of status with advancing age.

The value system of the United States is one which, like many of the societies in Mead's sample, stresses individual achievement and a low degree of security. Francis Hsu (1961) sees the American core value as "self-reliance," and he singles out dependency as the cardinal American sin. He believes that these ideas are rooted as deep as the Reformation and have therefore prevailed for more than 400 years in spite of modifications in technology, economics, family structure, and other factors that might affect the status and treatment of the aged. Philip Slater maintains that in the American ideological environment "everything . . . rests upon the assumption that the world does not contain the wherewithal to satisfy the needs of its human inhabitants. From this it follows that people must compete with one another for these scarce resources . . . . The key flaw is, of course, the fact that the scarcity is spurious—man-made in the case of bodily gratifications and man-allowed and man-maintained in the case of material goods" (1970:103).

What clearly is needed to understand the effects of modernization on a society's elderly population without the complications of having to deal with value variables is a longitudinal study in a society that has been transformed from a hunting or peasant culture to an industrial one. Something approaching a longitudinal study was carried out in 1976-1977 in American Samoa and California by Ellen Rhoads, who studied communities with varying amounts of modernization and then assessed what effects their varying conditions had on the elderly residents. Rhoads compared Ta'u village in the conservative and isolated Manu'a Group, Fagatogo (the port city and capital of American Samoa), and the Samoan migrant community of the San Francisco Bay area. She also compared her data with a 1962 study of Samoan aged made by Holmes (1972). The 1962 study was, however, somewhat general, and specific data comparisons were not always possible. Nonetheless, general impressions derived from a comparative analysis were valuable since a great deal of modernization was forced upon American Samoa between the years 1963 and 1976.

Using observation, information gleaned from government documents, and extended interviews with elderly and with younger family members (approximately 50 of each in each community) Rhoads found that although the level of community modernization varied from "low" in Ta'u to "medium" in Fagatogo to "high" in San Francisco, there was not a clear-cut or consistent decline in the status of the elderly in the more modern localities. She maintains that the status of the elderly in all three communities is relatively high but that "modernization is not without impact on the aged; there are indications in the data that problems do exist which appear to be related to modern change" (1981:123).

Rhoads' data show that despite a general decline in morale and in the authority of the aged and an increase in the old people's perception of problems associated with old age as one moves from the very traditional village of Ta'u to the urban community Fagatogo, this trend does not carry over to San Francisco. Rhoads writes:

> During the research in San Francisco in 1977, I was surprised to find that the migrants still seem as much Samoan as the people living in their homeland. The Bay area Samoans in the sample are still undeniably operating according to *fa'asamoa* . . . . Their ethnic identity seems to be a significant unifying principle. As other ethnic groups have sometimes done in the face of foreign influences, Samoans in San Francisco "compartmentalize" their lives to a great extent. They deal with the larger society at work or in other situations when they have to, but the larger part of their world is very much Samoan. (1981:140-141)

Part of this emphasis on Samoaness is a reaffirmation of traditions that place great value on old age and great emphasis on more than adequate concern for satisfaction of their social and material needs.

Although much more research is needed to acquire a complete understanding of the relationship between modernization and the status and support of the aged, some generalizations can be made based on what has been observed in a variety of third- and fourth-world countries and in the United States. These generalizations, borrowed in many cases from Cowgill and Holmes' *Aging and Modernization*, are:

1. *The concept of old age itself appears to be relative to the degree of modernization.* Even the definition of old age varies according to the degree of societal modernization. In preindustrial societies, where life spans tend to be shorter, people are inclined to perceive that old age comes earlier than in more modern societies; perhaps it does if life is hard and the life cycle has been characterized by strenuous labor, repeated periods of famine, and little effective medical care.

When the author investigated the chronological age at which people in Samoa began to be referred to as *matuaali'i* (old man) and *lo'omatua* (old woman) in 1962—when the society was still very traditional—he was told it was at age 50, whereas in 1976, after a decade and a half of intensive Western change, the Samoans responded that they thought of old age as beginning between the ages of 60 and 65. The Igbo of West Africa see the onset of old age as occurring between 40 and 50, and the Sidamo of Ethiopia (also a preindustrial society) consider a person old when he or she reaches 55. All modern Western nations, on the other hand, maintain that the threshhold of old age is between 65 and 70. Not only is there a decided tendency for the perception of when old age begins to be altered by modernization but there is a pronounced change in how old age is conceptualized. Most preindustrial societies hold a functional view of aging—that is, one is old when no longer able to perform normal adult duties. Modern societies have a chronological view, selecting an arbitrary year (65 or 70) as the threshhold.

2. *Longevity is directly and significantly related to the degree of modernization.* Cowgill believes that "longevity may well be the best index of modernization" (1972:8), since average age of life has steadily increased as societies have modernized. Neanderthals, who lived as hunters and gatherers 100,000 years ago, had a life expectancy of less than 20 years; Egyptians (based on mummy evidence) averaged 22.5 years of life, and Greeks in 400 BC could expect to live about 30 years. In North America, Late Woodland Indian populations in Maryland were averaging 20 years, Philadelphians in the 1780s had an average life span of 25 years, and Americans as a whole in 1900-1902 had a life expectancy of 48.2 years. By 1979 this figure had risen to 73.8. Although life expectancy has fluctuated in various places and at various times, the index has tended to accelerate rapidly as societies move toward urbanization and industrialization.

3. *Modernized societies have relatively high proportions of old people in their populations.* This phenomenon results from two interrelated factors—the reduction of birth rates and an increase in life span resulting from advances in medical technology—that tend to be associated with modern urban and industrial life. In 1977 the median age in America was 29.4; by the year 2030 the average age of Americans will be 38. In part, this is due to a "baby bust" that has driven birth rates downward since the 1960s and to a dramatic reduction in heart disease deaths that has boosted life expectancy well over a year since 1972. In 1969, 39% of the population of the United States

consisted of children and teenagers, but in the next 50 years that figure will drop to less than 27%.

Modern societies also have higher proportions of older women and consequently higher proportions of widows. In such areas of Africa as the Congo, Tanganyika, and Ituri the ratio of elderly men per 100 women varies from 108 to 194. In America the 1880 census recorded that for people 65 and older there were 101 men per 100 women; by the 1980 census, the figure had shrunk to 68 men per 100 women.

4. *The aged are the recipients of greater respect in societies where they constitute a low proportion of the total population.* Diamonds, gold nuggets, and the first editions are valued because there are so few of them. Perhaps the same applies to people. Some societies believe that very old people have special value because they are favored by the gods or because they have some superior innate quality that has allowed them to survive. Some very old men in Indian and Eskimo societies were believed to still be alive because of special supernatural power, and therefore they were the most appropriate people to serve as religious or medical practitioners.

Preindustrial societies seldom have more than 3% of the population over the age of 65; modern societies have between 9% and 12%. Some researchers propose a phenomenon called societal *carrying power,* and suggest that when a society reaches a point where dependent members cannot be supported comfortably the status and concern for these recipients decline. Some evidence indicates that this is what is occurring in America in regard to Social Security financing. When a few elderly were supported by the contributions of a large number of productive workers, little in the way of resentment was expressed, but when the percentage of recipients relative to contributors increased there were indications of both anxiety and resentment on the part of those members of the work force who were financially responsible for the continuation of the program. It is, however, difficult to establish cause-and-effect relationships in areas such as this. Actual numbers may have little to do with status considerations. Perhaps both the increase in number of elders and a decline in the status of old people are merely correlated with modernization and its many pervasive social, economic, and political manifestations.

5. *Societies that are in the process of modernizing tend to favor the young, while the aged are at an advantage in more stable, sedentary societies.* In the article "Aging in Modern Society," Simmons observed that "there is a pattern of participation for the aged that becomes relatively fixed in stable societies but suffers disruption with rapid social change" (1959:7). Press and McKool (1972) note that modernization causes breaks in the continuity of roles and results in reduced prestige for elderly. They maintain that the principal factors associated with reduced senior status are economic interests, minimization of number and importance of ascriptive roles, nuclear family independence, economic activity outside of the household, and early turnover of family resources from father to son.

In conservative, preindustrial societies, the aged, because they are custodians of both family property and cultural tradition, become entrenched in positions of power and authority, and their roles and status are guaranteed by seniority rights. Roles and statuses are well defined and well understood. Tradition provides security and that security is in part based on the fact that prediction is possible. There are few surprises.

The events of the past are repeated, and the elders who have been through these situations many times before can easily attend to them. The elders appear to be decisive, wise, and confident, and they are objects of admiration.

In situations of rapid change, social conditions become unstable and the old solutions to problems are not always adequate. Since the aged under these conditions cannot always continue to exhibit their wisdom and control, they become vulnerable and subject to replacement by younger people who are more flexible, less prone to call upon old solutions, more daring, and more willing to experiment and learn new solutions. Maxwell and Silverman further clarify the ramifications of modernization:

> Because of culture contact with a more dominant complex society, the information controlled by the aged becomes rapidly obsolete. This high rate of informational obsolescence is reflected in a decline in the social participation of the elderly. The low incidence of social participation in turn contributes to their loss of status. (1977:31-32)

6. *Respect for the aged tends to be greater in societies in which the extended family is intact, particularly if it functions as the household unit.* Rosow maintains that the position of aged in a society is relatively higher when the extended family is central to the social structure because "a clan can and will act much more effectively to meet crisis and dependency of its members than a small family. Mutual obligations between blood relatives—specifically including the aged—are institutionalized as formal rights, not generous benefactions" (1965:22).

The literature provides us with abundant examples of the supportive nature of the extended family. Munsell (1972) observed that among the Pima Indians, recent developments that have brought the nuclear family into prominence at the expense of the extended form have to a large extent deprived the elderly of decision-making functions and therefore resulted in loss of status and authority. Press and McKool found in Chinaulta, Guatamala, that "loss of extended family viability goes hand in hand with low, dependent status of the aged . . . . Where the economic unit is largely coterminous with the extended family, the elder members *de facto* remain economically active and may exert considerable control over the behavior of others" (1972:303).

Frances M. Adams, on the other hand, stresses the importance of the extended family as a socialization influence that provides family members with a positive attitude towards growing old. She writes:

> Changes in behavior expectations as a person gets older . . . are understood in advance through close association with older people who have already made the transitions. For example, a person knows how to be an old person because he has observed first his grandfather and then his father in this role. The emotional security developed in childhood in the context of the extended family is not lost in old age. (1972:110)

Shelton stresses still another aspect of extended-family organization that contributes to respect for the aged. This is the emphasis it puts on the cyclic flow of family members and spiritual forces. He notes:

> The dead are not buried and forgotten, but are "returners" who reappear in the patriline. The aged persons in the family, accordingly, are not simply individuals

who have served their brief span on earth and are soon due to disappear forever, but indeed are getting closer to the apogee of their cycle—they are soon to be ancestral spirits, in that most powerful condition in the endless cycle of existence. (1972:35)

Although extended-family household organization is somewhat rare in modern societies, McKain reports that in the Soviet Union at least a modified form is being preserved and that it is a key ingredient in the economic security of both young and old. He writes:

> Not many older persons in the Soviet Union live alone. For the most part unattached older persons live with their children, with older relatives or with an unrelated family.... Filial responsibility undoubtedly explains why most of the grandparents can find a home with their children should the need arise. Both the older persons and their children usually accept this arrangement without question and without a feeling of obligation.... The presence of grandparents in the house may also be prevalent for other more materialistic reasons. Since aged persons receive a pension, the added income is a very welcome supplement to the household budget. (1972:156)

In spite of great social and economic changes in the Soviet Union, the aged appear to be treated with great respect by family members, by trade unions, and by the general public. Their advice and counsel are valued, and obedience and esteem for the aged are values that are taught early in life.

Sheehan points out, however, that when a community turns away from an extended family emphasis and kinship loyalties are replaced by structures that emphasize peer allegiance and other-directed individualism, there is, in effect, a return to the less-binding ties associated with nomadic life. In such societies, he maintains, "social and geographic mobility become goals; individual autonomy emerges as a value" (1976:437). This is not unlike what happens with increased modernization. "As urban-industrial society increasingly technologizes, seniors ever more lose their family ties along with accompanying status, decision-making power and security" (ibid.).

7. *In nonindustrial societies the family is the basic social group providing economic security for dependent aged, but in industrial ones the responsibility tends to be partially or totally that of the state.* Although nonindustrial societies often provide for elderly through certain kinds of food-sharing practices and through certain food taboos, it is nearly impossible to find any traditional tribal society where support of the elderly is the primary responsibility of the greater society rather than the family or clan. There is one exception—Inca society. Although this group has usually been called a civilization, it certainly was not a modern industrial society. The Inca, whose government at one time controlled most of the Pacific coastal region of South America, divided the land under their control into sections to be worked communally by their subjects. These lands, under the administration of appointed government officials were designated as being (1) those to be cultivated for the support of the Inca (king) and his government officials, including a hierarchy of priests, (2) those that could be used for the support of the workers themselves and their families, and (3) those to be cultivated for the support of "soldiers, invalids, the aged and orphans" (Flornoy, 1956:111). Widows were to be taken care of by their brothers-in-law although war widows received

special help. Since national policy reserved the produce from some public lands for support of the elderly and other dependent individuals, the Inca represent a case of state-sponsored welfare within an indigenous Indian culture.

Some developing countries like Thailand have established programs that offer meager pensions for retired government employees and limited governmental assistance to elderly based on need, but such countries rarely have government-operated residences for the aged. In Samoa, Polynesia's first home for the aged is financed and operated by the Catholic Church under the Little Sisters of the Poor. On the other hand, in Japan (a world leader in industrialization and primarily an urban society), we find elaborate government pension, insurance, and assistance programs. Palmore writes that with the end of World War II and with increased industrialization has come the "belief that pensions or social security, rather than the children, should be primarily responsible for the support of older persons" (1975:90).

Of still another world leader in modernization and industrialization, the United States, Cowgill writes:

> Programs for the aged are many, varied and increasing. These include income maintenance programs, programs concerned with residence and living arrangements, educational and vocational programs, recreational and social programs, health and medical programs, and religious programs.
>
> The Federal Social Security Act provides for an Old Age Assistance program with the Federal Government providing, out of general tax funds, grants-in-aid to the states for assistance to needy old people. (1972:248)

In spite of these many programs, there is also an emphasis on social and financial independence, and there is definitely not a pattern of family support of elderly in the United States. In fact, says Cowgill, "As far as financial assistance is concerned, the flow is definitely from parents to children, although of course this varies with social classes" (1972:254).

8. *The proportion of aged who retain leadership roles in modern societies is lower than in preindustrial ones.* Vance Packard, whose book *The Pyramid Climbers* represents an analysis of American business leadership, maintains that "the management positions of a great many companies—and their recruiting consultants, take age very much into consideration in filling openings and weighing a man's future" (1962:212). He further states that most large companies pick men no older than 55 to fill their more important executive positions and he calculates that the age is even lower in Great Britain.

In modern societies, few people manage to retain leadership roles into old age. A few judges, owners of industrial or commercial businesses, and a handful of lawyers and physicians often manage to maintain their positions of authority and continue to command the respect of younger colleagues well into old age, but most elderly are subject to a great amount of prejudice and pressure to turn over leadership roles, and most are subject to mandatory retirement regulations.

On the other hand, among the Dusun of Borneo headmen are drawn from among the elderly and can never be removed or recalled; they remain in authority until they die or voluntarily retire (T. R. Williams, 1965). Charles Fuller maintains that the control of social organization in Bantu society has consistently been in the hands of elders. Old men have traditionally occupied positions with varying amounts of authority from lineage heads to tribal chiefs, but they have also held positions of leadership as judges, priests, teachers, and historians. Fuller writes:

> The most significant roles . . . are roles attained only at the more advanced years . . . . Almost every elder in most Bantu tribes . . . has a respected role as a wise counsellor. (1972:67)

The Hutterites, a North American subculture famous for its rejection of modernization, place great importance on age as a criterion for leadership. The oldest men occupy executive posts and serve as members of the village council. Elderly also hold leadership positions such as department heads for their various economic enterprises, and there is a general pattern of progress to higher and higher status positions as one grows older (Hostetler and Huntington, 1967).

9. *Religious leadership is more likely to be a continuing role of the aged in preindustrial than in modern societies.* Gerontologists disagree on whether or not people turn more to religion as they reach the end of their lives, but they do seem to agree that elders in preindustrial societies have a greater tendency to function in religious leadership roles than in modern societies. Ethnographers tell us that the majority of shamans among the Eskimo are old and that elderly West Africans are believed to have great power in dealing with spirits because they are "almost ancestors," but there is little evidence that it is appropriate for elders in America to play any kind of significant role in religious leadership. In fact, the first professional group to have mandatory retirement imposed upon them in America was New England ministers. Although many protestant churches have a group of congregation officers called "elders," such positions are rarely occupied by people over 40 or 50 years of age. Church congregations are more concerned with recruiting youth than recruiting the elderly, and youth ministries and youthful ministers abound.

A comparison of two religious groups with common doctrinal origins illustrates the point: the Amish maintain a leadership largely of elderly men and are renowned for their deliberate rejection of modernization. The Mennonites of America (Roth, 1981), on the other hand, have developed a youthful leadership and have openly and unashamedly adopted modernization.

Where ceremonialism and ritual are important, it is not uncommon for the elderly to be caretakers of procedure and protocol, but religion in modern societies has largely dispensed with ceremonialism and ritual, leaving little opportunity for participation or leadership by elders.

10. *Retirement is a modern invention found only in modernized high-productivity societies.* Preindustrial societies have less need for modifying and abandoning roles in old age than modern society, where retirement from economically productive roles has become expected. Advanced age in traditional societies often necessitates a shift from one kind of productive role to another—e.g., from the role of hunter to religious practitioner or from warrior to counsellor—but the role shift usually involves an increase in prestige and authority rather than a reduction in status. The role shifts in tribal societies are also more easily accomplished because there is often a traditional pattern of role shifts as in the case of formal age-grading systems.

In modern societies there "are no automatic roles awaiting many members of the society who must build new lives through their own efforts" (Lopata, 1972:276). Role shifts must be worked out by the individual with no help from the society. There are no rules and very little precedent for extending productivity after the age of formal retirement. Although traditional societies make provision for shifts to less strenuous but not necessarily less important or less honorific roles, modern society offers elders no role at all. Even when elders in traditional societies perform the same roles relegated to old people in modern society we find that they are valued in very different ways. Such menial tasks as housekeeping or babysitting are often viewed in preindustrial societies as vital social functions and activities that bring honor and respect. The role-adjustment problem particularly affects men in modern societies who must make the transition from respected work activities to purposeless inactivity, while women, particularly housewives, continue domestic roles well into old age.

In developing societies such as Samoa or Thailand there is today the concept of retiring at age 60 or 65 because a few people are now employed in civil service occupations and in modern commercial and industrial firms. However, in the rural areas of these societies where traditional occupations and subsistence economic activities prevail,

> retirement as a formal process is not common; instead there is only a gradual process of withdrawal from an occupation. Life in old age tends to be a continuation of living within a family context . . . . There are always useful things to do and old people are certainly not inactive. One of the types of activities that actually increases in the later years is religious activities. For the most part, the transition from middle age to old age is smooth and graceful, and older persons in this society usually are supported by a respectful and helpful circle of relatives and friends, stimulated and enlivened by continuing useful social roles, and comforted and encouraged by a religion which promises continuity of life. (Cowgill, 1972:100-101)

SALIENT ASPECTS OF MODERNIZATION

Having established in *Aging and Modernization* (1972) that there is a tendency for the status of the aged to decline when a society's degree of modernization increases, Cowgill next (1974) began an inquiry into the factors that cause such a phenomenon. Cowgill's theory is that certain aspects of modernization are more important than others in creating a sociological environment that places the elderly at a disadvantage. These aspects are (1) the application of modern technology in the fields of health and economics, (2) urbanization, and (3) education. The situation, which Cowgill has carefully described and diagrammed (Figure 9.1) can be described as follows:

Modernization invariably brings improvements in health and economic technology. Improvements in sanitation, medical diagnostic skills, and preventive and therapeutic medicine profoundly change the vital statistics of a population. Medical advances most noticeably affect infant and child mortality, but they also prolong life for everyone. Therefore, life-expectancy figures increase and life spans are generally lengthened. Mead suggests, however, that these life-extending medical advances may be a mixed blessing for the elderly, because before the advent of Western medicine they were

Figure 9.1. Cowgill's revised theory of the effect of modernization on the aged. (From Cowgill, Donald, "Aging and Modernization: Revision of the Theory," in Gubrium, J.F. (ed), *Late Life*, Springfield, Ill.: Charles C Thomas, 1974. Used by permission of the publisher.)

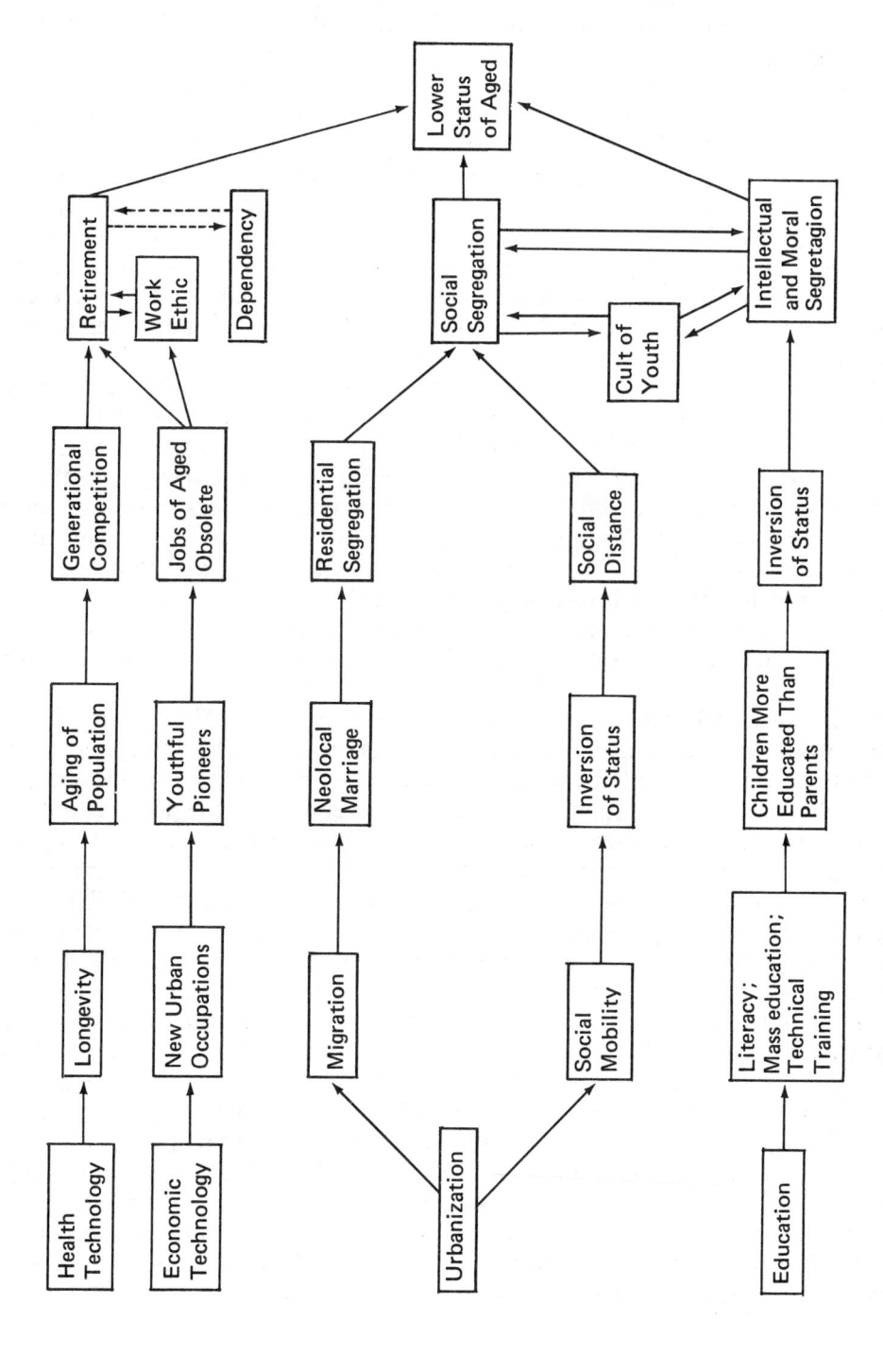

revered for their own resources for surviving while today they may be perceived as being kept alive by modern medicine. The smallness of their numbers in traditional societies automatically seemed to render them objects of admiration. Mead believes that in modern society "we are now developing a generation which is over-burdened with the care of old people who no longer have any relationship to the rest of the world, who are using up family funds, hospital beds, and social resources" (1967:36). She points out that old people in preindustrial societies are vigorous, active, and interesting people, and because of this, children in these societies have a positive attitude toward the elderly. Children in modern societies, on the other hand, often have very different experiences. Many of the aged they have observed have been reduced almost to a vegetable stage, kept alive by drugs and nursing homes. Understandably, then, children in modern societies perceive old age as a horror to be put out of their minds as long as possible.

Medical technology has not only brought more effective ways of curing disease and prolonging life, but it also has developed contraceptive devices that have made family planning possible. In time, a combination of longer life spans and a reduction in the birthrate will result in a "graying" effect in the population with the consequence that a considerable proportion of individuals will be in the productive work period of their lives. With greater numbers of working-age individuals in the society, fewer openings in the labor force will result, and there will be greater and greater competition between the older workers who hold the jobs and the younger workers who would like to take them over. Since medical science increases life expectancy, there will be social pressure from aggressive young people to open up the job market by substituting *retirement* for death.

Modern economic technology also changes the work situation. New technical processes result in the creation of new jobs and changes in old ones. The younger workers with their technologically oriented educations tend to be attracted to the new occupations, while older workers make minimal adjustments to cope with the new technology or attempt to carry on in the more traditional roles as long as possible. The steady reduction of traditional roles, however, represents still another pressure for retirement.

Since the new technology makes industrial expansion possible, there will be an increase in profits. The young pioneers in the new technology are well rewarded materially and psychologically for their productive efforts. The modernizing society reveres efficiency and evolves a work ethic that values work as the chief role in life and an important end in itself. In the case of America's modern development, this ethic has taken on the complexion of the Protestant ethic, which links Christianity and capitalism and interprets the material wealth of captains of modern industry as evidence of God's reward for diligent work. These ideas intensify the conflict and competition between generations and greatly affect the attitudes toward retired workers. At retirement the sudden and drastic reduction in material, psychological, and spiritual rewards is demoralizing. Since modern work-ethic societies commonly equate unemployment with sloth and failure, the retirement forced by competition for jobs is accompanied by a sense of dissatisfaction and depression. There is, therefore, a loss of both income and prestige and a dilemma concerning what one's role should consist of after one's work life is completed.

Attracted by the promise of high pay and prestigious positions that the new technology and economics produce, young people in modernizing societies flock to the cities. The young migrants come singly or as nuclear families, and their emigration has a decided effect on the social structure of the communities they leave. Extended-family units are weakened in the rural areas while in the city the emphasis is increasingly toward independent biological families. The rural areas have always been strongholds of traditional culture, with elders not only in control of property but of knowledge and prestige as well. In the city the young escape the control of the elders and begin to question their authority and priorities. Rowe (1961) relates that in India when young men return home from the cities where they have been employed they are impatient with the slow pace of life and outmoded procedures. The wealth they bring back disturbs the traditional association of affluence and old age. Similarly, Arth (1968) reports that among the Ibo of Nigeria young men can now acquire independent wealth from wage work in the cities and no longer have to depend on their fathers for bride price. All of this results in an inversion of status, which puts the young in roles of authority and leadership. As the young Ibos increase their participation and domination of the life-style of the city even the older urban residents will come to understand that old ideas are of less value than new ideas, old jobs are less lucrative than new, and old roles are less prestigious than new.

The elderly in the city do not have the same emotional support as the elderly in more traditional areas since the cross-generational kin networks are replaced by peer groups. In general, "cities are settled by young refugees liberated from the stifling control exercised in the small community by old men, religious leaders and omnipresent extended family" (Gutmann, 1977:320).

Traditional societies have a much greater proportion of illiterates than modern ones, for traditional skills—hunting, herding, and horticulture—can be passed on from generation to generation by word of mouth and through informal teaching by example. Furthermore, the wisdom and practical know-how of preindustrial societies has tended to remain valid for hundreds of years with minimal modification. In such societies, the people who exercise the greatest control and enjoy the greatest respect are those who have lived the longest and have experienced the most. Since conditions have remained much the same over long periods of time these people are most effective in advising, legislating, and administrating.

Modernization renders experience in traditional lifeways of little importance, since it changes the rules, challenges values, and alters the direction in which the society moves. Oral tradition and learning by imitation are inadequate in communicating the knowledge that people must have to function in a world of rapid change, urban life, and complex technology. No longer can individual heads carry the information requisite for a modern society. Modernization demands literacy, libraries, and formal education. Not only is more technical knowledge needed to function in a modernizing society but it is needed in a hurry and in large amounts. Thus, education in such societies is mass education—formal, impersonal, and designed to cultivate skills that will be called into play at some future time. Practical education is valued over general education, and education is primarily directed at the young. Since it is they who are attracted to the new jobs and new challenges of a technologically complex world, and since it is they who will carry the burden of modernization progress, education as an avenue to success is viewed as indispensable for young people. Parents strive to provide their children with better educations than they themselves were able to acquire.

In Western Samoa (a fourth-world country new to independence and modernizing influences), Rhoads and Holmes (1981) found that the establishment of a home for the aged in this society where families had always taken extreme pride in being able to care for their aged was related to increased emphasis on education. In this relatively poor country where most families have many children and all must pay tuition for schooling, there is often just not enough money for the needs of both the elderly and school-age children. Although families want to continue their generous support of their aged, medical bills and other special expense involved in their care are often beyond family means, and therefore they have reluctantly been forced to allow their elderly to enter the home.

Since mass formal education is prerequisite to industrialization, it takes on a special value in modernizing societies. In old Samoa, chiefs were elected to titles by their extended families based on a candidate's knowledge of ceremonial protocol and traditional lore, family service, and age (one had to be at least 40 to qualify), but in modern Samoa, many chief titles are held by young men who have good educations and consequently important jobs in government or industry. Harlan (1964) also found that in traditional Indian villages education and urban work experience were more important factors in village leadership than age.

In modern societies the young are, as a group, better educated than the old. Since the value system is tipped in favor of the better educated, and since better education is required for the more lucrative and prestigious jobs, the young are in a position to question old procedures and old symbols of respect and authority. A generation gap is created and tends to widen progressively as a "youth culture" and work ethic emerge. Conflict is introduced, and since the young in these new societies command the bulk of the resources for coping with modernization, they are the inevitable winners, monetarily, psychologically, and in terms of elevated prestige.

THE FUTURE OF AGING IN AMERICA

The "graying of America" is a phrase used by gerontologists to refer to changes in the age composition that has already begun and will continue well into the future. This development is primarily a matter of internal change brought about by triumphs in medical technology and by concomitant ideas about proper standards of living, which have resulted in adjustments to the size and composition of the American family. With more people living longer and fewer babies being born, the average age of American citizens progressively creeps upward. This has a number of obvious effects. There will be, in time, less need for classrooms and school teachers, and there will be continuing problems with Social Security financing, since relatively fewer young people will be entering the labor force and larger percentages of recipients will be eligible.

The graying phenomenon will, however, have much more widespread influences. First, all kinds of senior services will be in much greater demand. The needs of the elderly will become a major item in federal, state, and local government budgets, and there will undoubtedly be greater investment on the part of the private sector in retirement residences, nursing homes, and businesses that will cater to the special recreational and health needs of old people. Attempts to trim or do away with government benefits for the aged will run into more and more opposition as the percentage of citizens nearing 65 increases.

The future will also bring new ideas about the appropriate age of retirement. Pension plans will be modified to enable people to voluntarily retire at age 55, and there will be a successful movement to raise the mandatory retirement age to 70 or possibly do away with such an age limit altogether. This will not only appeal to many workers who dread the inactivity of retirement but it will also reduce the problems associated with financing Social Security. In regard to the legal aspects of mandatory retirement, Peterson, Powell, and Robertson believe that

> The Supreme Court will declare compulsory retirement at a fixed age unconstitutional. This development will remove the fixed age or length of service requirement now found in the working environment. This prediction will be realized as legal scholars, medical practitioners, and members of the gerontological community undertake revisions in present statutory and administrative laws which have developed over time in support of mandatory retirement. (1976:267)

Some social scientists see a potential for conflict in the society of tomorrow as the emphasis on youth gives way to emphasis on maturity. Philip M. House, for example, states:

> Now that the high expectations of . . . rising generations are starting to collide with reality the stage is set for a lot of social strife. The frustration is going to be especially acute among the fast-growing minority groups such as Hispanic and blacks. (Mann, 1977:5)

In 1981 the Reagan administration went out of its way to assure the elderly that their interests would be protected from budget cuts but liberally trimmed all funds that had supported minority youth employment projects and child-care benefits and services.

The change in population profile will have some positive aspects, however. For example, there should be a great reduction in traffic accidents and crime, since young people are principal causes of both. With the percentage of teenage and younger children expected to shrink from its present figure of 34% to 27% over the next 50 years, welfare costs for dependent children should decline and perhaps some of this tax money will help finance expanding benefits for aged.

With declining numbers of young people in the society, the nation's concern with youth will also decline. Advertising will begin to be directed more and more at an older market. There will be a trend away from short-lived clothing fads and meteoric careers of entertainment personalities. The rapidly fluctuating "top-ten" list of hit songs may once again include melodies that will become standards. Much of the success in the entertainment (concert and record) business today is due to adolescent interest and spending. There will also be a drastic decline in the popularity of "junk" food and in what critics are constantly assailing as infantile television programming.

The nature of recreation will change from an emphasis on the active sports and gaudy spectator events to the more sedate pastimes of mature adults—ballroom dancing, reading, hobby crafts, steamship cruises, and nature strolls. The choice of leisure time activities will in part be affected by the rapidly rising educational level. A generation ago less than one senior citizen in five had a high school diploma, but by 1990 at least 50% will hold that credential. Elderly will also have a new attitude toward leisure. A large share of the people who are over 65 today were raised in a world where a 50-hour work week was the average, where vacations were rare and never longer than two weeks, where unemployment was looked upon as a personal failure, and where idleness was a sin. Investing time and money in leisure activities is foreign to their thinking and their value system.

The elderly of the year 2000—now employed for only 40 hours or less a week, accustomed to three- and four-week vacations and numerous three-day long weekends—will be more interested in and more comfortable with leisure. America will probably never be able to shake off its deep-seated puritanical prejudice against idleness but there is good indication that in addition to honoring the work ethic we are also beginning to honor an activity ethic, particularly if it is seen in the light of therapeutic recreation to restore the individual's mental acuity and energy level.

The more accepting attitude toward leisure activities will also be influenced by the fact that the aged in the year 2000 will (1) have more free time (many will have retired at age 55) (2) will have better health, (3) should have more money compared with today's elderly, and (4) be more convinced that elderly should stay active.

While the middle and upper classes have been the main participants in leisure activities in the past, the future will open up participation to the masses. The shift may be gradual, however, with leisure activities tending to resemble work (through interest in home workshops, do-it-yourself home projects, and practical craft skills like sewing or knitting).

Although the retired of the future may want to spend their leisure becoming better educated, the national forecasts for the future of public education in the United States are not encouraging. With the decrease in the percentage of young people in the population and with funding in state-supported secondary and higher educational institutions to a large extent based on numbers of students served, we can expect a considerable decline in the availability and quality of educational opportunities. Mann writes, "Increasingly, these institutions, long the symbol of America's vitality as a young and growing nation, are being hit by budget cuts, layoffs of younger workers, aging staffs, flagging promotions and sagging morale" (1977:56).

Old people of the future will not only be more active; they will also be better organized politically and socially than their present day counterparts. Right now, the American Association of Retired Persons has an active membership of more than 12 million men and women, and more organizations of this type will no doubt be forthcoming. Stanford University gerontologist Alex Comfort warns that "businessmen, like politicians, are going to have to start taking old people more seriously. They are going to find out that these people aren't going to be tied down by old fashioned habits and 'product loyalties' any more" (Mann, 1977:6).

The next century will see the rise of a unique age grade which has been labeled the "young-old." These will be people between the ages of 55 and 75. At the present time this group numbers about 15% of the population but it will steadily grow in size and influence. Neugarten describes this age category: "As a group, they are already markedly different from the out-moded stereotypes of old age. They are relatively free from traditional social responsibilities of work and family, they are relatively healthy, relatively well off, and they are politically active . . . . With regard to work, some will opt for early retirement; some will want to continue to work beyond 65; some will want to undertake new work careers at one or more times after age 40" (1975:8).

Another characteristic of these "young-old," often overlooked by gerontologists, is that in the year 2000 these will be the people who were between the ages of 20 and 25 during the traumatic 1960s and early 1970s. They are the people who generated and sustained the Civil Rights, Consumer, Antipollution, Women's, Anti-war, and Ecology movements, and while these people have not been heard from for some time, the idealism can undoubtedly be revived along with the protest skills. Political administrations will need to pay attention to them.

Even though the future is expected to see the growth of a highly motivated and involved "young-old" group, the "old-old" will increase in number, in activity level, and in productivity. The bulk of them will continue to live independently, but many will need supportive social services such as elderly oriented public transportation, home health service and nutrition programs, drug and grocery delivery services, and special modification of their surroundings (e.g., home elevators, high volume phone receivers, better lighted streets) to compensate for their disabilities. There will also have to be special community-sponsored programs to provide the security that will allow old people to walk the city streets in safety. The elderly will have a growing desire for independence, and, based on present interest in aging programs, society will probably provide the means to make this possible.

By the year 2000 we will see four- and five-generation families, and this will bring about great social contact between the elderly and their children and younger relatives. A woman of 65 at the turn of the century will have many more surviving progeny than a woman of that age today. Right now 80% of elderly in America live in close enough proximity to permit visits from offspring more than once a week, and since Americans are a geographically mobile people the future should bring an increase in actual contacts between young and old family members.

The future of aging in America will involve a variety of changes in both type and locations of residence. A baby boom generation has produced a demand for apartments during the 1970s and 1980s but with increasing age and affluence these same people will turn their interest more and more to acquiring more private and more traditional housing—single-family homes, purchased perhaps at exorbitant prices. Not only will there be a shift away from apartment life but there will be increased mobility of some older citizens to particular parts of the country where their final years can be spent in greater comfort. During the next 15 to 20 years we can expect a great increase in migration of senior citizens to "sun-belt" states such as Florida and Arizona, where the population of elderly has already increased approximately 45% since 1970.

Migration to sun-belt states, however, depends greatly on economic and educational factors. Bultena and Wood have shown that elderly migrants to Florida and Arizona come, to a large extent, from the upper social and economic strata of American society. The majority of aged, however, are the least likely segment of the population to migrate. In fact, they are the ones most likely to be left behind when emigration begins. At first they were overrepresented in the older rural areas when the young people moved to the cities. Then they were the ones who were left behind in the inner city when the young and middle aged moved to the suburbs. Now it is believed that in the future they will be overrepresented in the city suburbs as the young move back into renovated inner city areas where residence involves less commuting time and less expenditure for gasoline or mass-transit fees.

Numerous aspects of our value system appear to devalue and oppress the aged, but there is also an indication that the future will produce a more secure and satisfying old age for citizens of the United States in spite of spiraling inflation.

In a study of the effects of modernization on the status and welfare of the elderly in 31 modernizing (mainly Western and third world) societies, Palmore and Manton (1974) discovered that when peasant societies first begin to move toward urbanization and industrialization and when the level of literacy and education begins to rise, the status of the elderly tends to decline. However, once the society is well into modernization, its valuation and support of old people increases. This involves increases in retirement benefits, inauguration of social and health services, increases in adult education opportunity, and a reversal of policies that had formerly discriminated against the old.

Considerable evidence indicates that the United States is well into this stage of modernization and that the future will bring even greater growth of industries and cities. Such developments should be accompanied by a trend toward fewer discrepancies between the young and the old in regard to educational level, technology and life experience. As a result, there will be a basis for greater understanding and greater empathy between generations and greater insight into the problems and needs associated with old age. The last two decades in America have been ones of urban and industrial growth, and they have been ones that have seen significant growth in services for the aged. A science of gerontology has emerged during this period; public interest has increased; new agencies to aid the elderly have come into being; the specialty of geriatrics has begun to expand and attract young physicians; and politicians have become acutely conscious of the senior segment of the population and their needs. No utopia is predicted for America's elderly, but the "graying of America" combined with an educational effort to communicate what the elderly want and need, plus an aggressive senior citizen population pressing for their own rights—to respect and a comfortable life-style—should result in a future with promise for everyone.

SUMMARY

The study of change has always been an important aspect of anthropology, and this emphasis continues among those who concern themselves with the elderly in this and other cultures. It is well documented that change can greatly influence societal attitudes toward senior status and role assignment and can alter traditional practices in regard to care and treatment. This is particularly true where there have been contacts between preindustrial and modern societies. Newly acquired values and institutional procedures often undermine age-old support systems for the elderly.

The effects of modernization have been studied by Cowgill and Holmes (1972) in 14 preindustrial and industrial societies, and they contend that there is an inverse relationship between the degree of modernization and the status of the aged. Status declines are particularly noticeable where there is emphasis on personal achievement, independence, private property, and security based on individual activity.

They also discovered that even the definition of old age varies according to the degree of modernization. In more modern societies, old age is seen as beginning later in life. Since modernization has the effect of increasing the average length of life in a society, longevity has been cited as an excellent index of modernization. Modern societies have greater proportions of old people than traditional societies, but the tendency is to favor the young and the mobile. This has, in turn, led to the demise of the extended family, always a refuge for the aged. The more flexible and mobile nuclear family is compatible with an urban, industrial life-style, but it represents a movement away from kin reliance. Consequently, in modern societies there is a shift away from family responsibility for the welfare of the aged to community or state responsibility. Cowgill (1974) has also postulated that some aspects of modernization have a more detrimental effect on the elderly than others, and he specifically cites modern technology (both in industry and in medicine), urbanization, and education. A combination of these factors results in a generation gap, the development of a youth culture, obsolescence of traditional knowledge and skills, and a decline in authority and leadership of older members of the society. Modernization also introduces entirely new cultural concepts, such as retirement, which tends to deprive senior people of any meaningful, productive role.

Cultural gerontologists have also investigated the probable trends in America's future development and how they will affect tomorrow's aged. Predictions are that (1) there will be a "graying of America," that is to say, an increase in the percentage of aged in the population, and consequently, (2) there will be a greater demand for services for senior citizens, (3) youth-oriented life-styles and public tastes will become more in tune with mature interests, (4) there will be two categories of aged—the young-old (55 to 75 and still active), and the old-old (75 and over and often in need of special supportive services), (5) there will be an increase in migration to sun-belt states and a trend toward residence in single-family dwellings, and finally, (6) there will be a general improvement in America's valuation and support of older people; this development will emanate in part from a change in the attitudes of the elderly toward themselves and in part from the pressure of their political influence.

Bibliography

Ablon, J. 1964. "Relocated American Indians in the San Francisco Bay Area: Social Interaction and Indian Identity." *Human Organization* 23:296-304.

——. 1971. "Retention of Cultural Values and Differential Urban Adaptation: Samoans and American Indians in a West Coast City." *Social Forces* 49:385-393.

Abrams, A. 1951. "Friends in Old Age Homes and Housing for the Aged in Various Parts of the World." In *No Time to Grow Old*. New York State Joint Legislative Committee on Aging, 19.

Acsadi, G. and Nemeskeri, J. 1970. *History of Human Life Span and Mortality*. Budapest: Akademiai Kiado.

Adams, F. M. 1972. "The Role of Old People in Santo Tomas Mazaltepec." In D. Cowgill and L. Holmes (eds.), *Aging and Modernization*. New York: Appleton-Century-Crofts.

Aiken, L. 1978. *Later Life*. Philadelphia: W. B. Saunders Co.

Amoss, P. T. 1981. "Coast Salish Elders." In P. Amoss and S. Harrell (eds.), *Other Ways of Growing Old*. Stanford, Calif: Stanford University Press.

Amoss, P. T. and Harrell, S. 1981. *Other Ways of Growing Old, Anthropological Perspectives*. Stanford, Calif.: Stanford University Press.

Anderson, B. G. 1964. "Stress and Psychopathology Among Aged Americans: An Inquiry into the Perception of Stress." *Southwestern Journal of Anthropology* 20:190-217.

——. 1972. "Deculturation Among the Aged." *Anthropological Quarterly* 45:209-216.

Anderson, E. N., Jr. 1972. "Some Chinese Methods of Dealing with Crowding." *Urban Anthropology* 1:41-50.

Angrosino, M. V. 1976. "Anthropology and the Aged, A Preliminary Community Study." *Gerontologist* 16:174-180.

Arensberg, C. and Kimball, S. 1968. *Family and Community in Ireland*. Cambridge, Mass.: Harvard University Press.

Arensberg, C. M. and Niehoff, A. H. 1964. *Introducing Social Change*. Chicago: Aldine Publishing Company.

Arth, M. 1968. "Ideals and Behavior. A Comment on Ibo Respect Patterns." *Gerontologist* 8:242-244.

———. 1968a. "An Interdisciplinary View of the Aged in Ibo Culture." *Journal of Geriatric Psychiatry* 2:33-39.

Bailey, T. 1857. *Records of Longevity*. London: Darton and Co.

Baker, P. T. and Lieberman, L. S. 1976. *The Samoan Migrant Project*. (Unpublished Report) University Park, PA.: Human Biology Program, Pennsylvania State University.

Banik, A. E. and Taylor, R. 1960. *Hunza Land*. Long Beach, Calif.: Whitehorn Publishing Company.

Barnes, J. A. 1972. *Social Networks*. Reading, Mass.: Addison-Wesley (Module in Anthropology, 26).

Barwick, D. E. 1971. "Changes in the Aboriginal Population of Victoria, 1863-1966. In D. J. Mulvaney and J. Golson (eds.), *Aboriginal Man and Environment in Australia*. Canberra: Australian National University Press.

Bateson, G. 1950. "Cultural Ideas About Aging." In H. E. Jones (ed.), *Proceedings of a Conference Held in August 7-10, 1950 at the University of California, Berkeley*. New York: Pacific Coast Committee on Old Age Research, Social Science Research Council.

Beaubier, J. 1975. "Culture Categories and High Life Expectancy in the Paros Community, Greece." In E. S. Watts, F. E. Johnston, and G. Lasker (eds.), *Biosocial Interrelations in Population Adaptation*. The Hague: Mouton.

———. 1976. *High Life Expectancy on the Island of Paros, Greece*. New York: Philosophical Library.

———. 1980. "Biological Factors in Aging." In Christine Fry (ed.). *Aging in Culture and Society*. New York: J. F. Bergin Publishers.

de Beauvoir, S. 1972. *Coming of Age*. New York: G. P. Putnam's Sons.

———. 1972a. "The Harsh Arithmetic of Old Age in America." *Saturday Review of Society*, April 8:262-264.

Becker, E. 1973. *The Denial of Death*. New York: Free Press.

Benedict, R. 1934. *Patterns of Culture*. Boston: Houghton Mifflin.

Benedict, R. 1971. "A Profile of Indian Aged." In *Minority Aged in America*. Ann Arbor: Institute of Gerontology, University of Michigan-Wayne State University.

Benet, S. 1974. *Abkhasians, the Long-Living People of the Caucasus*. New York: Holt, Rinehart and Winston.

———. 1976. *How to Live to be 100; the Life-Style of the People of the Caucasus*. New York: Dial Press.

Berdyshev, G. D. 1968. *Ecologic and Genetic Factors of Aging and Longevity*. Leningrad: Nauka Publishing House.

Biesele, M. and Howell, N. 1981. "The Old People Give You Life; Aging Among !Kung Hunter-Gatherers." In P. Amoss and S. Harrell (eds.), *Other Ways of Growing Old*. Stanford, Calif.: Stanford University Press.

Billingsley, A. 1968. *Black Families in White America*. Englewood Cliffs, N.J.: Prentice-Hall.

Block, M. 1979. "Exiled Americans: The Plight of Indian Aged in the United States." In D. Gelfand and A. Kutzik (eds.), *Ethnicity and Aging*. New York: Springer Publishing Co.

Boissevain, J. 1969. *Hal-Farrug: A Village in Malta*. New York: Holt Rinehart and Winston.

Boyd, R. R. 1973. "Preliterate Prologues to Modern Aging Roles." In R. Boyd and C. Oakes (eds.), *Foundations of Practical Gerontology*, 2nd ed. Columbia, S.C.: University of South Carolina Press.

Boyer, E. 1980. "Health Perception in the Elderly: Its Cultural and Social Aspects." In C. Fry (ed.), *Aging in Culture and Society*. New York: J. F. Bergin Publishers.

Brass, W. 1968. *The Demography of Tropical Africa.* Princeton, N.J.: Princeton University Press.

Bronfenbrenner, U. 1977. "The American Family in Decline." *Current* 189 (January):39-47.

Brown, M. S. 1978. "A Cross-Cultural Look at Aging." *Health Values* 2 (Mar./Apr.):96-100.

Bultena, G. and Wood, V. 1969. "Normative Attitudes Toward the Aged Role Among Migrant Retirees." *Gerontologist* 9:204-208.

Burch, E. S., Jr. 1975. *Eskimo Kinsmen.* (AES Monograph) St. Paul, Minn.: West Publishing Co.

Burton, R. F. 1864. *A Mission to Gelele, King of Dahomey.* 2 vols. London: Routledge & K. Paul.

Cahn, E. (ed.). 1969. *Our Brother's Keeper: The Indian in White America.* New York: New Community Press.

Cantor, M. 1975. "Life Space and the Social Support System of the Inner City Elderly of New York." *Gerontologist* 15:23-27.

Cattell, S. H. 1962. *Health, Welfare and Social Organization in Chinatown, New York City.* New York: Community Service Society of New York.

Cheng, E. 1978. *The Elder Chinese.* San Diego, Calif.: Campanile Press.

Cherry, R. and Cherry, L. 1974. "Slowing the Clock of Age." *New York Times Magazine,* May 12:20-22, 78, 80, 82, 84, 86, 92.

Clark, J. 1956. *Hunza: Lost Kingdom of the Himalayas.* New York: Funk and Wagnalls Co.

Clark, M. 1967. "The Anthropology of Aging: A New Area for Studies of Culture and Personality." *Gerontologist* 7:55-64.

———. 1968. "The Anthropology of Aging: A New Area for Studies of Culture and Personality." In B. L. Neugarten (ed.), *Middle Age and Aging.* Chicago: University of Chicago Press.

———. 1971. "Patterns of Aging Among the Elderly Poor of the Inner City," *Gerontologist* 11:58-66.

———. 1972. "An Anthropological View of Retirement." In Frances Carp (ed.), *Retirement.* New York: Human Sciences Press.

———. 1973. "Contributions of Cultural Anthropology to the Study of the Aged." In L. Nader and T. W. Maretzki (eds.), *Cultural Illness and Health.* Washington, D. C.: American Anthropological Association (Anthropological Studies, No. 9).

Clark, M. and Anderson, B. G. 1967. *Culture and Aging.* Springfield, Ill.: Charles C Thomas, Publisher.

Cool, L. 1980. "Ethnicity and Aging: Continuity Through Change for Elderly Corsicans." In C. Fry (ed.), *Aging in Culture and Society.* New York: J. F. Bergin Publishers.

Committee on the Family. 1970. *The Case History Method in the Study of Family Process.* Vol. III, Report No. 76 (Mar.): New York Group for the Advancement of Psychiatry.

Connelly, J. R. 1980. "An Expanded Outline and Resource for Teaching a Course on the Native American Elderly." In G. A. Sherman (ed.), *Curriculum Guidelines in Minority Aging,* Pt. IV. Washington, D. C.: National Center on Black Aging.

Cowgill, D. O. 1972. "The Role and Status of the Aged in Thailand." In D. Cowgill and L. Holmes (eds.), *Aging and Modernization.* New York: Appleton-Century-Crofts.

———. 1972. "Aging in American Society." In D. Cowgill and L. Holmes (eds.), *Aging and Modernization.* New York: Appleton-Century-Crofts.

———. 1974. "Aging and Modernization: A Revision of the Theory." In J. F. Gubrium (ed.), *Late Life: Communities and Environmental Policy.* Springfield, IL: Charles C Thomas, Publisher.

———. 1974a. "The Aging of Populations and Societies." *Annals of the American Academy of Political and Social Sciences* 415:1-18.

Cowgill, D. and Holmes, L. 1972. *Aging and Modernization.* New York: Appleton-Century-Crofts.

Crandall, R. C. 1980. *Gerontology: A Behavioral Science Approach.* Reading, Mass.: Addison-Wesley Co.

Crane, J. G. and Angrosino, M. V. 1974. *Field Projects in Anthropology: A Student Handbook.* Morristown, N.J.: Central Learning Press.

Crawford, M. 1978. "Focus." *Gerontology Review* 1:1.

Crawford, M. H. and Oberdieck, L. 1978. "Aging, Longevity and Genetics." *Dialogue* (Kansas Journal of Health Concerns) 4:37-40.

Cuellar, J. B. 1978. "El Senior Citizens Club." In B. Myerhoff and A. Simic (eds.), *Life's Career–Aging.* Beverly Hills, Calif.: Sage Publications.

———. 1980. *Minority Elderly American, A Prototype for Area Agencies on Aging.* San Diego, Calif.: Applied Home Health Association.

Cumming, E. and Henry, W. E. 1961. *Growing Old, The Process of Disengagement.* New York: Basic Books.

Cutler, N. E. 1977. "The Aging Population and Social Policy." In R. Davis (ed.), *Aging: Prospects and Issues.* University Park: University of Southern California.

Cutler, R. G. 1975. "Evolution of Human Longevity and the Genetic Complexity Governing Aging Rate." *Proceedings of the National Academy of Science U.S.A.* 72:4664-4668.

———. 1978. *Frontiers of Aging Research: Biological Aspects.* In press. Switzerland: Elsevier Dequoro.

———. 1978a. "Evolutionary Biology of Senescence." In J. Behnke, C. Finch and G. Moment (eds.), *The Biology of Aging.* New York: Plenum Press.

Dart, R. A. 1957. *The Osteodonto Keratic Culture of Australopithecus Africanus.* Transvaal Museum Memoir No. 10.

Davies, D. 1975. *The Centenarians of the Andes.* Garden City, N.Y.: Anchor Press/Doubleday.

Davis, D. L. 1971. "Growing Old Black." In *The Multiple Hazards of Age and Race.* U.S. Senate Special Committee on Aging, Sept. 1971. Washington, D. C.: U.S. Government Printing Office.

Douglass, F. 1855. *My Bondage and My Freedom.* New York: Miller, Orton and Mulligan.

Dozier, E. P. 1971. "The American Southwest." In E. Leacock and N. Lurie (eds.), *North American Indians in Historical Perspective.* New York: Random House.

Driver, H. 1969. *Indians of North America,* 2nd ed. Chicago: University of Chicago Press.

Dukepoo, F. 1980. *The Elder American Indian.* San Diego, Calif.: Campanile Press.

Eisenstadt, S. N. 1956. *From Generation to Generation.* Glencoe, Ill.: Free Press.

Ellis, A. B. 1887. *The Tshi-Speaking Peoples of the Gold Coast of West Africa.* London: Chapman and Hall.

Ellis, G. W. 1914. *Negro Culture in West Africa.* New York: Neale Publishing Co.

Encyclopedia of Japan. 1982. "Old Age and Retirement." Tokyo: Kodansha, Ltd.

Eribes, R. A. and Bradley-Rawls, M. 1978. "The Underutilization of Nursing Home Facilities by Mexican-American Elderly in the Southwest. *Gerontologist* 18:363-371.

Ericksen, M. F. 1976. "Cortical Bone Loss with Age in Three Native American Populations." *American Journal of Physical Anthropology* 45:443-452.

———. 1976a. "Some Aspects of Aging in the Lumbar Spine." *American Journal of Physical Anthropology* 45:575-580.

Evans, F. G. 1977. "Age Changes in Mechanical Properties and Histology of Human Compact Bone." *Yearbook of Physical Anthropology,* Vol. 20 (1976). Washington, D. C.: American Association of Physical Anthropologists.

Feagin, J. R. 1968. "The Kinship Ties of Negro Urbanities." *Social Science Quarterly* 49:660-665.

Firth, R. 1958. *Human Types.* New York: Mentor Books.

Fischer, D. 1978. *Growing Old in America.* Oxford: Oxford University Press.

Flornoy, B. 1958. *The World of the Inca.* Garden City, N.Y.: Doubleday/Anchor Books.

Foster, G. 1965. "Peasant Society and the Image of Limited Good." *American Anthropologist* 67:298-318.

Frazier, E. F. 1939. *The Negro Family in the United States.* Chicago: University of Chicago Press.

———. 1959. "The Negro Family in America." In R. N. Anshen (ed.), *The Family: Its Function and Destiny.* New York: Harper and Row.

Freuchen, P. 1961. *Book of the Eskimos.* Greenwich, Conn.: Fawcett Crest Book.

Frolkis. V. V. 1973. "Mechanisms of Longevity." In D. F. Chebotarev (ed.), *Gerontology and Geratrics 1972 Year Book: Longevous People.* Kiev: Institute of Gerontology.

Fromm, E. 1962. "Alienation Under Capitalism." In E. Josephson and M. Josephson (eds.), *Man Alone.* New York: Dell Publications.

Fry, C. L. 1980. "Cultural Dimensions of Age: A Multidimensional Scaling Analysis." In C. L. Fry (ed.), *Aging in Culture and Society.* New York: J. F. Bergin Publishers.

———. 1981. *Dimensions: Aging, Culture and Health.* New York: J. F. Bergin Publishers.

Fry, C. L. and Keith, J. (eds.). 1980. *New Methods for Old Age Research.* Chicago: Loyola University, Center for Urban Policy.

Fujii, S. M. 1976. "Elderly Asian Americans and Use of Public Services." *Social Casework* 57:202-207.

Fuller, C. E. 1972. "Aging Among Southern African Bantu." In D. Cowgill and L. Holmes (eds.), *Aging and Modernization.* New York: Appleton-Century-Crofts.

Galston, A. W. 1975. "In Search of the Antiaging Cocktail." *Natural History,* (Mar.):14-19.

Ganschow, T. W. 1978. "The Aged in a Revolutionary Milieu: China." In S. Spicker, K. Woodward, and D. Van Tassel (eds.), *Aging and the Elderly: Humanistic Perspectives in Gerontology.* Atlantic Highlands, N.J.: Humanities Press.

Garn, S. 1975. "Bone-Loss and Aging." In R. Goldman and M. Rockstein (eds.), *The Physiology and Pathology of Human Aging.* New York: Academic Press.

Gide, A. 1931. *The Counterfeiters.* New York: Modern Library.

Gillimore, R., Boggs, J. W., and Jordan, C. 1974. *Culture, Behavior and Education, a Study of Hawaiian Americans.* Beverly Hills, Calif.: Sage Publications.

Glascock, A. P. and Feinman, S. L. 1980. "Toward a Comparative Framework: Propositions Concerning the Treatment of the Aged in non-Industrial Societies." In C. L. Fry and J. Keith (eds.), *New Methods for Old Age Research.* Chicago: Loyola University, Center for Urban Policy.

———. 1980a. "A Holocultural Analysis of Old Age." *Comparative Social Research,* No. 3.

Glazer, N. and Moynihan, D. P. 1963. *Beyond the Melting Pot.* Cambridge, Mass.: M.I.T. Press and Harvard University Press.

Goldman, R. and Rockstein, M. 1975. *The Physiology and Pathology of Human Aging.* New York: Academic Press.

Goldschmidt, W. 1954. *Ways of Mankind.* Boston: Beacon Press.

Goody, J. 1976. "Aging in Nonindustrial Societies." In R. H. Binstock and E. Shanas (eds.), *Handbook of Aging and the Social Sciences.* New York: Van Nostrand Reinhold.

Gorer, G. 1967. "The Pornography of Death." In G. Gorer, *Death, Grief and Mourning.* New York: Doubleday.

Gots, D. E. 1977. "The Long Life Diet." *Family Circle* 90(9):14, 20, 166, 168, 170.

Graburn, N. H. H. 1969. *Eskimos Without Igloos.* Boston: Little, Brown and Company.

Grattan, F. J. H. 1948. *An Introduction to Samoan Custom.* Apia, Samoa: Samoa Printing and Publishing Company.

Gutmann, D. L. 1964. "An Exploration of Ego Configurations in Middle and Late Life." In B. L. Neugarten (ed.), *Personality in Middle and Late Life.* New York: Atherton Press.

———. 1976. "Alternatives to Disengagement: The Old Men of the Highland Druze." In J. Gubrium (ed.), *Time, Roles and Self in Old Age.* New York: Human Science Press.

———. 1977. "The Cross-Cultural Perspective." In J. E. Birren and K. W. Schaie (eds.), *Handbook of the Psychology of Aging.* New York: Van Nostrand Reinhold.

Halsell, G. 1975. "The Viejos." *Human Behavior,* (Oct.):25-29.

———. 1976. *Los Viejos, Secrets of Long Life from the Sacred Valley.* Emmaus, Penn.: Rodale Press.

Harlan, W. H. 1964. "Social Status of the Aged in Three Indian Villages." *Vita Humane* 7:239-252.

Harrell, S. 1981. "Growing Old in Rural Taiwan." In P. Amoss and S. Harrell (eds.), *Other Ways of Growing Old.* Stanford, Calif.: Stanford University Press.

Hays, W. C. and Mindel, C. H. 1973. "Extended Kinship Relations in Black and White Families." *Journal of Marriage and the Family* 35:51-57.

Hendricks, J. and Hendricks, C. D. 1977. *Aging in Mass Society.* Cambridge, Mass.: Winthrop.

Henry, J. 1963. *Culture Against Man.* New York: Vintage Books.

Hentoff, N. 1966. "The Other Side of the Blues." In H. Hill (ed.), *Anger and Beyond: The Negro Writer in the United States.* New York: Harper and Row.

Herskovits, M. J. 1938. *Dahomey,* Vol. I. New York: J. J. Augustin.

———. 1941. *Myth of the Negro Past.* New York: Harper and Brothers.

———. 1949. *Man and His Works.* New York: Alfred A. Knopf.

———. 1967. *The Backgrounds of African Art.* New York: Biblo and Tannen.

Himes, J. H. and Mueller, W. H. 1977. "Aging and Secular Change in Adult Stature in Rural Colombia." *American Journal of Physical Anthropology* 46:275-280.

Hochschild, A. R. 1973. *The Unexpected Community.* Berkeley: University of California Press.

Hollis, A. C. 1909. *The Nandi.* Oxford: Clarendon Press.

Holmes, L. D. 1958. *Ta'u: Stability and Change in a Samoan Village.* Reprint No. 7. Wellington New Zealand: Polynesian Society.

———. 1967. *The Story of Samoa.* Cincinnati: McCormick-Mather.

———. 1972. "The Role and Status of the Aged in a Changing Samoa." In D. Cowgill and L. Holmes (eds.), *Aging and Modernization.* New York: Appleton-Century-Crofts.

———. 1979. "The Aging Jazz Musician: Creativity and Adaptability." Paper presented at the American Anthropological Association Annual Meetings, Cincinnati.

Holmes, L. D. and Parris, W. 1981. *Anthropology: An Introduction.* New York: John Wiley and Sons.

Hostetler, J. A. and Huntington, G. E. 1967. *The Hutterites in North America.* New York: Holt, Rinehart and Winston.

Howell, S. C. and Loeb, M. B. 1969. "Culture, Myths, and Food Preferences Among Aged." *Gerontologist* 9:31-37.

Hrachovec, J. P. 1969. "Aging Research—Coming of Age." *Industrial Research,* (Sept.):78-80.

Hsu, F. 1953. *Americans and Chinese: Two Ways of Life.* New York: Schuman.

———. 1961. "American Core Values and National Character." In F. Hsu (ed.), *Psychological Anthropology*. Cambridge Mass.: Schenkman Publishing Co.

———. 1969. *The Study of Literate Civilizations*. New York: Holt, Rinehart and Winston.

———. 1971. "Filial Piety in Japan and China: Borrowing, Variation and Significance." *Journal of Comparative Family Studies*, Spring:67-74.

Hughes, C. C. 1960. *An Eskimo Village in the Modern World*. Ithaca, N.Y.: Cornell University Press.

Huntington, R. and Metcalf, P. 1979. *Celebrations of Death*. New York: Cambridge University Press.

Ikels, C. 1980. "The Coming of Age in Chinese Society: Traditional Patterns and Contemporary Hong Kong." In C. Fry (ed.), *Aging in Culture and Society*. New York: J. F. Bergin Publishers.

Ishikawa, W. 1978. *The Elder Samoan*. San Diego, Calif.: Campanile Press.

———. 1978a. *The Elder Guamanian*. San Diego, Calif.: Campanile Press.

Ishizuka, K. C. 1978. *The Elder Japanese*. San Diego, Calif.: Campanile Press.

Jacobs, J. 1974. *Fun City*. New York: Holt, Rinehart and Winston.

———. 1974a. "An Ethnographic Study of a Retirement Setting." *Gerontologist* 14:483-487.

———. 1975. *Old Persons and Retirement Communities*. Springfield, Ill.: Charles C Thomas Publisher.

Jalavisto, E. 1951. "Inheritance of Longevity According to Finnish and Swedish Genealogies." *Annals Medical Internal, Fenniae* 40:163-274.

Jeffers, F. C. and Verwoerdt, R. 1977. "How the Old Face Death." In E. Busse and E. Pfeiffer (eds.), *Behavior and Adaptation in Late Life*. Boston: Little, Brown and Co.

Jeffries, W. R. 1972. "Our Aged Indians." In *Triple Jeopardy—Myth or Reality*. Washington, D.C.: National Council on the Aging, April.

Johnson, C. S. 1934. *Shadow of the Plantation*. Chicago: University of Chicago Press.

Jones, F. C. 1973. "The Lofty Role of the Black Grandmother." *The Crisis* 80:19-21.

Jones, K. and Wellin, E. 1980. "Dependence and Reciprocity: Home Health Aid in an Elderly Population." In C. Fry (ed.), *Aging in Culture and Society*. New York: J. F. Bergin Publishers.

Josephson, E. and Josephson, M. 1962. *Man Alone*. New York: Dell Publications.

Josephy, A. Jr. 1976. *The Indian Heritage of America*. New York: Bantam Books.

Jurmain, R. D. 1977. "Stress and the Etiology of Osteoarthritis." *American Journal of Physical Anthropology* 46:353-365.

Kagan, D. 1980. "Activity and Aging in a Colombian Peasant Village." In C. Fry (ed.), *Aging in Culture and Society*. New York: J. F. Bergin Publishers.

Kahn, C. 1979. "What Really Happens When we Get Old?" *Family Health*, (Sept.):20-24, 44, 57.

———. 1979a. "Why We Age: The Toughest Puzzle of All." *Family Health*, (Oct.):42-45, 56.

———. 1979b. "Forever Young?" *Family Health*, (Nov.):50-54.

Kallmann, F. J. and Sander, H. 1948. "Twin Studies on Aging and Longevity." *Journal of Heredity* 39:349-356.

Kastenbaum, R. and Aisenberg, R. 1972. *The Psychology of Death*. New York: Springer Publishing Co.

Katz, S. H. 1978. "Anthropological Perspectives on Aging." *Annals of the American Academy* 438(July):2-12.

Keesing, F. 1953. *Cultural Dynamics and Administrative Proceedings*. Auckland, New Zealand: Seventh Pacific Science Congress.

Keith, J. (ed.). 1979. "The Ethnography of Old Age." *Anthropological Quarterly* 52(1).

———. 1980. "Old Age and Community Creation." In C. Fry (ed.), *Aging in Culture and Society.* New York: J. F. Bergin Publishers.

———. 1980a. "The Best is Yet to Be: Toward an Anthropology of Age." In B. Siegel (ed.), *Annual Review of Anthropology,* Vol. 9. Palo Alto, Calif.: Annual Reviews.

———. 1982. *Old People as People.* Boston: Little, Brown and Co.

Kerns, V. 1980. "Aging and Mutual Support Relations Among the Black Carib." In C. Fry (ed.), *Aging in Culture and Society.* New York: J. F. Bergin Publishers.

Kiefer, C. W. 1971. "Notes on Anthropology and the Minority Elderly." *Gerontologist* 11:94-98.

———. 1974. *Changing Cultures, Changing Lives.* San Francisco: Jossey-Bass Publishers.

Kimball, S. T. 1946. "Review of Leo Simmons." *The Role of the Aged in Primitive Society. American Journal of Sociology* 52:287.

Kinzer, N. S. 1974. "The Beauty Cult." *The Center Magazine* 7 (Nov./Dec.):2-9.

Kitano, H. L. 1969. *Japanese Americans: The Evolution of a Sub Culture.* Englewood Cliffs, N.J.: Prentice-Hall.

Kneller, G. F. 1965. *Educational Anthropology.* New York: John Wiley and Sons.

Koty, J. 1933. *Die Behandlung der Alten und Kranken bei den Naturvölkern.* Stuttgart: W. Kohlhammer.

Kroeber, A. L. 1948. *Anthropology.* New York: Harcourt, Brace and World, Inc.

Kroeber, T. 1961. *Ishi in Two Worlds; a Biography of the Last Wild Indian in North America.* Berkeley: University of California.

Lambing, M. L. B. 1971. "A Study of Retired Older Negroes in an Urban Setting." Ph.D. dissertation, University of Michigan. Ann Arbor, Mich.: Dissertation Abstracts #71-12759.

Landor, A. H. S. 1893. *Alone with the Hairy Ainu.* London: J. Murray.

Lawton, M. P. 1978. "Leisure Activities for the Aged." *Annals of the American Association of Political and Social Science,* (Jul.):71-80.

Leaf, A. 1973. "Every Day is a Gift When You Are Over 100." *National Geographic* 143 (Jan.):93-119;

———. 1973a. "Getting Old." *Scientific American,* (Sept.):291-299.

———. 1975. *Youth in Old Age.* New York: McGraw-Hill.

Lebon, J. H. G. 1952. *An Introduction to Human Geography.* London: Hutchinson.

Legesse, A. 1979. "Age Sets and Retirement Communities." In J. Keith (ed.), *The Ethnography of Old Age.* Special Issue of *Anthropological Quarterly* 52(1).

Lehman, H. 1953. *Age and Achievement.* Princeton, N.J.: Princeton University Press.

Leonard, O. E. 1967. "The Older Rural Spanish-Speaking People of the Southwest." In E. G. Youmans (ed.), *Older Rural Americans: A Sociological Perspective.* Lexington: University of Kentucky Press.

Levkoff, S., Pratt, C., Esperanza, R., et al. 1979. *Minority Elderly: A Historical and Cultural Perspective.* Corvallis: Oregon State University.

Levy, J. E. 1967. "The Older American Indian." In E. G. Youmans (ed.), *Older Rural Americans.* Lexington: University of Kentucky Press.

Little, V. 1979. "Open Care for the Aging: Alternative Approaches." *Aging* (Nov./Dec.): 10-23.

Lopata, H. Z. 1972. "Role Changes in Widowhood: A World Perspective." In D. Cowgill and L. Holmes (eds.), *Aging and Modernization.* New York: Appleton-Century-Crofts.

Lorge, I. 1963. "The Adult Learner." In W. C. Hallenbeck (ed.), *Psychology of Adults.* Washington, D. C.: Adult Education Association of the U.S.A.

Lozier, J. and Althouse, R. 1975. "Retirement to the Porch in Rural Appalachia." *International Journal of Aging and Human Development* 6:7-16.

McKain, W. C. 1972. "The Aged in the U.S.S.R." In D. Cowgill and L. Holmes (eds.), *Aging and Modernization.* New York: Appleton-Century-Crofts.

McKinley, K. R. 1971. "Survivorship in Gracile and Robust Australopithecines: A Demographic Comparison and a Proposed Birth Model." *American Journal of Physical Anthropology* 34:417-426.

Maduro. R. 1974. "Artistic Creativity and Aging in India." *International Journal of Aging and Human Development* 5:303-329.

Mainliner Staff. 1977. "Creativity." *Mainliner,* (Jul.):25-31.

Maldonado, D., Jr. 1975. "The Chicano Aged." *Social Work,* (May):213-216.

———. 1979. "Aging in the Chicano Context." In D. E. Gelfand and A. J. Kutzik (eds.), *Ethnicity and Aging.* New York: Springer Publishing Co.

Mann, A. E. 1968. "The Paleodemography of Australopithecus." Ph.D. dissertation, University of California, Berkeley.

Mann, J. 1977. "End of Youth Culture." *U.S. News and World Report,* (Oct.) 3:54-56.

Martin, P. 1976. "The Old Men and Women of the Mountains." *Parade,* (Apr.) 4:10, 12.

Matula, L. 1969. Testimony, U.S. Senate Hearing in San Antonio.

Maxwell, J. A. (ed.). 1978. *America's Fascinating Indian Heritage.* Pleasantville, N.Y.: Readers Digest Association.

Maxwell, R., Bader, J. E., and Watson, W. 1972. "Territory and Self in a Geriatric Setting." *Gerontologist* 12:413-417.

Maxwell, R. J. and Silverman, P. 1970. "Information and Esteem: Cultural Considerations in the Treatment of the Aged." *Aging and Human Development* 1:361-392.

Mazess, R. and Forman, S. H. 1979. "Longevity and Age Exaggeration in Vilcabamba, Ecuador." *Journal of Gerontology* 34:94-98.

Mead, M. 1928. *Coming of Age in Samoa.* New York: William Morrow and Co.

———. 1937. *Cooperation and Competition Among Primitive Peoples.* New York: McGraw-Hill.

———. 1951. "Cultural Contexts of Aging." In *No Time To Grow Old.* Albany, N.Y.: Legislative Committee on the Problems of Aging, Legislative Document No. 12.

———. 1967. "Ethnological Aspects of Aging." *Psychosomatics* 8 (July./Aug.):33-37.

———. 1971. "A New Style of Aging." *Christianity and Crisis* 31:240-243.

Medawar, P. B. 1957. *The Uniqueness of the Individual.* London: Methuen and Co.

Medvedev. Z. A. 1974. "Caucasus and Altay Longevity: A Biological or Social Problem?" *Gerontologist,* 14:381-387.

Melnick, N. 1975. "You Don't Have to Grow Old Before Your Time." *Mainliner,* Jan.:24-26.

Messer, M. 1968. "Race Differences in Selected Attitudinal Dimensions of the Elderly." *Gerontologist* 8:245-249.

Miall, W. E., Ashcroft, M. T., Lovell, H. G., and Moore, F. 1967. "A Longitudinal Study of the Decline of Adult Height with Age in Two Welsh Communities." *Human Biology* 39:445-454.

Mintz, S. W. and Price, R. 1976. *An Anthropological Approach to the Afro-American Past.* Philadelphia: Occasional Papers, Institute for the Study of Human Issues.

Montoye, H. J. 1975. *Physical Activity and Health: An Epidemiologic Study of an Entire Community.* Englewood Cliffs, N.J.: Prentice-Hall.

Moore, C. D. 1979. "The Native American Family: The Urban Way." In *Families Today*. Vol. 1. Washington, D. C.: National Institute of Mental Health Science Monograph 1, U.S. Dept. of Health, Education and Welfare.

Morris, J. N., Heady, J., Raffle, P. A. B., et al: 1953. "Coronary Heart Disease and Physical Activity of Work." *Lancet* 2:1053-1057.

Munsell, M. 1972. "Functions of the Aged Among the Salt River Pima." In D. Cowgill and L. Holmes (eds.), *Aging and Modernization*. New York: Appleton-Century-Crofts.

Murdock, J. 1887-1888. "Ethnological Results of the Point Barrow Expedition." *Annual Reports of the Bureau of American Ethnology*, Vol. 9.

Murillo, N. 1971. "The Mexican American Family." In N. N. Wagner and M. J. Haug (eds.), *Chicanos: Social and Psychological Perspectives*. St. Louis: C. V. Mosby Co.

Myerhoff, B. 1978. "Aging and the Aged in Other Cultures: An Anthropological Perspective." In E. E. Bauwens (ed.), *The Anthropology of Health*. St. Louis: C. V. Mosby Co.

Myerhoff, B. and Simic, A. (eds.). 1978. *Life's Career–Aging: Cultural Variations on Growing Old*. Beverly Hills, Calif.: Sage Publications.

Nahemow, N. and Adams, B. 1974. "Old Age among the Baganda: Continuity and Change." In J. Gubrium (ed.), *Late Life: Communities and Environmental Policy*. Springfield, Ill.: Charles C Thomas, Publisher.

Nash, M. 1967. *Machine Age Maya*. Chicago: University of Chicago Press.

Nason, J. D. 1981. "Respected Elder or Old Person: Aging in a Micronesian Community." In P. Amoss and S. Harrell (eds.), *Other Ways of Growing Old*. Stanford, Calif.: Stanford University Press.

National Indian Conference on Aging. 1978. *Final Report*. Aug. Washington, D. C.

National Institute of Aging. 1978. *Final Report on the National Indian Conference on Aging*. Aug. Washington, D. C.

Neugarten, B. L. 1975. "The Future and the Young-Old." *Gerontologist,* Supplement (Feb.):4-9.

Osako, M. M. 1979. "Aging and Family Among Japanese Americans: The Role of Ethnic Tradition in the Adjustment to Old Age." *Gerontologist* 19:448-455.

Packard, V. 1962. *The Pyramid Climbers*. New York: McGraw-Hill.

Palmore, E. 1975. *The Honorable Elders*. Durham, N.C.: Duke University Press.

Palmore, E. B. and Manton, K. 1974. "Modernization and Status of the Aged: International Correlations." *Journal of Gerontology* 29:205-210.

Payne, E. H. 1954. "Islands of Immunity, Medicine's Most Amazing Mystery." *Readers Digest,* (Nov.):11-13.

Pearl, R. D. and Pearl, R. D. 1934. *The Ancestry of the Long-Lived*. London: Humphrey Milford.

Peterson, D. A., Powell, C., and Robertson, L. 1976. "Aging in America, Toward the Year 2000." *Gerontologist* 16:264-275.

Peterson, R. 1978. *The Elder Pilipino*. San Diego, Calif.: Campanile Press.

Plath, D. 1973. "Ecstasy Years-Old Age in Japan." *Pacific Affairs* 46(3):421-429.

———. 1982. "Old Age and Retirement." In *Encyclopedia of Japan*. Tokyo: Kodansha.

Pollard, L. J. 1978. "Age and Paternalism in a Slave Society." *Perspective on Aging* 7(6):4-8.

Powdermaker, H. 1936. *After Freedom*. New York: Viking Press.

Prescott, J. W. 1975. "Body Pleasure and the Origins of Violence." *The Futurist* (Apr.):64-74.

Press, I. 1967. "Maya Aging: Cross-Cultural Projective Techniques and the Dilemma of Interpretation." *Psychiatry* 30:197-202.

Press, I. and McKool, M. 1972. "Social Structure and Status of the Aged: Toward Some Valid Cross-Cultural Generalizations." *Aging and Human Development* 3:297-306.

Priest, P. N. 1966. "Provision For the Aged Among the Siriono Indians of Bolivia." *American Anthropologist* 68:1245-1247.

Quain, B. 1948. *Fijian Village.* Chicago: University of Chicago Press.

Queen, S. A. and Habenstein, R. W. 1974. *The Family in Various Cultures,* 4th ed. New York: J. B. Lippincott.

Rasmussen, K. 1908. *The People of the Polar North.* Philadelphia: J. B. Lippincott Company.

Rattray, R. S. 1923. *The Ashanti.* Oxford: Clarendon Press.

———. 1927. *Religion and Art in Ashanti.* Oxford: Clarendon Press.

Ray, P. H. 1885. *Report of the International Polar Expedition to Point Barrow, Alaska.* Washington.

Redfield, R. 1947. "The Folk Society." *American Journal of Sociology* 52:293-308.

———. 1960. *The Little Community and Peasant Society and Culture.* Chicago: University of Chicago Press.

Red Horse, J. G. 1980. "American Indian Elders; Unifiers of Indian Families." *Social Casework* 61:490-493.

Reichard, G. A. 1928. *Social Life of the Navajo Indians.* New York: Columbia University Contributions to Anthropology, 7.

Reynolds, D. K. 1971. "Japanese-American Aging: A Game Perspective." Paper presented at the Society for Applied Anthropology Meeting, Miami, Florida, April 16, 1971.

Rhoads, E. C. 1981. *Aging and Modernization in Three Samoan Communities.* Ph.D. dissertation, University of Kansas.

Rhoads, E. C. and Holmes, L. D. 1981. "Mapuifagalele, Western Samoa's Home for the Aged—a Cultural Enigma." *International Journal of Aging and Human Development* 13:121-135.

Rockstein, M. and Sussman, M. 1979. *Biology of Aging.* Belmont, Calif.: Wadsworth Publishing Co.

Rogers, C. J. and Gallion, T. E. 1978. "Characteristics of Elderly Pueblo Indians in New Mexico." *Gerontologist* 18:482-487.

Rogers, T. 1976. "Manifestations of Religiosity and the Aging Process." *Religious Education* 71:405-415.

Rose, A. M. 1965. "The Subculture of the Aging: A Framework in Social Gerontology." In A. R. Rose and W. A. Peterson (eds.), *Older People and Their Social World.* Philadelphia: F. A. Davis Co.

Rosow, I. 1965. "And Then We Were Old." *Transaction* 2(2):21-26.

Ross, J. Keith. 1977. *Old People, New Lives.* Chicago: University of Chicago Press.

Roth, D. 1981. *Aging and Modernization Among the Yoder Amish and Hesston Mennonites.* Master's thesis, Wichita State University.

Rowe, W. 1961. "The Middle and Later Years in Indian Society." In R. Kleemeier (ed.), *Aging and Leisure.* New York: Oxford University Press.

Ruffini, J. L. and Todd, H. F. 1979. "A Network Model For Leadership Development Among the Elderly." *Gerontologist* 19:158-162.

Salamon, S. and Lockhardt, V. 1979. "Land Ownership and the Position of Elderly in Farm Families." Unpublished paper presented at the annual meeting of the American Anthropological Association, Cincinnati, December 1979.

Shulz, C. M. 1980. "Age, Sex, and Death Anxiety in a Middle-Class American Community." In C. Fry (ed.), *Aging in Culture and Society*. New York: J. F. Bergin Publishers.

Shahrani, M. N. 1981. "Growing in Respect; Aging Among the Kirghiz of Afghanistan." In P. T. Amoss and S. Harrell (eds.). *Other Ways of Growing Old*. Stanford, Calif.: Stanford University Press.

Shakespeare, W. 1957. *As You Like It*. In John Munro (ed.), *The London Shakespeare*. New York: Simon and Schuster.

Sharp, H. S. 1981. "Old Age Among the Chipewyan." In P. Amoss and S. Harrell (eds.), *Other Ways of Growing Old*. Stanford, Calif.: Stanford University Press.

Sheehan, T. 1976. "Senior Esteem as a Factor of Socioeconomic Complexity." *Gerontologist* 16:433-440.

Shelton, A. J. 1965. "Aging and Eldership: Notes for Gerontologists and Others." *Gerontologist* 5:20-23.

——. 1972. "The Aged and Eldership among the Igbo." In D. Cowgill and L. Holmes (eds.), *Aging and Modernization*. New York: Appleton-Century-Crofts.

Sichinava, G. N. 1965. *On the Question of the Character and Range of Work Done by the Aged People of Abkhasia; Anthology of Papers by Physicians of Ostroumov Republican Hospital*. Sukhumi, Russia: Alashara Publishing House.

Siemaszko, M. 1980. "Kin Relations of the Aged: Possible Consequences to Social Service Planning." In C. Fry (ed.), *Aging in Culture and Society*. New York: J. F. Bergin Publishers.

Simic, A. 1977. "Aging in the United States and Yugoslavia: Contrasting Models of Intergenerational Relationships." *Anthropological Quarterly* 50:53-63.

Simic, A. and Myerhoff, B. 1978. "Conclusion." In B. Myerhoff and A. Simic (eds.), *Life's Career-Aging: Cultural Variations on Growing Old*. Beverly Hills, Calif.: Sage Publications.

Simmons, L. 1945. *The Role of the Aged in Primitive Society*. New Haven, Conn.: Yale University Press.

——. 1945. "A Prospectus for Field-Research in the Position and Treatment of the Aged in Primitive and other Societies." *American Anthropologist* 47:433-438.

——. 1959. "Aging in Modern Society." In *Toward Better Understanding of the Aging*. Seminar on the Aging, Aspen, Colorado, September 8-13, 1958. New York: Council on Social Work Education.

——. 1960. "Aging in Pre-industrial Societies." In C. Tibbits (ed.), *Handbook of Social Gerontology*. Chicago: University of Chicago Press.

——. 1962. "Aging in Primitive Societies: A Comparative Survey of Family Life and Relationship." *Law and Contemporary Problems* 27 (Winter):36-51.

Slater, P. 1970. *Pursuit of Loneliness, American Culture at the Breaking Point*. Boston: Beacon Press.

Smith, R. 1961. "Cultural Differences in the Life Cycle and the Concept of Time." In R. Kleemeier (ed.), *Aging and Leisure*. New York: Oxford University Press.

Smith, T. L. 1950. "The Aged in Rural Society." In M. Derber (ed.), *The Aged and Society*. Champaign, Ill.: Industrial Relations Research Association.

Sokolovsky, J. and Cohen, C. 1978. "The Cultural Meaning of Personal Networks for the Inner-City Elderly." *Urban Anthropology* 7:323-339.

Spencer, R. and Jennings, J. D. 1977. *The Native Americans*. New York: Harper and Row.

Stanford, E. P. 1978. *The Black Elder*. San Diego, Calif.: Campanile Press.

Stenning, D. J. 1958. "Household Viability Among the Pastoral Fulani." In J. Goody (ed.), *The Developmental Cycle in Domestic Groups*. Cambridge, Mass.: Cambridge University Press.

Stephen, A. M. 1936. *Hopi Journal of Alex Stephen.* E. C. Parsons (ed.), New York: Columbia University Contributions to Anthropology. Vol. 33.

Taylor, R. and Nobbs, M. J. 1962. *Hunza, the Himalayan Shangri-la.* El Monte, CA: Whitehorn Publishing Company.

Thomlinson, R. 1976. *Population Dynamics.* 2nd ed. New York: Random House.

TIAA Cref. 1974. "New TIAA-Cref Study Profiles Retired Educators." *The Participant* (Oct.):1-4.

Time. 1978. "High Hoax. Those Not-so-Old Ecuadorians," *Time* Mar. 27:87.

de Tocqueville, A. 1899. *Democracy in America.* 2 vols. New York: Alfred A. Knopf.

Trela, J. and Sokolovsky, J. 1979. "Culture, Ethnicity, and Policy for the Aged." In D. Gelfand and D. Fandetti (eds.), *Ethnicity and Aging.* New York: Springer Publishing.

Turner, G. 1884. *Samoa, A Hundred Years Ago and Long Before.* London: Macmillan.

Turner, L. M. 1894. "Ethnology of the Ungava District, Hudson Bay Territory." Washington, DC: *Annual Reports of the Bureau of American Ethnology.* Vol. II.

Ubelaker, D. H. 1974. Reconstruction of Demographic Profiles from Ossuary Skeletal Samples; A Case Study from the Tidewater Potomac. *Smithsonian Contributions to Anthropology,* No. 18, Washington, DC.

———. 1978. *Human Skeletal Remains.* Chicago: Aldine Publishing Co.

Underhill, R. 1953. *Red Man's America.* Chicago: University of Chicago Press.

Valle, R. and Mendoza, L. 1978. *The Elder Latino.* San Diego, Calif.: Campanile Press.

Van Stone, J. 1967. *Eskimos of the Nushagak River.* Seattle: University of Washington Press.

Vatuk, S. 1980. "Withdrawal and Disengagement as a Cultural Response to Aging in India." In C. Fry (ed.), *Aging in Culture and Society.* New York: J. F. Bergin Publishers.

Voegelin, C. F. 1941. "North American Indian Languages Still Spoken and Their Genetic Relationships." In L. Spier (ed.), *Language, Culture and Personality.* Menasha, Wisc.: Sapir Memorial Fund.

Ward, R. 1961. *Islands of the South Pacific.* London: Educational Supply Association.

Watson, W. 1971. "Aging and Race." *Social Action* 38(3):20-30.

Watson, W. and Maxwell, R. 1977. *Human Aging and Dying.* New York: St. Martin's Press.

———. 1977. "The Internal Order of a Home for the Jewish Elderly." In W. Watson and R. Maxwell (eds.), *Human Aging and Dying.* New York: St. Martin's Press.

———. 1977."Social Interaction in a Home for the Black Elderly." In W. Watson and R. Maxwell (eds.), *Human Aging and Dying.* New York: St. Martin's Press.

Wechsler, D. 1958. *The Measurement and Appraisal of Adult Intelligence.* Baltimore: Williams and Wilkins.

Weyl, N. 1977. "Survival Past the Century Mark." *Mankind Quarterly* 17:163-175.

Whiting, J. W. M. and Child, I. L. 1953. *Child Training and Personality.* New Haven, Conn.: Yale University Press.

Williams, G. C. 1966. *Adaptation and Natural Selection.* Princeton, N.J.: Princeton University Press.

Williams, Gerry C. 1980. "Warriors No More: A Study of the American Indian Elderly." In C. Fry (ed.), *Aging in Culture and Society.* New York: J. F. Bergin Publishers.

Williams, T. R. 1965. *The Dusun: A North Borneo Society.* New York: Holt, Rinehart and Winston.

Wu, F.Y.T. 1975."Mandarin-Speaking Age Chinese in the Los Angeles Area." *Gerontologist* 15:271-275.

Wylie, F. M. 1971. "Attitudes Toward Aging and The Aged Among Black Americans: Some Historical Perceptions." *Aging and Human Development* 2:66-69.

Young, B. B. C. 1980. "The Hawaiians." In J. F. McDermott, Jr., W. S. Tseng, and T. W. Maretzki (eds.), *People and Cultures of Hawaii.* Honolulu: University of Hawaii Press.

Index

Abkhasians, people and culture, 68, 69-73, 80
Ablon, Joan, quoted, 147
Abrams, Albert, 25
acculturation, 166
Adams, Bert, 14
Adams, F. M., quoted, 148, 172
Aegyptopithecus, 57
aged, as minority, 116-117
age exaggeration among Vilcabamba, 76
age grades, 23-25
    among Nandi, 23
Aging and Modernization, vii, 13, 176
aging as a career, 30
Aiken, Lewis, 68
Althouse, R., 34
American aging, history of, 104
American family system, compared to Yugoslavian, 36-37
American ceremonial life, 105
American culture, 102-111
American Indians, vii, 120, 122, 131, 140-147, 166
    cultural tendencies of, 141-142
Amish, 175
Amoss, Pamela, quoted, 122
Anderson, Barbara G., 34, 45
    quoted, 34-35
Anderson, E. N., quoted, 79
Andres, Rubin, 70

Angosino, M., 27
anthropology, defined, 1-2
    physical, 2
    scope of, 2
applied anthropology, 9, 48-51
archeology, 2
Arensberg, C., quoted, 167
Arth, Malcolm, 46, 179
Australopithecus, 57, 60

Bader, J., 49
Baganda (East Africa), 14
Baker, P. T., 159
Bateson, Gregory, quoted, 4-5
Beaubier, Jeff, quoted, 77, 81
de Beauvoir, Simone, 129
    quoted, 114-115, 116, 118, 120, 121, 124, 125
Becker, E., 47
Benedict, Ruth, 34
    quoted, 6, 142
Benet, Sula, 68
    quoted, 70
Berdyshev, G. D., 69, 73
Biesele, M., quoted, 128
Billingsley, A., 135, 139
Black-American aged, viii, 49, 134-140
    differences from whites, 135
Black Caribs, 15-16

Block, M., quoted, 142, 143-144
Boas, Franz, 1
Boggs, J. W., quoted, 162
Bojaca, Columbia, 28-29
Bradley-Rawls, Martha, 50
Brown, Marie Scott, quoted, 124
Burch, Ernest, 89
    quoted, 87, 90, 91-92
Burton, Richard F., 137

Cahn, E., quoted, 143
case study method, 4, 8-9
cell division theory of aging, 63-64
ceremonial knowledge of the aged, 121-122
Chagga (Tanzania), 30
change, 9, 13, 166-185
Cheatham, Doc, 42-43
Cheng, E., 153
Child, I., 125
Child, Julia, quoted, 42
Chinese (Taiwan), 132
Chinese-American aged, 151-154
Chinese-American family, 115-116
Chinese revolutionaries, 120
Chippewyan Indians, 131
chronological definition of aging, 27, 103
Clark, Margaret, 27, 32, 34, 44, 45
    quoted, 44, 51
Coast Salish Indians, 122
Cohen, C., 21-22
Colonel Sanders, 32, 51
Committee on the Family, 8
community, common characteristics of, 20
    factors involved in formation of, 20
    studies of, 9, 17-21
comparative perspective, 4, 5
Connelly, J. Richard, 141
Cool, Linda, 22, 40
    quoted, 22
Corsicans in Paris, 22, 40
Counterfeiters, The, 5
Cowgill, Donald, 13, 16, 27, 117, 167, 170, 176
    quoted, 170, 174, 176
Crane, J., 127
Crawford, Michael, quoted, 69, 71
creativity, 9, 41-43
    defined, 42
Cro-Magnon, 59-60

Cuellar, José, 149
culture, 4, 58
    defined, 4
Culture Against Man, 48
Cumming, E., 37
    quoted, 35
Cutler, Richard, 63
    quoted, 65

death and dying, 9, 47
deculturation, viii, 34-35
democracy and age status, 111
diachronic studies, 5
diet, 50
diffusion, 167
disengagement, 18, 35-39
Douglass, Frederick, quoted, 138

Early *Homo sapiens. See Homo sapiens,* early
ecological factors, 11
Eisenstadt, S. N., 24
emic, 4, 6-7
enculturation, 34, 58
Eribes, Richard, quoted, 50
Eskimos, viii, 7, 84-92, 175
    cultural change among, 91-92
esteem for aged, 15
Etalese (Caroline Islands), 126-127
ethnicity, 5, 39-41, 49-50
    and diet, 50
ethnocentrism, 8
ethnography, 4
ethnology, 4
etic, 4, 6-7
extended family and status of the aged, 172

Feagin, J., 140
Feinman, S., quoted, 118
filial piety, 15, 152
Firth, Raymond, quoted, 166
Fischer, David H., quoted, 2, 104, 105
Flornoy, B., quoted, 173
"The Folk Society," 18
Forman, Sylvia, quoted, 76
Foster, George, 51
Frazier, E. Franklin, quoted, 135, 139
free radicals, 64
Freuchen, Peter, quoted, 90, 91
Frolkis, V. V., quoted, 73

Fry, Christine, quoted, 28
Fulani (West Africa), 126
Fuller, Charles, quoted, 175
Fun City, 18-19, 33-34, 37-39
functional age, 27
future of aging in the United States, 180-194

Gallion, T., 145
    quoted, 146
Garn, Stanley, quoted, 46
Ganschow, Thomas, 120
generational reciprocity, 124-125
genetic master-plan theory of aging, 63-64
gerontocide
    Eskimo, 90-91
    Samoan, 99-100
gerontology, cultural, 134
Gide, André, 5
Gillimore, R., quoted, 162
Glascock, A., quoted, 118
Glazer, N., quoted, 134
Goldschmidt, Walter, 115
    quoted, 116
Goody, James, quoted, 122, 126
Gorer, Geoffrey, 47
grandmother in Black-American culture, 138
Grandparent-Teacher Associations, 50
Graburn, Nelson, 90, 91
    quoted, 89-90
Grattan, F. J. H., quoted, 97
"graying of America," 166, 184
Guamanians, 160-161
Guarneiri, John, 42
Gutmann, David, 129
    quoted, 37, 114, 119, 179

Habenstein, R., quoted, 139
Hamer, John, quoted, 129
Harlan, W., 180
Harrell, S., quoted, 132
Hawaiians, viii, 162-163
Hayflick, Leonard, 63
Hays, William, 140
Henry, Jules, quoted, 48, 49
Henry, W., 37
    quoted, 35
Hentoff, Nat, 135
hereditary factor in longevity, 65

Herskovits, M. J., 135, 138
    quoted, 136, 137
High Haven, 18
Hochschild, Arlie, 19
holistic perspective, vii, 4, 6, 8
Hollis, A. C., 23
Holmes, Lowell D., 13, 16, 27, 42, 117, 167, 169, 170
    quoted, 26, 168
homes for the aged in non-Western cultures, 25-27
Homo erectus, 59
Homo habilis, 57
Homo sapiens, early, 59
Hong Kong, 15
    noise in, 79
Hostetler, J., 175
House, P., quoted, 181
Howell, N., quoted, 128
Howell, S. C., 50
Hsu, Francis, 168
    quoted, 106-107, 152, 153
Hughes, Charles C., quoted, 86
Huntington, G., 175
Hunza society and culture, viii, 68, 73-75, 80
Hutterites, 175

Ibo culture, 45, 179
Ikels, Charlotte, 15
immune system, 65
Inca, state sponsored welfare program of, 173
Indian folk painters, 41, 42-43
information control, 12-13
Ishikawa, W., quoted, 160, 161
intergenerational conflicts, 39
Ireland, 13
Israel, 13
Issei, 39, 156

Jacobs, Jerry, 18-19, 37
    quoted, 19, 33, 39
Jalavisto, E., 65
Japanese-American aged, 154-157
jazz musicians, aged, 42
Jeffries, W. R., quoted, 143
Jeffers, F. C., 47
Jennings, J., quoted, 122
Jonas, K., 22

Jordan, C., quoted, 162
Josephson, Eric and Mary, quoted, 107
Josephy, Alvin M., 141

Keesing, Felix, 137
Keith, Jennie, quoted, 20, 21
Kagan, Dianne, 28
    quoted, 29
Kallmann, Franz, 65
Kerns, Virginia, 15
    quoted, 16
Kiefer, Christy, 39
    quoted, 155
Kimball, Solon T., 11
King Lear, 126
Kinzer, Nora Scott, quoted, 108
Kirghiz (Afghanistan), 127, 132
Kneller, George, quoted, 58
Koty, J., 11
!Kung Bushmen, 128

Lambing, Mary L. Brooks, 140
Landor, A. H. S., quoted, 125
Leaf, Alexander, 63
    quoted, 68, 70, 74, 76
Lebon, J. H. G., 102
Legesse, Asmarom, 23-24
    quoted, 23
Lehman, Harvey, 41
Leonard, O., quoted, 149
Les Floralies (French retirement home), 20-21
Levy, J., quoted, 145
Lieberman, L. S., 159
life-cycle analysis, 9, 27-30
life-cycle stages, 117-120
Life's Career - Aging, 30
life expectancy, 54
lifespan, maximum (MLP), 54
linguistics, 2
Linton, Ralph, 34
Little Community, The, 18
Lockhardt, V., 127
Loeb, M. B., 50
longevity, 9, 54-81
    cultural factors in, 79-81
    desire for, 128
    formulas for, 80
    studies of, 41
Lopata, Helen, quoted, 176
Lozier, J., 34

McKain, W., quoted, 173
McKool, Mike, 13, 171
    quoted, 172
Machine Age Maya, 168
Madura, Renaldo, quoted, 41, 42-43
Maldonado, D., quoted, 149, 150
Mann, J., quoted, 182
Manton, Kenneth, 184
    quoted, 17
Mapuifagalele (Samoan home for the aged), 25-27
Matula, L., quoted, 151
Maxwell, Robert, 12-13, 49, 121
    quoted, 172
Mazess, Richard, quoted, 76
Mead, Margaret, 34, 41, 50-51, 168, 177
    quoted, 35, 58, 59, 96-97, 178
Meals on Wheels, 7
Medawar, P. B., 64
Medvedev, Zhores, quoted, 69, 71
memory, value of, 119-121
Mende culture (West Africa), 120-121
Mendoza, L., 149
Mennonites, 175
Merrill Court, 19-20
Messer, M., 135
Mexican-American aged, 30, 50, 147-151
Mindel, C., 140
Mingus, Charles, quoted, 42
Mintz, Sidney, quoted, 138
mock funeral, Samoan, 100
modernization, 13-17, 27, 167-180
    defined, 167
    salient aspects of, 176
Montoye, H. J., 46
Moore, C., quoted, 147
Moore, Sally, 30
Morris, J. N., 70
Moynihan, D., quoted, 134
multidimensional life-cycle analysis, 28
Muni San nursing home, 48
Munsell, Marvin, 146, 172
Murdock, J., quoted, 86
Murillo, N., quoted, 150
Myerhoff, Barbara, 30, 129
    quoted, 30, 112-113, 115, 119

Nahemow, Nina, 14
Nandi age grades, 118
Nash, Manning, 168

Nason, James, quoted, 126
Native Americans. *See* American Indians
Navaho aged, 144-145
Neanderthal, 59-60, 170
network creation, 22-23
networks, 21-23
Neugarten, Bernice, quoted, 183
Niehoff, A., quoted, 167
Nisei, 39, 156

Oberdiech, L., quoted, 69
Oklahoma Indians, 120
Older Persons and Retirement Communities, 18
Oriental-American aged, 151-157
Osako, M., quoted, 154, 157
osteoarthritis, 47
osteoporosis, 46

Pacific-American aged, 157-163
Packard, Vance, quoted, 174
Page, Satchel, formula for staying young, 80
Paget's Disease, 47
paleodemography, 2
Palmore, Erdman, 17, 184
    quoted, 174
Paros, Greece, viii, 76-79
participant observation, 9
Payne, Eugene, quoted, 75
Pearl, Raymond, 65
performance, 54
personality and culture, 9
personality change in old age, 37
Peterson, R., quoted, 161, 162
Peterson, D. A., quoted, 181
phonemic analysis, 6
phonetic analysis, 6
Pilipinos, viii, 161-162
Plath, David, 154
pleiotropic damage, 64
Polish-Americans, 40
political leadership, 122-123
Pollard, L. J., 135
postulates, American, 102-103
Powdermaker, Hortense, quoted, 139
Powell, C., quoted, 181
Prescott, James, quoted, 125
Press, Irwin, 13, 171
    quoted, 172
prestige generating components, 13

Price, R., quoted, 138
Priest, Perry, quoted, 114-115
process analysis, 4, 9
productivity of aged artists, scientists, and scholars, 41
property, control of, 12, 125-128

Queen, Stuart, quoted, 139

radical scavengers, 64
Ramapithecus, 57
Rasmussen, K., quoted, 86, 89
Rattray, R. S., 137
Ray, P. H., 88
Reagan, Ronald, 32, 122
recreation in the future, 182
Redfield, Robert, 18
Reichard, Gladys, quoted, 144
relativism, cultural, 4, 7-8
religion in America, 105-106
residence patterns in the United States, 103-104
retirement, 9, 32-39, 175-176, 178, 181
retiring to the porch, 34
Rhoads, Ellen C., 101
    quoted, 16, 26, 169
Rio Grande Pueblo aged, 145-146
Robertson, L., quoted, 181
Rogers, C., 145
    quoted, 146
role changes in old age, 119
Role of the Aged in Primitive Society, 11, 111, 113, 128
Rosemont nursing home, 48
Rosow, Irving, 12
    quoted, 172
Roth, Dwight, 175
Rowe, W., 179
Russia, 13

Salamon, S., quoted, 127
Salt River Pima, 146
Samoan islanders, viii, 7, 16, 25-27, 28-29, 92-102, 127, 169, 170, 174, 180
    cultural change among, 101-102
    in the United States, 158-160
Sander, Gerhard, 65
Sansei, 39, 156-157
Santo Tomas Mazaltepec, Mexico, 148

self-reliance in America, 106
senescence, 63
sex ratio among aged, 117
sex roles of aged, 129-132
sexual maturation and MLP, 61
Shahrani, M., 132
Shakespeare's seven ages, 27, 118
Shangri-las, viii, 68-76
Sharp, H., quoted, 131
Sheehan, Tom, 173
    quoted, 15
Shelton, Austin, 45
    quoted, 172-173
Shore, Bradd, 28-29
Sichinava, G. N., 70
Sidamo culture (Ethiopia), 129-130
Silverman, Phillip, 12-13, 121
    quoted, 172
Siemaszko, Maria, quoted, 40
Simic, Andrei, 30, 129, 132
    quoted, 30, 36-37
Simmons, Leo, 11-12, 111, 113, 115, 128, 129, 141, 167, 171
    quoted, 99, 116, 121, 122-123, 124, 129-130
Siriono food taboos, 114-115
Slater, Philip, quoted, 169
social alienation in America, 107-108
social anthropology, 2
societal complexity, levels of, 15
sociolinguistics, 2
Sokolovsky, Jay, 21-22
    quoted, 40
Spencer, Robert, quoted, 122
SRO (single room occupancy) hotels, 21
Stanford, Percil, quoted, 140
status and role, 9, 11-17
Stenning, D. J., quoted, 126
subsistence activities, Eskimo, 85
Sun Chief, 12
synchronic studies, 5

de Tocqueville, Alexis, 102, 138
Tower nursing home, 48
Trela, J., quoted, 40
Turner, George, quoted, 100
Turner, L. M., quoted, 87
twin studies, 65-66

Ubelaker, Douglas, 2
universal interests (Leo Simmons concept), 113
universals (Cowgill and Holmes concept), 116
universals, defined, 112
universals in aging, 112-132
urban Indian aged, 146-147
urban Mexican-American aged, 150-151

Valle, R., 149
values (American) affecting the aged, 106
Van Stone, James, quoted, 85, 86
Vatuk, Sylvia, quoted, 37
Vilcabamba society and culture, viii, 68, 75-76, 80

Watson, Wilbur, 49
    quoted, 40
"wear and tear" theory of aging, 63-64
Wellin, E., 22
Weyl, N., quoted, 128
Whiting, J., 125
widowhood, 117
Williams, C. G., 64
Williams, Gerry, quoted, 120
Williams, T. R., 174
work ethic, 178-179
Wu, F., 153
    quoted, 154
Wylie, F. M., 135, 137

Yankelovich survey, 139
Young, B., quoted, 162, 163
youth culture in the United States, 108-109

Student Survey

Other Cultures, Elder Years: An Introduction to Cultural Gerontology
by Lowell D. Holmes

Students, send us your ideas!

The author and the publisher want to know how well this book served you and what can be done to improve it for those who will use it in the future. By completing and returning this questionnaire, you can help us develop better textbooks. We value your opinion and want to hear your comments. Thank you.

Your name (optional) _____ School _____

Your mailing address _____

City _____ State _____ ZIP _____

Instructor's name _____ Course title _____

1. How does this book compare with other texts you have used? (Check one)
   - ☐ Better than any other
   - ☐ Better than most
   - ☐ About the same as the rest
   - ☐ Not as good as most

2. Circle those chapters you especially liked:

   Chapters   1   2   3   4   5   6   7   8   9

   Comments:

3. Circle those chapters you think could be improved:

   Chapters   1   2   3   4   5   6   7   8   9

   Comments:

4. Please give us your impressions of the text. (Check your rating below)

	Excellent	Good	Average	Poor
Local organization	( )	( )	( )	( )
Readability of text material	( )	( )	( )	( )
General layout and design	( )	( )	( )	( )
Match with instructor's course organization	( )	( )	( )	( )
Illustrations that clarify the text	( )	( )	( )	( )
Up-to-date treatment of subject	( )	( )	( )	( )
Explanation of difficult concepts	( )	( )	( )	( )
Selection of topics in the text	( )	( )	( )	( )

OVER PLEASE

5. Please list any chapters that your instructor did not assign. _____
   _____

6. What additional topics did your instructor discuss that were not covered in the text? _____
   _____

   Do you feel that these topics should have been covered in the text? _____
   _____

7. Did you buy this book new or used?   ☐ New   ☐ Used
   Do you plan to keep the book or sell it?   ☐ Keep it   ☐ Sell it
   Do you think your instructor should continue to assign this book? ☐ Yes   ☐ No

8. After taking the course, are you interested in taking more courses in this field? ☐ Yes ☐ No
   What is your major? _____

9. **GENERAL COMMENTS:**

May we quote you in our advertising?   ☐ Yes   ☐ No

To mail, remove this page and mail to: Mary L. Paulson
                                          Burgess Publishing Company
                                          7108 Ohms Lane
                                          Minneapolis, MN 55435

THANK YOU!